"Manu Bazzano's *Nietzsche and Psychotherapy* is not just 'a breath of fresh air' in contemporary psychotherapy. It is what Nietzsche would call a full 'gale.' It blows open windows and doors on vistas of which most of those concerned with 'mental health,' 'behavioral science,' and 'wellness' – those handmaidens of social-political hygiene – have no clue. Nietzsche rightly considered himself the first of a new type of psychologist that had yet to be imagined, and said that it would take a century and more before his writings would begin to be understood. Today, some hundred plus years later, we are seeing an emerging Nietzschean type of psychology. Bazzano's *Nietzsche and Psychotherapy* is a major contribution to that development. It is an important and challenging work, because Nietzsche is an important and challenging thinker, and because applying him to psychotherapy is an important and challenging enterprise. This book is not for psychotherapists who, faint of heart and without realizing it, labor for the sake of social-political hygiene rather than for the life that animates their clients. It is for psychotherapists who dare to be bold and, most importantly, willing to dignify the lives of their clients by inspiring and encouraging the same boldness and daring in them."

– **Daniel Chapelle**, author, *Nietzsche and Psychoanalysis; The Soul In Everyday Life;* and (forthcoming) *Nietzsche and the Buddha: Different Lives, Same Ideas – How Nietzsche May Yet Become the West's Own Buddha*

"With curiosity, skill and mischievousness, Bazzano taps the bell of psychotherapy with Nietzsche's hammer. The resulting sound is something I wish for every therapist to hear – it dispels Gods and their shadows, and resonates with the beauty of engagement. Read it at your peril – the more rigorous your therapeutic worldviews, the deeper they will crack."

– **Dr Niklas Serning**, Senior Lecturer University of the West of England, Consultant Psychotherapist OTR, Chartered Psychologist, Existential and Child psychotherapist, Registered Supervisor

NIETZSCHE AND PSYCHOTHERAPY

Drawing on over a century of international Nietzschean scholarship, this ground-breaking book discusses some of the unexplored psychological reaches of Nietzsche's thought, as well as their implications for psychotherapeutic practice.

Nietzsche's philosophy anticipated some of the most innovative cultural movements of the last century, from expressionism and surrealism to psychoanalysis, humanistic psychology and phenomenology. But his work on psychology often remains discarded, despite its many insights. Addressing this oversight, and in an age of managerialism and evidence-based practice, this book helps to redefine psychotherapy as an experiment that explores the limits and intricacies of human experience. It builds the foundations for a differentialist psychology: a life-affirming project that can deal squarely with the challenges, joys and sorrows of being human.

Nietzsche and Psychotherapy will be of great interest to researchers interested in the relationship between psychotherapy and philosophy, Nietzschean scholars, as well as to clinicians grappling with the challenges of working in the so-called "post-truth" age.

Manu Bazzano is a psychotherapist in private practice and a visiting lecturer at Roehampton University, London. He facilitates seminars and workshops internationally on Zen and Phenomenology. His books include *Buddha is Dead* (2006); *Spectre of the Stranger* (2012); *After Mindfulness* (2014); *Therapy and the Counter-tradition* (2016); *Zen and Therapy* (2017); and *Re-visioning Person-centred Therapy* (2018). www.manubazzano.com.

NIETZSCHE AND PSYCHOTHERAPY

Manu Bazzano

Routledge
Taylor & Francis Group

LONDON AND NEW YORK

First published 2019
by Routledge
2 Park Square, Milton Park, Abingdon, Oxon OX14 4RN

and by Routledge
52 Vanderbilt Avenue, New York, NY 10017

Routledge is an imprint of the Taylor & Francis Group, an informa business

British Library Cataloguing in Publication Data
A catalogue record for this book is available from the British Library

Library of Congress Cataloging-in-Publication Data
A catalog record has been requested for this book

ISBN: 978-1-138-35121-9 (hbk)
ISBN: 978-1-138-35125-7 (pbk)
ISBN: 978-0-429-43542-3 (ebk)

Typeset in Bembo
by Taylor & Francis Books

To the memory of Ralph Oppenheimer (1941–2016)

CONTENTS

Acknowledgements   *x*

Introduction   1

1   "You get burned either way"   12

2   Love and the uncontested life   44

3   Fables of identity   64

4   Against humanism   75

5   *Homo natura*   100

6   Poison and remedy   127

7   Ambiguous legacies   143

8   Tears of joy   159

References   *179*
Index   *190*

ACKNOWLEDGEMENTS

I am greatly indebted to Julie Webb for her encouragement, invaluable comments, edits of an early draft, and shrewd suggestions.

The following friends and colleagues have, knowingly and unknowingly, helped me develop some of the ideas present in this book:

Nigel Armistead, Shani Bans, Emily Corrie, John Davis, Nancy Hakim Dowek, Katy Driscoll, Nick Duffell, Hank David Earl, Subhaga Gaetano Failla, Barbara Godoy and the participants to the Labyrinth & the Mask course, Hugh Knopf, Anna Kruger, Tim Lott, John Mackessy, Beatrice Millar, Andrew Miller, Michael Montgomery, Glenn Nichols, Joy Schaverien, Andrew Seed, Anthony Stone, Yana Trichkova, Devang Vaidya, Rodney Wilson, Emily Woof.

The work of the following writers has been instrumental in helping me rethink Nietzsche's thought in a more naturalistic frame, invaluable to an embodied psychotherapeutic theory and practice:

Cristina Acampora, Babette Babich, Christopher Cox, Sarah Kofman, Duncan Large, Ferruccio Masini, Brian Massumi, Graham Parkes, Keith Ansell Pearson, Jacqueline Rose, Richard Schacht, Joy Schaverien, Alan Schrift, Gianni Vattimo.

I am forever grateful to Sarita Doveton, without whom – nought.

INTRODUCTION

1.

Nietzsche *and*: despite its original meaning, the conjunction in this book's title cannot designate union. Countless comparative studies were written with those first two words in the title – innumerable texts comparing Nietzschean thought to everything under the sun. Given that it is to some degree comparative, this book inevitably joins that long list. Nietzsche derided exercises of this kind: "the one thing I can't stand to hear" – he wrote in relation to the German scholarship of his time – "is the notorious *and*" (1888/1998, p. 60). Wary of joining the academic chorus, and aware of how unfeasible a task is producing an extensive 'comparative study', I will focus instead on a handful of Nietzschean thought experiments that are pivotal to an investigation of psychotherapeutic theory and practice today.

Nietzsche is a little more than our contemporary. It is tempting to say that it may take until the end of this century to begin to get closer to the psychological reaches and cultural implications of his thought. But that implies a linear view of history. It assumes that intelligibility of a particular oeuvre is a given. It ignores Walter Benjamin's "now of recognisability" (2007, p. 463), the subtle view that real understanding of an image, an event or, in this case, an innovative philosophical corpus will elude us without the fortuitous occurrence of an 'opening' in time that makes them recognizable to us.

Is our time receptive to Nietzsche's ideas? It would seem that his thought is destined to remain *untimely*, even more so at a time when psychology and psychotherapy are being increasingly dominated by neopositivism and managerialism instead of the key Nietzschean notions of experiencing and experimentation. If that is the case, and until a genuine opening occurs, one can prepare the ground. And this is what this book attempts to do. In itself, this exercise has been nothing short of exhilarating. My hope is that the reader will be affected by Nietzsche's vibrant, unruly thought and stirred to carry the experiment further into the heart of psychotherapy, a discipline that began to arise in the 1890s, around the time of his mental collapse (1888) and death (1990).

2.

The first time I opened the door marked 'Nietzsche', aged 20, it was a detour – a jubilant escape from the beaten track. I never made it back, for that's when I began to lose not only my religion but, one by one, most of its surrogates – what Nietzsche calls *shadows of God*. The door stayed ajar, and from time to time I'd give in to the temptation and wilfully open it; other times, a blast of air would throw it wide open. I'm invariably compelled to walk in and then whatever is central to my life undergoes a re-evaluation. Religion, art, love, literature, sex, politics, nationality, spirituality and now therapy – can all be 'sounded out' under Nietzsche's hammer. The hammer is not there to 'smash' personal or public idols, as it is commonly held, but to investigate them by testing their soundness – in the same way as one sounds out a bell to see if it still retains its pitch. It is high time for me to sound out what has become central to my life – therapy – by making use of my own, homespun version of Nietzsche's hammer, namely a 'life-denigration detector'. The first thing Nietzsche invites us to look for when examining a system of thought, a religion, or psychological and scientific method, is not whether these are 'true' or 'false', for in his view this would be an idle task fit for pedants or dispensers of blame. What matters to him is whether a method *affirms* life, or is animated instead by the *instinct of revenge*, i.e., by an overriding tendency to resent life and denigrate it.

In relation to psychotherapy, the question then is whether a particular form of therapeutic practice is life-affirming, or whether it is fuelled by the instinct of revenge – by the need to justify, amend, and redeem life. In sounding out the bells of therapy, the intention is, as the poet said, to ring the bells that still can ring. Do they still reverberate? Or have they morphed into muffled incantations uttered in the vain hope of finding solace from life's beauty and terror?

The task at hand would be relatively easy if the instinct of revenge were a psychological trait, a particular defect in need of a cure. But for Nietzsche *the instinct of revenge is the fundamental principle of psychology itself*. In this, psychology follows metaphysics, science and religion, all animated by the very same spirit. In a posthumous fragment he wrote:

> Wherever responsibilities have been sought, it was the *instinct of revenge* that sought. This instinct of revenge has so mastered mankind in the course of millennia that the whole of metaphysics, psychology, conception of history, but above all morality, is impregnated with it. As far as man has thought, he has introduced the bacillus of revenge into things. He has made even God ill with it, he has *deprived existence* in general *of its innocence*; namely, by tracing back every state of being thus and thus to a will, an intention, a responsible act. The entire doctrine of the will, this most fateful *falsification* in psychology hitherto, was essentially invented for the sake of punishment.
>
> (Nietzsche, 1968, pp. 401–402)

Ressentiment, as he also likes to call the instinct of revenge in his beloved French, implies both a *topology*, i.e. a place, or *topos* – as well as a *typology*, that is to say, it manifests concretely through particular *types* of individuals in whom reactive forces, forces inimical to life, triumph. *Ressentiment* is integral to *nihilism*. What is nihilism? It is the notion that life in and by itself is nothing (*nihil*) or next to nothing without some form of justification, elevation, explanation, or redemption. Thus understood, nihilism happens to be the chief assumption behind *all* metaphysical claims. All metaphysical systems denigrate life in the name of something placed outside the sensuous perception of life itself, in the name of a psychological/spiritual/scientific explanation. In this sense, nihilism does not constitute a *particular* worldview or category of thought. Instead, "the categories of thought" and "reasonable thought" in particular – "identity, causality, finality" – themselves presuppose an interpretation of force which is that of *ressentiment*" (Deleuze, 1962/2006, p. 32).

What the above calls for is, effectively, a reversal of metaphysics; in our case, it calls for a reversal of psychotherapy. None of us has the faintest idea of what a human being devoid of the instinct of revenge would be like. This is because the instinct of revenge has dominated and continues to dominate human history. Would a human who does not blame or devalue life still be called human? Or would she/he tilt towards the threshold of experience that Nietzsche calls the *overhuman*?

3.

Another important factor of the 'Nietzsche effect' is that it can free us from the trap of synthesis and the compulsion of recoding. The trajectory of his thought is exemplary in this regard, though maddening to those among us who are hungry for systems and the institutionalization of knowledge. Unlike the work of the other two masters of suspicion, Marx and Freud, Nietzsche's thought cannot be *recoded* and for that reason wholly belongs to a genuine *counter-tradition* (Bazzano & Webb, 2016). With Marx, it was the State that wrecked us and a (socialist) State that will make us well. With Freud, it was the family that twisted us and the family that will put us straight. But it is not so easy to recode Nietzsche, though many have tried. He mixes up all the codes leaving us (thankfully in my view) without a single chance to conjure up a 'Nietzschean remedy'.

A welcome side effect to Nietzsche's irreducibility is an eruption of *laughter*. His uncoding is so thorough that it is simply impossible to build a new model on its premise. What we inherit instead is the encouragement to venture boldly into the wide expanse left uncharted by the death of God. To acknowledge the death of God means (a) recognizing our condition of *groundlessness*; (b) acknowledging the demise of the old "horizon of meaning and ontological stability" (Viriasova, 2016, p. 225); (c) abolishing "the cosmological distinction between two worlds, the metaphysical distinction between essence and appearance, the logical distinction between the true and the false" (Deleuze, 2004, p. 74).

After Nietzsche, the task is to clear the view for new horizons to appear – a task that is as urgent in psychotherapy as it is in science, art and also religion. Will the creation of new landscapes mean the end of psychotherapy as we know it? Or will it mean the creation of new forms? It remains to be seen. My hope is that to attuned readers this book will signal a possible route towards the radical re-visioning of psychotherapy as an art and a science geared towards experimentation and experiencing and less burdened by normative dictates.

The limits of psychotherapy were inbuilt from its (psychoanalytic) beginnings. Psychotherapy was and still largely is a contractual bourgeois association based on the trading of words and money. Even that image looks charmingly archaic and daringly enfleshed in a psychic landscape ruled by digital solitary confinement. But psychotherapy's inherent limits were duly noted and commented upon long before the ascent of humanistic psychology and the concerted reaction against psychoanalysis. In their own unique ways Rank, Taft, Winnicott, Lacan (among others) hinted at the need to explode this contractual straitjacket and widen its confines onto a terrain that is neither legal nor institutional.

It is widely held that Nietzsche's writings deliberately refuse to present us with a system, and that he is the one thinker who introduced *perspectivism* in modern thought. What is often forgotten, however, is one important reason that motivates his reluctance towards system-building, namely a close connection with the world *outside* the page, something that is confirmed by his aphoristic style. Nietzsche often formulated his ideas while walking, and it is as if his writings are "traversed by a movement which comes from the outside, which does not begin in the page of the book" (Deleuze, 2004, p. 256). To be even momentarily affected by his thought, as it dances across the page, implies establishing a fleeting, complicit alliance with the vitality, wit and passion that animate it. It means becoming contaminated by the same force, in itself a potential catalyst for transformation. This carries more weight than the intellectual understanding of his ideas, for it deals with concrete, contingent *life* rather than with the abstract *being* of philosophers. For that reason alone, Nietzsche's work bears an immediate and intimate link to psychotherapy, a practice that so far contends with living subjects and living matter.

For instance, aiding the logical understanding or unveiling the alleged untruth of a self-destructive pattern of behaviour in a client is not the same as evaluating the cluster of natural forces that animates that pattern. The former pertains to a rationalist as well as onto-theological investigation, while the latter is, properly speaking, *psychological* as well as *axiological*, i.e. relating to questions of *value*. Axiology, so central in the therapeutic endeavour and strangely absent in contemporary psychotherapeutic discourse, is one of the central themes of this book, particularly in relation to evaluating the life-affirming or life-denying attributes of the natural forces at play in the psyche.

4.

Nietzsche's philosophy is exploration, experiment, and temptation. He himself describes his work as *experiment*. This term is unpopular in our current cultural climate, superseded by the surrogates of evidence and consensus – by the (neo)positivism of allegedly friendly 'facts' and the intimidation of ready-made, seemingly objective theories. Yet experimentation is essential to the psychotherapeutic endeavour. The route towards individuation (i.e., towards authorship of one's life, self-direction, towards finding one's internal locus of evaluation, modifying/expanding one's self-concept/self-construct and so forth) implies the creation of certain conditions that facilitate change, a situation in which one is diverted from the highway of blind obeisance to the rules of what Nietzsche calls 'the herd' and to the dictates of *fate* and onto the more uneven, less trodden path of personal *destiny*. Those coming to therapy are more or less consciously inviting a creative crisis into their life. Whatever the presenting issues might be, clients are in a sense requesting to be diverted from a route that has so far brought suffering, stuckness and discontent, and onto a path that may better reflect their present and contingent 'truth'. The transformation this calls for cannot occur without experimentation, for neither the client nor the therapist knows beforehand what that route might be, nor whether this path may bring, instead of 'happiness' and 'integration', greater affirmation of difference, more solitude and pain.

To follow this line of enquiry is ill-timed – which is why I like to pursue it. Integration is the buzzword in the current political landscape: a consensus-driven demand for assimilation of difference, migrancy and otherness within all parameters set by institutional power. Bizarrely, mainstream psychotherapies and the bodies that represent them appear to have cheerfully joined the bandwagon. In the name of happiness and wellbeing, they have bypassed the vital step of individuation while paying lip service to diversity, internal loci of evaluation and imbalance of power in therapy.

To become an individual is, however, only the first step for Nietzsche. The next step is coming to recognize our existence as *dividuals*. Individuation must be followed by *dividuation*. The first step is hard enough for any one of us living in an age when we are often lonely but not alone, isolated yet inescapably 'connected'. One clear message emerging from Nietzsche's writings is that *individuation takes first place over integration*. Another is that individuation is the springboard for an investigation that leads us away from individualism and the narcissistic search for authenticity, towards a fuller recognition of the fundamentally plural, non-atomistic nature of the self, what Nietzsche calls "dividuum" (Nietzsche, 1984, p. 54). In this instance he reframes subjectivity in terms of "impersonal individuation rather than personal individualization" (Deleuze, 2001, p. 8). This amounts to the re-description of *my* life in terms "*a life*" (ibid.) – or, in the language of humanistic psychotherapy, a never-ending movement from self-concept or self-construct to *organism*.

The above implies an unapologetically *naturalistic* reading of Nietzsche which, supported by various strands of contemporary scholarship and discussed at various points in the book, will, it is hoped, present psychotherapists with exciting new avenues of inquiry. 'Naturalistic' here means *founded on* biology but *not bound* by it; it implies an exploration that is *body-oriented* yet not *shackled* to the body. For Nietzsche *physis* itself ('nature', both animate and inanimate) is *interpretation*. I find this thought experiment Nietzsche invites us to consider astonishing and it bears repeating: *the organism itself is interpretation* rather than the final ground. Therefore a form of psychotherapy inspired by Nietzsche's ideas cannot be only body psychotherapy.

The notion of interpretation, pervasive in Nietzsche's writings, is, however, profoundly different from diagnostic and psychoanalytic ideas of interpretation; it does not hark back to a cause but is there instead to clarify what forces are at play at any given time. It is more akin to a process of evaluation that knowingly selects and discerns in an ongoing deconstructive and freeing process.

5.

Nietzsche's famous declaration *God is dead* was sombre recognition of the groundlessness of existence and at the same time exultation for the deep blue sea open at last to seekers and explorers. As he writes in *The Gay Science*, in a section titled *The meaning of our cheerfulness*:

> Indeed, we philosophers and "free spirits" feel, when we hear the news that "the old god is dead", as if a new dawn shone on us; our heart overflows with gratitude, amazement, premonitions, expectation. At long last the horizon appears free to us again, even if it should not be bright; at long last our ships may venture out again, venture out to face any danger; all the daring of the lover of knowledge is permitted again; the sea, our sea, lies open again; perhaps there has never yet been such an "open sea".
>
> *(Nietzsche, 1882/1974, p. 280)*

It is common today to interpret 'God is dead' univocally as the affirmation of exalted humanism that simply replaces the deity with the human. This is a mistake; as it happens, the seismic shift signalled by the statement has been more accurately registered by Nietzsche's critics. For some Jungians (e.g., Frey-Rohn, 1988; Tedeschi, 2000), preserving the notion of God is central to a notion of 'mental health' that upholds the archetype of God as pivotal in propping up the archetype of the self. For Klossowski (1969/1997) the death of God similarly produces the collapse of the self, sole assurance of its identity. But Nietzsche had reversed the equation from the start: it was *because* of the superstitious psychological prejudice that ascribes separate existence to the self (the 'doer' behind the deed) that the notion of God (the creator behind creation) arose in the first place. When one of them goes, the other too vanishes; from then on, both of them assume a merely functional, 'grammatical' role. With the demise of God, the self not so much dies as reveals itself to be constituted of an intricate cluster of affects: not a 'place' where affects meet, but a composite – an aggregate with no separate existence. This is one of the facets of Nietzsche's *multiplicity*, a far more radical stance than the current fashionable pluralistic spin-offs on Jung's notion of *personifying* will allow. Nietzsche's notion of multiplicity insinuates a radical transformation; it lures us inside a labyrinthine process of unmasking that reveals and evaluates different forces at play. It is a psychology of the *mask*.

6.

Nietzsche's thought offers profound insights into the practice of psychotherapy because it is at heart a philosophy of affirmation. To affirm means to say *yes*. Historically, one way of saying yes is voluntarily carrying a burden – professing in one's life that 'acceptance' of suffering, the bearing of one's cross that has been inculcated in our minds by 2,000 years of Christianity and that made of humans so many beasts of burden. Later, with the increasing influence of secularism, the burden changed shape and colour. With transcendental values in some societies gone or hiding, it was now time to carry on one's own shoulders "the burden of the real" (Deleuze, 2004, p. 120), which often meant the burden of a morality that is integral to the religion that had been allegedly outwitted. The effect was (is) equally poisonous to human flourishing, with an ever-present guilt sha-dowing, under the guise of social conscience and 'responsibility', the coercive needs of 'the herd' whose norms aim at keeping itself alive. Various therapeutic orientations gradually abandoned notions (e.g. the unconscious, the organism, actualization, indi-viduation, autonomy, cultivation of vulnerability and creativity, etc.) that were at variance with the bearing on one's shoulder the burden of the real and the dictates of dominant ideologies. From that moment on, psychotherapy and psychology themselves began to play a pivotal role (marginal at first, but increasingly influential) in aiding the ongoing process of coercion and social conformity. They did so by providing a set of ready-made formulas – e.g. mental health, integration, social adjustment and so on – that attempted to fill the space left empty by the demise of religion and its moral injunctions. In a cultural landscape where saying 'yes' is roughly on a par with the *y-a* of the beast of burden and the spiritual vanity of noble self-effacement, Nietzsche's words, through his character Zarathustra, sound positively incongruous, for Zarathustra's 'yes' is an invitation to unburden life, to make ourselves light by dancing and creating. Not the yes-saying of donkeys, but the yes-saying of dancers.

And what about saying 'no'? This can be, and often is, plain resentment, petulance, despondency – even aggression. But then again aggression is *aggredi* = to step forward decisively, the first essential manifestation in the human subject of a 'will to power' that is for Nietzsche another word for the incessant, excessive and mysterious move-ment of life itself.

7.

Nietzsche's influence in the wider world of culture is extraordinary. His thought anticipated psychoanalysis, expressionism, existentialism, phenomenology, surreal-ism, humanistic psychology, post-structuralism and several other innovative cultural movements of the twentieth century. In the area of philosophy, it created the foundations for the development of both the *Lebensphilosophie* of Klages (and the *philosophische Anthropologie* of Scheler and Plessner that came out of it), as well as the *Existenzphilosophie* of Jaspers and the onto-phenomenology of Heidegger.

Even more marked was Nietzsche's impact on the artistic avant-garde of the early years of the twentieth century, particularly the literary experimentations in remarkable novels and essays that (alongside psychoanalysis but without the pres-sure of scientific verification imposed by the medical profession on the latter) freely explored and exploded the once untouchable notion of the atomistic human self.

Gradually, Nietzsche's influence even began to extend to the 'no-go area' of Anglo-American analytic thought which has for a long time chosen to trace in Nietzsche the heterodox origins of a derogatorily named 'continental' philosophy. And yet, as a letter of September 1888 to his 'Indologist' friend Paul Deussen testifies, Nietzsche was the first to be alert to his own heterodoxy. In his writings we find a seemingly boundless production of metaphors that, given the refreshing lack in them of both moral prejudice and the cult of 'left-brain' reasoning that are arguably the staple of our way of being and thinking, end up subverting any explicit and implicit hierarchy and open the horizon to new explorations.

In relation to psychology and psychotherapy, he posited a strong challenge to the conventional notion of the self, a challenge that is still valid today. This is because the idea of a unitary, undivided/individual self is arguably regaining traction in contemporary psychology and in a contemporary culture dominated by neoliberal values. This is in many ways an updated, post-modern version of the bourgeois notion of identity that was all the rage in the post-war years. It substitutes the old-fashioned belief in a self propped up by property, moral certainty and encircled self-identity (one that was threatened by early psychoanalysis's notion of the unconscious) with the hypermodern, liquid mode of entrepreneurial risk that thrives on uncertainty. The apparent difference is only in the method of survival. Whereas the bourgeois self preserves itself by standing still, the neoliberal self does so by moving fast.

A sign of the enduring importance of the notion of the self in contemporary culture is the popularity of biography and autobiography. It is not surprising that both are now thriving industries, given that they provide a form of consolation, a conduit even for the mourning of a self that even in life continues to evade us. It is partly for these reasons that I want to resist the fashionable temptation of psychologizing Nietzsche, by attempting to read between the lines of his life: it would feel inappropriate. At the same time, even a casual glimpse at facets of his biography affords so many enticing and rich details that not to mention any of them could be seen as an unforgivable omission. In the light of this consideration, I scatter some of these here and in other chapters, in the hope of giving the unacquainted reader a glimpse of the person.

Some of those who knew him as a young man derided at times the overly serious countenance of his early years. But how could he not be sombre? He lost his beloved father and then his brother within the space of a few months at the age of five; not long after that, he witnessed the death of his aunt and grandmother and was forced to leave behind the tranquillity of his village parsonage (his father was a pastor) for Naumburg (Safranski, 2003). In adolescence he became deeply religious and at the same time excited by reading Byron and Hölderlin. Thanks to his natural gifts, he was appointed at the young age of 24 as Professor of Classical Philology at the University of Basel. His acquaintance with the writings of Schopenhauer in 1865 began to shift his attention from philology to philosophy, but a keynote to both was undoubtedly his great love of music. At any rate, and despite a momentary, ecstatic derailment occasioned by his meeting with Wagner and despite his decision, prompted by illness (and welcomed as a chance for relinquishing his rummaging through old books), to give up philology, the *style* and the very ambiance of philology left an indelible mark on his future work. He chewed, as it were, the flesh of philology and spat out its bones, discarding the ingrained pedantry whilst retaining its essential invitation to read well and to read slowly, to cultivate a taste for a mode of interpretation – something that, I believe, can prove useful to the art and science of psychotherapy.

As we shall see, Nietzsche's interpretative style is at variance with the hermeneutical orthodoxy that later emerged and that was to gain ascendancy, via Heidegger and Gadamer, within existential psychotherapy. The philological method is, in Nietzsche's case, no mere scholarly exercise. In due course it gave birth to a distinctly genealogical line of attack that will help disrupt the complex construction of subjectivity erected by Christian and bourgeois morality and by conventional philosophy.

He had finished writing the beginning of volume two of *Human, all too Human* when his illness prompted him in March 1879 to cancel his lectures. He sent a letter of resignation to the university and left Basel for good, after having been granted an annual pension. This is when his wandering period begins, a time spent between Sils Maria (Switzerland), Nice, and Italy among other places, a period marked by a creative loss of national identity.

Nietzsche considered attachments to any so-called fatherland, with their "lapse and regression into old loves and narrow views" (Nietzsche, 1978, p. 152), as a form of "lunacy" (ibid., p. 169). His initial pan-Europeanism eventually morphed into trans-Europeanism: a good European, it turns out, is for him one who gazes at Europe from the viewpoint of exile and statelessness; one who, like himself, has no homeland. Believing that Europe found itself at a time of difficult transition, in the mid-1880s he wrote words that are resonant today:

> How can those of us who are children of the future be at home in this house of today? We are averse to all the ideals in which anyone today, in this brittle and broken time of transition, might feel at home; but as far as the "realities" of our times are concerned, we do not believe that they will last. The ice that barely continues to bear our weight has become very thin: thawing winds are blowing, and we ourselves, we who have no homeland, are something that breaks up ice and all those "realities" that have become too thin.
>
> *(cited in Krell & Bates, 1997, p. 2, translation modified)*

The nomadic period was also punctuated by an extraordinary creative output. Nietzsche wrote a book per year from 1878 to 1888. 1888 was also the year of his mental collapse in Turin which brought to an end the ambitious project, conceived two years earlier in Switzerland, to write a major work in four volumes whose working title was *The Will to Power: Attempt at a Transvaluation of Values*. This is all the more poignant, considering how marred by illness and a painful lack of like-minded people this long period was, a life bearable in the morning and unendurable by the afternoon and evening, a life that several times he contemplated leaving honourably, feeling, in the mid 1880s, that he had achieved enough under very difficult circumstances.

8.

In discussions with friends and colleagues the question has come up a few times as to whether the area of investigation I found myself involved with through the writing of this book truly belongs to psychology or, rather, whether it skirts a wider area that includes philosophy, spirituality, politics and aesthetics. The perplexity arises, I believe, because we have by and large acquiesced to regard psychology within the narrow parameters set by academic discourse. The agendas of a self-appointed 'scientific community' rule the roost, almost entirely operating within the remit of the dominant neoliberal ideology. 'Mental health' is the buzzword here; measuring, computing and assessing it are the tasks of a wide contingent of 'mental health workers' whose task is to ensure that people are made fit to go back to work. The very wide field of 'psychology' – comprising academic psychology, counselling, psychotherapy, counselling psychology – has become wholly instrumental to a neoliberal agenda. Pockets of resistance and autonomous discourse are forced into the elite ghettos of psychoanalysis and psychotherapeutic private practice.

Yet psychology can be, in Nietzsche's definition, the "queen of the sciences" with the other sciences "serv[ing] and prepar[ing] for it"; it can effectively be "the road to the fundamental problems" (Nietzsche, 1886/1978, p. 36). This, however, can happen only on condition that psychology will be ready to venture "into the depths" instead of remaining "anchored to moral prejudices and timidities" (ibid., p. 35). At a crucial moment in his life – the time of creative disillusionment and crisis characterized by his middle works – Nietzsche turns to psychology (defined in his own terms) and away from both art and philology, at least in the way he had hitherto conceived of them. One of the first to recognize the tremendous value of Nietzsche's effort for the future of psychology and psychotherapy was Otto Rank:

> Nietzsche, who experienced thoroughly the whole tragedy of the creative man and admitted in his "amor fati" the willingness to pay for it, is in my opinion the first and has been up to now the only psychologist.
>
> *(Rank, 1929/1978b, p. 18)*

9.

William Blake's unorthodox and radical poem *Jerusalem* was turned, a little more than a century after it was written, into a hallowed anthem of blatant conformity, sung among other places at Ronald Reagan's state funeral in Washington National Cathedral in 2004 and at the royal wedding of Kate Middleton and Prince William in Westminster Abbey in 2011. Greater ignominy than this was bestowed on Nietzsche's work, despite the fact that it is hard to convincingly bend his poetic passages or fragments in the service of a conventional ethos. Do people need reminding that the association of Nietzsche's thought with Nazism is unfounded, idiotic, and unsubstantiated? Sadly, yes. This is because, despite a hundred-plus years of sophisticated European, Anglo-Saxon, Eastern and Far-Eastern Nietzschean scholarship – the great majority of it allied to progressive, innovative hermeneutics and epistemologies and to cultural movements such as existentialism, psycho-analysis, phenomenology, abstract expressionism, surrealism, deconstruction, post-structuralism (not to mention direct and indirect influence on the contemporary activism of groups such as Occupy and Pussy Riot) – there still are writers and philosophers who insist on a bizarre reading of Nietzsche that ominously coincides with the wackiest and most fascistic misconceptions of his thought. These were partly set in motion by that Frankenstein of a book, *Will to Power*, arbitrarily and manipulatively cobbled together from notes and fragments not meant for publication by his sister Elizabeth (whose anti-Semitic husband and friends Nietzsche unceremoniously referred to as 'scum'), and culminating in the ravings of dangerous and ignorant demagogues such as Mussolini and Evola.

Some of this anti-Nietzschean crusading is sadly becoming dominant with Anglo-Saxon theorists on the left, all too happy to enlist Nietzsche with the "neoclassic ... and [the] reactionary" (Bull, 2014), and missing out entirely on the emancipatory and progressive aspects of his thought that are discussed in the present work. Some of these debates and their links to psychotherapy will be discussed in relation to the charges of Nietzsche as forerunner of post-modernism and, by association, with the disastrous emergence of 'post-truth' in current politics.

What is crucial to assert at this point is that the very notion of *identity* and its correlatives in nationality, ethnicity and territorialism, on which fascist ideas (as well as contemporary far-right populist manifestations) rely, are subverted to the core by Nietzsche – something which those among us tempted to walk the path outlined by this great writer can find out for themselves.

1

"YOU GET BURNED EITHER WAY"

Blinkered

On 3 January 1889, Nietzsche went out of his lodging house in Via Carlo Alberto, n. 6, in Turin, Italy, where for the last eight months he had been renting a room in the large house of the Fino family. Within the urbane surroundings of this elegant, Baroque city, the loveless, stateless writer had found solace and, as he wrote in a letter to his mother, a "courage for life … waxing again" (Chamberlain, 1996, p. 21). He had found a quiet space to think and, with access to the family piano, a chance to compose and extemporize. Walking along the nearby Via Po that morning, he noticed that outside the university gates a cab driver was having difficulties with his wilful horse. The horse did not want to move, so at one point the driver lost his patience and whipped the horse. Nietzsche promptly stepped in, snatched the whip from the man's hands and threw his arms around the horse's neck, sobbing uncontrollably. He slumped to the floor and was nearly arrested for disrupting the peace.

This was the beginning of Nietzsche's mental collapse – a place of no return. He had exhibited eccentric behaviour in the few weeks and months before the event, but it is this occurrence – tragic and affecting – that lingers in the collective imagination to this day, inspiring artists, writers and also film directors; for example, Béla Tarr's *The Turin Horse* (Tarr, 2012) is an unrelenting and deeply affecting journey into inevitable darkness, shot in a desolate nowhere-land where God has long left the scene.

It may be worth pausing a moment longer on this film, for it presents us with an atmosphere that responds to important aspects of Nietzsche's thought scattered in his oeuvre up until book IV of his *Gay Science*, that is to say, just before, around 1881, his ecstatic affirmation of becoming, before the courageous declaration of *amor fati*, or love of destiny. Tarr's is a *Dostoyevskian* Nietzsche, and it may be that Dostoyevsky played an indirect role in Nietzsche's collapse in Turin. In *Crime and Punishment* (Dostoyevsky, 1866/2003), Raskolnikov dreams that he is a child, walking with his father in a small town, when they come across a noisy and inebriated crowd surrounding an old horse who cannot pull the heavy cartload he is harnessed to. The owner is cruelly beating the horse, sometimes across the eyes and muzzle. A few people even climb into the cart to make it heavier and when someone protests, the owner shouts back that the horse is his property and that he can do what he likes. Raskolnikov, a child in the dream, begs him in his childish voice to stop, and as he runs towards the horse he catches a lash from the whip. He then flings his arms around the wounded muzzle and kisses the horse's eyes, crying out through the tears for the cruelty to stop. As his father gets hold of him and takes him away, Raskolnikov wakes up in a cold sweat.

Some moments in life become decisive in giving us, in *condensed* and *poetic* form (the German word *Dichtung* means both), a hint of the emblematic sense of our existence, or at least of one of the stages we are living through. It is very likely that Nietzsche, who loved Dostoyevsky's writings, had read the above passage and that it lay dormant somewhere in his mind.

I cannot resist the temptation to read his humane, impulsive decision on that cold January morning as a tragic signal of how he would have wanted to be remembered. He had repeatedly stated in his writings that he had no part in the tradition of sensible philosophers, dull scholars, and dispensers of wisdom within whose folds many later tried hard to embalm him. Instead, a spontaneous feeling of pity for a mistreated animal, paired to some vital autobiographical yearning made him rush in, in such a way that "the shock of willing his own life to the last conscious moment, that momentary exciting flush of power, precipitated his collapse" (Chamberlain, 1996, p. 209).

It is all the more poignant that of all sentient beings a horse should be part of Nietzsche's last conscious act. These sensitive, powerful animals look at the world through the "seemingly limitless gaze of their large, dark eyes" (Klinkenborg, 2018, p. 46), with a mind that, some say (Hyland, 1990), never adjusts to history and modern thinking, but belongs instead to a perpetual present. Horses were sacrificed on a massive scale during two World Wars; while carrying heavy machinery, their attentive gaze reflected like a mirror the terror and devastation of the battlefield. Already by the end of World War I,

> the horse at war was no longer an embodiment of "terrifying power", as it was in the days of mounted cavalry. It was a drudge, a labourer in a dire landscape. The terror it experienced was simply gratuitous, a change for the worse in working conditions.
>
> *(Klinkenborg, 2018, p. 46)*

During World War II, horses were pulling heavy machinery through snow and mud, and a change for the worse happened in the overall way they were perceived. That time signalled what Ulrich Raulff (2018) calls the end of the centaurian pact, a dramatic shift that altered irreversibly the relationship between humans and horses. To speak of 'centaurian' and centaurs gestures towards a symbiosis between human and animal that is customarily the stuff of ancient myth and, less interestingly, of New

Age lore. But a centaur, a half-human, half-horse creature, is a clumsy being, Xenophon tells us in his *Cyropedia* through the mouth of Chrysanthas (Xenophon, 2012). It is certainly no substitute for a horse *and* a rider, especially when the latter is humbly attuned to the docile and invincible nature of the former, to the tremendous sensitivity and intelligence of the animal. And it is this link, neither symbiotic nor severed, but signalling instead a *continuum* between animal and human, that is of interest here. The human rider is neither the crown of creation nor is she the linear descendant of the Darwinian ape. She is "as alert and attentive as the horse is, as present in the world" (Klinkenborg, 2018, p. 47). This vital link between animal and human was lost in the machine horse of the nineteenth century, as it was in the way the horse had been later employed, until the mid 1950s, in agriculture. Humans had no time for this animal's attentive mind, instinct and intelligence. One thing only was appreciated: its muscular power. To put blinkers on a horse is to restrict its range of attention.

Reducing a living organism to a machine is also what we humans are doing to ourselves. Has psychotherapy reached a similar point? By accepting a neopositivist view of the human organism as unruly and unpredictable, it may have narrowed its range and scope to the drudgery of quantifiable, measurable data. Only by turning the human into a machine can the human be understood, accepted and financed by State and government, and made to serve forces of control and coercion instead of forces of freedom and experimentation. In a scenario where all theoretical orientations supinely accept the managerialism and standardization of an art and a science once designed to explore the inherent complexity of human experiencing, rushing in to snatch the whip in defence of the horse and embrace the animal in a desperate expression of compassion is an act of necessary madness.

Compassion in the face of suffering was also one of the main feelings behind a dream that my client Joanna brought to one of our sessions one winter evening. It had left her bewildered, she said, partly because it was a recurring dream – with one important variation.

In the dream, she is driving a carriage with six horses along a dusty, windy road. Alive with excitement, she notices cars on the road, but not a single person. She knows that the brakes – a square, sticky metal thing – don't work, and that this can be dangerous. At some point, overcome by worry and wanting to avoid a crash, she decides to 'take control' and slams the brakes down. This provokes a terrible accident. The carriage leaps forward, there is blood everywhere; the horses are wounded. She is horrified and wakes up with an awful feeling that lingers after the dream. She feels deep sadness for the poor horses that were so hurt, perhaps mortally wounded, and also feels regret for having caused the accident.

She explained that in past versions of the same dream there were no horses; she was driving a car instead. In the conversation that followed – dreaming the dream onwards – a few things came up. It was her desire to take control that caused the accident. Could greater trust in the instinctual, animal life be a better option? What would that mean? I know this well, she said: it's a kind of relinquishment. She described – movingly, I thought – going on a horse up a mountain trail, daydreaming, relaxed yet fully present, horse and rider enjoying each other in the stillness and beauty of the place. We dreamt on: there is a danger that comes (paradoxically?) with exerting control. Instead, choosing to let go and gaining … *what?* mastery? skill? artistry? She looked for the right word to express both relinquishment of the tight grip on experiencing and that feeling of direction and purpose that is gained when one can afford faith in the intelligence of the body, in the intelligence of feeling and emotions.

Against Socratism

What is at the origins of the managerialism and standardization to which psychotherapy is subjected in our day and age? And what are these two overriding tendencies trying to tackle or avoid? At this point in our investigation, these key questions can only be addressed obliquely.

Before ushering in this chapter's central topic – the link between Nietzsche's early writings on Greek tragedy and the dimension of affect in therapy – it will be useful to consider one of the most pervasive oppositions to the above: *Socratism*. One important aspect of Socratism is what has come to be known as Socratic questioning. This has become popular in psychotherapy over the last two decades, especially among practitioners working from cognitive-behavioural and Adlerian perspectives (e.g. Padesky, 1993; Millar, 2015, among others). Even when reduced to interviewing techniques, the underlying assumption behind Socrates' way of questioning is *maieutics* or midwifery. Socrates' method went on to become the founding and widely accepted principle of education (from *educere* = to lead out or draw out) as we know it. According to this view, the 'soul' comes into the world having forgotten all it knew. The wealth of knowledge and wisdom it had gathered from time immemorial is integral, ingrained – so goes the story – and can be drawn out by a skilful 'midwife', whose task is to help the soul remember and reassemble its primary sense of discernment. There is, admittedly, a little more to the Socratic method than this Platonist perspective would allow. Equally central to it, as we shall see, is *agon* or conflict, which in Socrates' case comes with generous helpings of dialectical reasoning.

The assumption has long been that dialectical reasoning is by nature *dialogic* – an interpretive error that bore consequences in the development of the art of psychotherapy. But Socrates' dialectical reasoning, the to and fro in his way of questioning, is not, properly speaking, *dialogical*. Or: it is dialogical only in the predominant meaning of the term, i.e. dialectical. In other words, Socratic dialogue may use dialectics, but there is *no real encounter taking place*. The interviewer asks questions in order to draw out (*educere*) an allegedly pre-existing truth from the interviewee. The therapist/interviewer is the one who knows best, even when she might be paying lip service to the now fashionable theoretical stance of 'not-knowing'.

Secondly, dialectical reasoning is an essential part of what can be identified as a *reactive* force. In dialectical reasoning, the natural exuberance of the life force is already waning and nearly spent. Socrates' shrewd, articulate questioning aims at *justifying* life, whereas *active* forces celebrate it. There are ways of conceiving the therapeutic encounter *outside* dialectical reasoning, ways that are refreshingly non-dialectical. The non-dialectical domain has been referred to as the domain of accident (Bazzano, 2012a; Webb, 2018). This idea is already latent in the writings of Buber (2004) himself, the champion of the Philosophy of the Meeting, and is radically different from the popular misconception that imagines the I-Thou encounter as something that two people can manufacture once the right conditions are created.

Against dialectical reasoning and even, I would add, against the more appealing notion of encounter, Nietzsche's early writings (1872/2000, 1872/2006b) point towards a quality of meeting that is more akin to what I have variously described as *poetry* (Bazzano, 2012a) as well as *grace* (Bazzano, 2018a) – drawing, respectively on the primacy of aesthetics and of immanent spirituality. In Nietzsche's terms, this equals a threefold re-affirmation: (a) of the *tragic* in human life; (b) of ancient *Greek drama* as representational model; and (c) of *Dionysus* as the presiding (affirmative/affirming) god. The difficult task for a philosophical/psychotherapeutic practice consists in retrieving this (un)holy trinity from the concerted onslaught at the hands of reactive forces.

a   Affirmation of the *tragic* means, at its basic level, developing the ability to embrace the joys and sorrows of existence. This is the beginning of a gradual process of leaving behind the human for the overhuman, which, in this particular context, means recognizing the indissoluble link between the self and the world, and gradually coming to the great affirmation, what Nietzsche calls, improving on Spinoza's *amor Dei* (love of God), *amor fati* (love of destiny).
b   Affirmation of *tragedy*, as in the ancient dramas of Aeschylus and Sophocles, invites 'mystical participation'. The intensity set free by the action on the stage viscerally unifies actors and spectators. It becomes direct expression of the god who presides over the event and to whom the dramas are dedicated: Dionysus.
c   *Dionysus* is an elusive, ambivalent incarnation of immanence, reminding us that transformation – in art, in life, as in therapy – happens through a process of dismemberment, fragmentation (for instance of the atomistic self) and an opening to the sublime ordinariness of being in the world.

Retrieving even only a glimpse or taste of the tragic spirit is almost impossible. The tragic has died so many deaths that it is now almost vanished from the world and survives in everyday language only as reference to what is extremely distressing or sad. It suffered three separate, lethal blows at the hands of, respectively, Socratism, Christianity, and (Hegelian) dialectics. These three cultural phenomena together represent the quintessence of reactivity or, in Nietzsche's parlance, *decadence*, i.e., an attitude of life denigration. However, finding possible openings within each of these three cultural tendencies is far more preferable to either dreaming up an implausible return to the Arcadia of pre-Socratic 'Being' as well as to taking on the attractive, cosy stance of the principled outsider. Furthermore, active engagement with each of these life-denying stances will allow us to know these dominant narratives intimately, so as to subvert them more effectively. Let us look at each of them separately.

a   In the case of *Socratism*, the task is to bypass the Platonism of maieutics and give greater emphasis to the element of agon already present in Socratic dialogue. This implies decentring power away from the philosopher/midwife and placing the heart of education in *exteriority*, i.e. in the genuine disorientation and truer learning that comes with being exposed to otherness. For this task – a political one before being psychological – the radical ethics of hospitality championed by Levinas (1961), Derrida (Derrida & Dufourmantelle, 2000) and Jankélévitch (2005) offer inspiring developments to the deconstruction of morality boldly initiated by Nietzsche.

b   In the case of *Christianity*, the death of God can be reformulated as the end of transcendence and affirmation in its place of *immanent spirituality*. This entails that for self-proclaimed atheists the field of perception is potentially widened and can reclaim experiences conventionally precluded to the non-religious. This would make some of us more able to work more effectively with clients who bring the numinous dimension into the therapy room. It also opens one's exploration to subversive readings of Christianity and immanent theology (e.g. Yoder, 1994; Barber, 2014).

c   Hegelian *dialectics*, representing modernity's proverbial last straw that breaks the tragic spirit, can also be reversed in favour of the tragic. It is true, for example, that from a Nietzsche-inspired perspective, power is in Hegel's master/servant dialectic still only representational, rather than being immediate or 'true' power. Crucial to Hegel is *Anerkennung* (recognition/acknowledgement). In Nietzsche's terms, this implies that in order to fully accept myself, I first need recognition from others. But this is already an improvement from the current cult of the relationship in which therapy is currently enmeshed, for inherent in Hegel's *Anerkennung* is the reality of conflict, essential in shaping an under-standing of self and kinship alongside love and kinship. It is from the active acceptance of the inescapable presence of conflict in human relations that access can be found back to the tragic spirit. The same conflict and struggle found in encounter are also found at the heart of the contested life.

In a way, it does not matter which pathway to the tragic we choose. What is crucial is gaining a glimpse of it. What is common to all routes is, at first, the indistinct per-ception of *intensity* that is subsequently translated into subjective feeling, passion and emotion, both 'positive' and 'negative'. This is a first glimpse, through the domain of affect, of Dionysus – a 'god' who does not justify or redeem existence but affirms it. Dionysian affirmation goes beyond the need to resolve life's inherent suffering, whether in Schopenhauerian or 'Buddhist' fashion. It also bypasses the rationalism of Socrates and his famous daimon, a voice that at all times "dissuades" (Nietzsche, 1872/2000, p. 75). For the young Nietzsche, writing in 1872, the above is an example of Socrates' perversion. But what is it exactly that Socrates' daimon *perverts*? It is the natural "instinct" that characterizes "all productive people". The "creative-affirmative force" is criticized, dissuaded, and exposed by the Socratic daimon and its "uncontrolled" rationalism – a particularly virulent form of rationalism, one that is "developed in excess" (Nietzsche, 1872/2000, p. 75).

Socrates is for Nietzsche the first great decadent thinker. *Decadence* in Nietzsche's vocabulary does not indicate the enjoyment of forbidden pleasures in opium dens among velvety pillows, as the colloquial use of the term may suggest. It designates instead detachment from life, and in Socrates' case viewing it as something one needs to judge and redeem. This is the decadence of rationalism, i.e. the elaborate strategy of elevating reason to the highest value as a rampart against the intensity of life – a rationalism born out of the fear of being incapable of upholding this intensity.

Another influential form of decadence which those wishing to apply Nietzsche's ideas to psychotherapy must contend with is Christianity, a truly formidable opposition to the tragic spirit. The Christian worldview looks at life as needing redemption, this time not through dialectical reasoning but through suffering. It presents us with a double bind: life is "blameworthy because it suffers" and "it must suffer since it is blameworthy" (Deleuze, 1962/2006, p. 14). Life has to be crucified, than resurrected. Nietzsche's Dionysian thought presents us instead with a *tragic* perspective: it states that with all its exhilarating joys, agonizing sorrows – with its tedium, anguish and limitless power – life is both *innocent* and *fair*.

This very same notion was already present in Heraclitus. Life does not need validation, explanation, or deliverance. This perspective is not animated by the spirit of revenge but embraces life's plural joy. In this sense, the alternative to crucifixion is *dismemberment* – no less painful, no less poignant, but ultimately life-affirming. In the mythological account that will much later reverberate in the crucifixion, Dionysus Zagreus is dismembered and eaten by the Titans; but Zeus ground up his heart, put it in a concoction, and gave it to Semele to drink, who then was pregnant with Dionysus (Grant, 1960). While the crucifixion speaks of purging and death, dismemberment stands for the tragic joy of existence's inherent multiplicity.

Carrying the cross

Despite feeling a lot better lately, Dan often referred to the noonday demon of depression he had experienced years ago. Once or twice he described how bad it had been: the utter desolation, the sense of being terminally wrong. Above all, the unbearable pressure from what he called the 'inner judge'. At times he felt unsure, he said, and even suspicious of his current serenity and of those moments of real contentment he had experienced lately. As if you don't deserve it? – I asked. No, it wasn't quite like that. It was a real solace, he added, being able to talk freely here, expressing whatever came up without the strong pressure of the inner judge. When growing up, being emotional and expressing feelings was seen as self-pity and looked down upon in his family. He learned self-compassion and became interested in art. He became an artist, very successful at one point, experiencing what he called 'the illusion of fame'.

In later sessions, the recurring question was: Where is my moral compass? His main worry now was that he didn't feel worried. He just couldn't stand people who rationalized their behaviour, he said. Was he becoming like them? In the past, the critical voice was externalized – the one person voicing it loud and clear was his ex, Roxanne. Now that they had split up, now that Roxanne was no more around, the same critical refrains had become louder inside his head. The punishing voice, Dan called it. What is it? Why does it show up? His fear, voiced more clearly as sessions went on, was that without this self-punishing, critical voice, now inside his head, he would lose his moral compass. It didn't matter that this very same voice had brought him misery and depression in the past, he said, because depression had been a crucifixion, and when he had come out of it he was a new person, a better person, a more moral person. Stories like the crucifixion, he said, surely had a deep meaning, even if one was not religious.

Nietzsche saw clearly that the blow to the tragic spirit dealt by Christian morality cuts deep and leaves its mark even among artists like my client Dan who, despite having long left behind the trappings of religion, find the seed of life denigration in their heart and mind. There is one thing, Nietzsche writes, that "triumphed over the Christian god: Christian morality itself" (1882/1974, p. 307). It was "Christian conscience [that became] translated and sublimated into a scientific conscience, into intellectual cleanliness at any price" (ibid.). He goes on to say:

> Looking at nature as if it were proof of the goodness and governance of a god; interpreting history in honour of some divine reason, as a continual testimony of a moral world order and ultimate moral purposes; interpreting one's own experiences as pious people have long enough interpreted theirs, as if everything were providential, a hint, designed and ordained for the sake of the salvation of the soul – that is *all over* now.
>
> *(Nietzsche, 1882/1974, p. 307)*

All of the above has been overcome, he writes, by the "good Europeans" (ibid.), who have brought a new courageous and generous spirit that has, among other things, questioned the legitimacy of nationalism and anti-Semitism in the name of an inspired cosmopolitanism. His is a vision of Europe as cradle of open-minded scepticism, and was later to become a deconstructive force of critical thought, fostering the blossoming of writers who fled wars and holocausts, or left voluntarily: Joyce, Beckett – the latter preferring France at war to Ireland at peace; a Europe that gave us, among other things, existentialism and phenomenology. Nietzsche's optimism in this matter sounds sadly quaint now, with far-right bigotry and intolerance gaining traction all over Europe and elsewhere.

Bad players and good players

"It is necessary" – Nietzsche writes in his posthumous fragments – "to disperse the universe, to lose respect for the whole" (cited in Deleuze, 1962/2006, p. 21). What is affirmed in Nietzsche through the revival of the tragic spirit is *innocence* – the innocence of becoming. Innocence is "the truth of multiplicity" (Deleuze, 1962/2006, p. 21). How would a first glimpse of innocence manifest in relation to human psychology? We would need to suspend our belief in a free will existing in a neutral subject that we imagine as separate from her actions. With the deed, comes the ability to interpret it. Both deed and interpretation are innocent as well as infinite. Innocence is broken when we decide to hold on to a particular interpretation that bolsters our sense of separate entities endowed of free will. We then create misshapen images of force and will; "we separate force from what it can do". We label it as "'worthy' when it holds back from what it cannot do" (Deleuze, 1962/2006, p. 21), and 'blameworthy' when it manifests fully. We become bad players in the innocent game of existence, calling evil those manifestations of force whose intensity we are incapable of sustaining.

Heraclitus, the first thinker of becoming, helps us retrieve a vital glimpse of innocence. For him – against the entire philosophical tradition instigated by Socrates and Plato – there is *no being behind becoming*; also, there is nothing beyond phenomena. The latter are not 'illusions', nor are they mere 'appearance': phenomena are semblance (*Schein*), 'that which arises' (the literal meaning of 'phenomenon'), and their manifestation is invariably multiple. They are not interconnected by cause and effect, but promiscuously linked by what the Buddhist philosopher Nagarjuna (150–250 AD) called dependent co-arising (Park, 2006). What is convincingly denied by these thinkers of becoming is the alleged *unity* of an imaginary *whole*. What begins to emerge in our investigation is that these intimately linked factors – appreciation of becoming, celebration of the innocence of existence – also constitute a necessary adjunct to any endeavour that is inspired by phenomenology. The latter cannot be mere prelude to an investigation about 'Being', but needs to be alive through active participation in multiplicity. The phenomenologist then becomes a *good player*. What makes a good player? Thinking that the universe has no purpose whatsoever, no sense of 'evolution' and 'progress', no sense of 'loss' and 'gain', and abandoning these notions when playing our part in the throwing of the dice. What makes a good player? Substituting the venerable old pairs of causality/finality and probability/finality with the Dionysian pairs of chance/necessity and chance/destiny (Nietzsche, 1883/2006a).

Madness and love of wisdom

As 'love *of* wisdom' (*philo-sophia*), philosophy, a term coined by Plato, suggests that the love in question is for something that is at a slight remove, and that one's love of it may recover that wisdom. There is, in other words, a *rupture* between wisdom and the love of wisdom that is philosophy (Colli, 1975). This rupture is between an oral tradition that in 600 BC and 500 BC was one with poetry, divination, and myth, and the more systematized attempts at retrieving it that take place with Plato and Socrates and the birth of dialectical reasoning – of philosophy as we know it.

There appears to be a fundamental split in Plato's psyche, and consequently at the origins of the Western philosophical tradition. Himself a gifted poetic spirit, he was contemptuous of poetry, in his view, an imitation of things about which the poet knows nothing about, as well as a craft that appeals to our inferior faculties and distracts us from the pursuit of truth. He dissociated dialectical reasoning from poetic imagination and reverie, giving primacy to the former. This dissociation has proved fatal to Western civilization and culture. In Nietzsche's version of its history, Platonism – "the worst, most wearisomely protracted and most dangerous of all errors" (Nietzsche, 1886/1978, p. 14) – paved the way for the Judaeo–Christian model of religion which is *the* way we still understand religion today (in the West and beyond) and, consequently, for how we understand ourselves and our experience in the world. Plato and his teacher Socrates inherited a culture that had elevated divination – practised by other peoples and civilizations before them – to the highest level of refinement and to the role of vital symbolic power. Delphi, home to the legendary oracle of the god Apollo, represented the very peak of this culture. The god spoke in riddles – seemingly malevolent at times, at all times ambivalent – and his riddles had to be interpreted because, in the words of Nietzsche's favourite philosopher of antiquity, Heraclitus, the god neither reveals nor conceals, but *hints*. The differentiation between enigma and decoding of the enigma is a fairly modern phenomenon, whose articulation we partly owe to Schopenhauer and later, to Nietzsche himself. This distinction between 'raw' reality and representation is self-evident to us. Obvious reverberations can be found, for instance, in psychotherapy and supervision practice. It is the distinction between the client's 'direct' experience and how this becomes filtered and articulated further in therapy and via the therapist's and the client's inevitable interpretative layers. But for the ancients, this differentiation was neither clear-cut nor feasible. The god Apollo, whose name, lest we forget, means 'the one who destroys completely', is referred to in the *Iliad* as 'the archer who brings death' (through sickness). He spoke through the enigmatic pronouncement of the priestess at Delphi. Apollo strikes from afar; his message may be mediated but is communicated to us through the *madness* of the oracle; the priestess or prophetess communicates it in a state of trance. Socrates' own view on the madness of the priestess in *Phaedrus* is of a divine gift for individuals and communities alike. There are, according to this view expounded by Plato, four types of madness: prophetic, mysteric, poetic and erotic, with the last two being variations of the first two.

From all of the above it could be inferred that Apollo is at heart the god of madness, and that, at variance with the commonly held view, there is a fundamental similarity between him and Dionysus. This would allow, as it were, a 'division of labour' between Apollonian poetic folly and Dionysian erotic folly. At any rate, there appears to be much more complexity to pre-Socratic thought and the multi-layered world it mirrors than one would suspect at first. By flinging open that mysterious back door held tightly shut by Socrates, Plato and the entire Western tradition, the young Nietzsche unlocked our perception to a world hitherto unknown. This is an unprecedented act of daring in the history of thought that bears important consequences, with some of the implications directly concerning the world of psychotherapy. The first thing it does is to confirm in philosophical language what we had already hazily glimpsed via the work of the great tragedians Sophocles and Aeschylus. Not only does it give us a peek into the magnificent and terrifying world of the pre-Olympian gods. Not only does it recreate the link, severed by the Platonist tradition and so vital for contemporary psychotherapy, between philosophy, art, and poetry. It also gives us a mythical narrative that, being so imaginably removed from the Bible's, allows us to partake of another psychic landscape. At this point in our investigation, a brief foray into the pre-Socratic cultural and mythical milieu that Nietzsche draws upon, may help grasp more fully the importance of his contribution.

Old and new gods

Prometheus Bound (Aeschylus, 1978) was the first of a trilogy of plays written by Aeschylus (525–456 BC). Of the other two, *Prometheus Unbound* and *Prometheus the Fire-Bringer*, sadly only a few fragments remain. In the opening scene, Prometheus is chained to a rock; he has been so for a long time – a punishment administered by Zeus, son of Cronos, for daring to steal a spark of divine fire and bring it to humans. He is one of the Titans, gigantic sons of Earth created by gods and endowed with great strength. He is unusual among them in that he possesses intelligence and a love of justice. He is an immortal, but moved by the human plight; he understands the sadness and tragic irony of our situation as transient beings.

Humans had been created by the gods during the pre-Olympian reign of Cronos, following the reign of his father Ouranos. Until that moment, we had lived servile and squalid lives; the gods realized that creating us had been a mistake, and nevertheless decided to keep us alive because our species provided them with an unadulterated source of amusement. Prometheus helps human beings by teaching them agriculture, language, mathematics, harnessing of animals, and sailing. He also taught medicine, divination, and mining. Towards the end of the play, he speaks of an ancient prophecy according to which Zeus will be destroyed unless he is warned beforehand. Hermes, the messenger god sent by Zeus, appears and tries in vain to negotiate with Prometheus. As the latter proudly refuses, the thunder gathers around him and the earth begins to shake, while Prometheus calls on the elements to witness his plight.

Towards the beginning of the play, just before he hears a sound in the "fragrant air", the Chorus of Oceanids, daughters of Ocean, approaching on a winged chariot to soothe him and console him, Prometheus calls nature to witness the fact that he will not see "the star of [his] deliverance" (Aeschylus, 1978, p. 24) rise; that his gift of prophecy grants him the knowledge of "exactly everything that is to be; no torment will come unforeseen", adding: "my appointed fate I must endure as best I can" (ibid.). He asserts a fundamental theme present in all of Greek tragedies. No one, not even the gods, not even Zeus, is immune to necessity or fate.

Oresteia, or the Oresteian trilogy, is considered not only Aeschylus' most accomplished work, but one of the greatest achievements in art. The three plays – *Agamemnon, The Libation Bearers*, and *The Eumenides* – depict in their trajectory the quintessence of the pre-Socratic world that inspired Nietzsche.

Agamemnon begins hours after the eponymous king's capture of Troy and ends with his assassination at the hands of his wife Clytemnestra. As with other plays, glory and ignominy, rise and fall are all within the arc of fate; they are two sides of the same coin. 'Nothing fails like success' was, back in the day, a popular slogan among hippies and dropouts or among those who, like me, spent part of their youth in India. In Greek tragedies, success and glory are themselves dangers. What the heroes and heroines of Aeschylus' and Sophocles' tragedies have in common is that they fully understand and accept their fate, for they play an active role in shaping the destiny/destination of their fate.

With the throne, Agamemnon inherited the curse of the house of Atreus. This is another familiar theme in Greek tragedies; it tells us that our fate, though individualized, is embedded within complex family structures and dynamics that go way back for generations. The larger ancestral psychic domain clients carry with them is relevant to psychotherapy but is seldom explored, despite our profession's avowed intention of paying heed to embedded social relatedness. The presence of fate, its silent course through generations, its dramatic surfacing at crucial moments when individuals are asked to respond by making difficult choices – all this is vividly portrayed throughout the Oresteia trilogy and is relevant to our present investigation. What is also evident, and equally relevant, is the centrality of justice. For what is justice, at heart? And how much is justice related to vengeance?

The changes that the notion of justice undergoes through the three plays are momentous. It begins with brutal vengeance and it ends, by the final scene of the trilogy's third play, *The Eumenides*, with the casting of a vote in the Athenian court – with the redirection of the violent 'eye for an eye' stance into the court room presided over by the goddess Athena and the acquittal of Orestes for the murder of his mother Clytemnestra. In many ways, this charts an arc of progress, one that reflects the coming into life of the new Athenian democracy, some 30 years after the Persians' defeat at Marathon and the expulsion, by the end of 600 BC, of most tyrants. By this point Aeschylus, who had spent his youth in the midst of wars and tyrannies, is celebrating with his contemporaries the birth of a new and difficult democracy. But the old question on the nature of justice had not gone away and is played out in the tragedies. Above all, the difficult conundrum to be explored through the medium of art was whether the new notion of democratic justice could easily sit with the complex and competing demands of religion, with the power of human feelings and the obstinate presence of fate. What is meant here by 'competing demands' are the radically different claims of *two* religions: (a) the old, pre-Olympian, chthonian religion of the underworld dealing with the dark forces, working at appeasing them, and predominantly associated "with fear and mourning" (Vellacott, 1977, p. 16); (b) the new, Olympian religion that came into life through *theomachy*, i.e., the struggle and competition of the new gods against the old ones (above all, of Zeus against Cronos), and whose main characteristics, as the enduring presence of the Olympic Games testifies to this day, are "dancing, athletic and dramatic performances [as well as] feasting" (ibid.). Indeed, all the dramas mentioned here were written and performed under the auspices of the new religion. The same applies to the establishing of laws, military traditions and recognized dynasties. Old and new religion – or worldview – coexisted in the new world of Athenian democracy, at times uneasily. But the (near) taming of the Furies or

Erinyes in the trilogy's last play (almost) testifies to the victory of the new order. Within the old chthonian worldview, the role of the Furies – infernal goddesses, personified curses, or ghosts of the murdered – was to chastise those who had committed either acts of sacrilege against the gods, deceitfulness towards guests or hosts, or the shedding of familial blood. All three transgressions threatened human society, and the Furies' hounding of wrongdoers rebalanced the scale of justice through vengeance, and was considered a service, hence their epithet *Eumenides*, or 'Kindly Ones'– both tribute to them and desire to appease them. Vengeance then turns into the rule of law and the Furies are called upon to bring their case within a court: a democratization that is also candid recognition of an even thread between lust for gruesome revenge and the cool administration of justice in court.

Enter the counsellor

Written some 30 years after the battle of Marathon in 490 BC, which signalled the birth of democracy in Athens, Aeschylus' tragedies are still relevant today. Robert Icke's 2016 adaptation of the Oresteia at the Almeida in London (Icke, 2015) tried to make it even more contemporary by adding bold changes to the original. Among these is the cinematic device of young Orestes recounting the events that befell his family, including his own crime, to a female counsellor. Orestes has killed his mother Clytemnestra who in turn killed her husband Agamemnon who had killed his daughter Iphigenia. The play asks profound questions about the relation between vengeance and justice. Orestes was spurred on by no less than a god, Apollo, and Clytemnestra in turn avenged the murder of her daughter by killing her husband, an act that also manifests her indignation as a woman in a society that granted personal liberty and social and political responsibility to men alone.

In the dialogues between Orestes and the counsellor, Orestes tries to understand, make out truth from falsity, story from reality. We witness familial scenes around the dinner table which resemble a depraved version of a Marks & Spencer's catalogue, designed to highlight the eminently current dilemmas of any male politician consumed by skirmishes, terror and vainglory, with little time for the wife and kids.

As the play progresses, the counsellor gradually turns into an investigator. Towards the end, she then turns into a full-blown accuser. This is both remarkable and disturbing, for it unwittingly hints at what the new role of the therapist has become in our society. A counsellor is normally committed to helping her clients explore and process traumatic experience in order to gain insight into destructive and self-destructive thoughts and behaviours. This in turn may prepare the ground for rehabilitation and healing. What the counsellor is doing here instead is effectively preparing her client to be slaughtered. She gathers evidence for the trial against Orestes, for the courtroom scenes that constitute the last part of the trilogy, *The Eumenides*. The kindly Furies, the true protagonists of this section of the Oresteia, are fiercely terrifying creatures unleashed on Orestes and ready to tear him to shreds. They may or may not represent his inner terrors and torments for having done something irretrievably dreadful. Orestes has committed a most heinous crime. He is of course guilty, and to assume that a therapist should merely help a murderer "explore his feelings" would amount to a vilification of the psychotherapist's role. And yet, as any practitioner who has counselled violent men will tell you, the therapy room is often the only place where difficult things can be explored, which in turn opens the door to healing. But what if the therapist turns into an investigator? First of all this is a caricature, attuned with a rather quaint notion of the shrink as detective, Freud as the Sherlock Holmes of the psyche. Secondly, investigation rather than opening unbiased exploration is on its way to becoming ammunition for indictment. In this case, the therapist simply holds a normative role, alongside judges, lawyers and prison wardens. She will uphold the dominant values of a particular society and enforce them on the troubled and the deviant – even when those values are not entirely noble or humane, or even common sense.

I am frankly dismayed at how therapy is increasingly being summoned in order to fulfil a normative role. But then we live in a culture where punishment still rules over rehabilitation. No wonder prisons in England and Wales are in a bad state, with inmate deaths and self-harming on the rise. I have supervised counsellors who work in prisons and had friends who worked as chaplains. Their work is besieged with difficulties, to put it mildly, and part of the problem is that they are often being seen as integral part of an institution that exists solely for punishment. How can therapy be effective in a society where the dominant mode towards offenders is punishment?

Therapy in an age of no culture

Writing specifically about supervision in art psychotherapy, Joy Schaverien (2007) considers situations where the psychotherapist is "spellbound and ... in need of the vision of another in order to break that spell". Supervision, she writes, helps "extract[ing] both therapist and patient from the spell that has woven them together" (p. 45). As a form of "framed experience" (Schaverien, 2007, p. 46), supervision resembles the theatre. There are, however, different ways of thinking about the theatre. Normally, the audience is in the auditorium and the actors are on the stage; both participate to some degree to the shared endeavour of make-believe. If anyone in the audience were to interpret the action on stage literally rather than symbolically, and decided to intervene in the action, he or she would contravene the implicit rules of drama. Similarly in psychotherapy:

> When the symbolic attitude collapses – the projection is taken for real – then there is a temporary loss of the "as if" meaning of the transference. Like our hypothetical member of the audience, the client, and sometimes the therapist, becomes identified with the transference and cannot separate from the unconscious projection.
>
> (Schaverien, 2007, p. 47)

It is important to emphasize (despite and maybe *because* of the canonical belief in the 'relationship' imposed by the current zeitgeist) that psychotherapy is first and foremost a *symbolic* domain. This alone grants the freedom and autonomy of the client in an atmosphere of openness and welcoming *neutrality*. For that reason alone, the theatre is a fitting metaphor for therapy.

However, from such an enlivening premise, Schaverien reaches a conclusion that is wholly aligned with conventional theatre as well as conventional therapy and supervision. She writes:

> Supervision plays a part in reinstating the symbolic attitude by helping the therapist regain a conscious stance. Supervision is then an essential form of *emotional cleansing*, offering separation from the projections and *restoring reality*.
>
> *(Schaverien, 2007, p. 47, emphasis added)*

What the writer has in mind is, I assume, an alignment of therapy with the theatre conceived in the *Aristotelian* mode. Earlier on in the text, in differentiating different types of drama, she had mentioned "tragedy [as a mode that] moves the spectator to tears, whilst aggression may induce fear" and so forth. Referring to Aristotle, she adds that tragedy constitutes "vicarious enjoyment in witnessing an intimate drama but being removed from it" (ibid., p. 47). There is an entirely different way to understand drama – and ancient Greek tragedy in particular – that does *not* resort to Aristotle's canonical beliefs. The opposite of emotional cleansing or catharsis takes place in the sort of drama Nietzsche is interested in: affective contamination and co-participation in the life of the magnificent monsters, i.e. of those powerful emotions and feelings that tend to overwhelm the self. For it is only by being affected first that deeper understanding can emerge – in the theatre as in therapy.

In his *Poetics*, Aristotle (1996) says the peak of Greek drama is reached with *anagnorisis*, the moment of self-recognition when the central character comes to understand something fundamental about herself. Borges toyed with a similar idea:

> Although a man's life is compounded of thousands and thousands of moments and days, those many instants and those many days may be reduced to a single one: the moment when a man knows who he is, when he sees himself face to face. I suppose that when Judas kissed Jesus (if indeed he did so), he felt at that moment that he was a traitor, that to be a traitor was his destiny and that he was being loyal to that evil destiny.
>
> *(Borges, 2000, pp. 99–100)*

For Nietzsche, this moment of self-knowledge is simply unattainable. He refuses Aristotle's notion of anagnorisis in the same way as he refuses the other, even more influential Aristotelian idea of *catharsis*, universally thought as a key aspect of drama. As he sees it, in tragedy there is transformation or transfiguration but no self-recognition: "the self is not found but *achieved*" (Strong, 2004 p. 197, emphasis added). This liberating idea is incomprehensible in contemporary culture as in the world of psychotherapy. As a result, we may fail to honour the self that the client or patient has managed to construct until now in favour of our own fantasy of an authentic or true self that will emerge one fine day. We call therapy successful if it helps the person shed one layer of personality that we deem false and inauthentic in favour of another construct, another layer that we applaud as genuine and congruent. The reasons we do this are embedded in the culture, or rather 'no culture': for "ours is not … a time readily available to tragedy" (ibid., p. 198).

If it is true, as Tracy Strong says, that it is "tragedy [that] made the growth of Greek culture possible", in comparison "we live in an age of 'no culture'" (Strong, 2004, p. 198). The first urgent question for a psychotherapeutic tradition worth its salt may then be the following: How can we help *create* a culture? This might entail a process of education as much as of psychic exploration and healing. Above all, it could mean an "involved distance … from one's own world" (ibid., p. 198).

An *involved distance* is the very opposite of what is taking place at present. Neoliberal ideology has been formidably successful in selling us the idea that, as consumers, we are no longer under the influence of any ideology and that psychology, as a science, is a matter of expertise, knowledge and academic specialization. As with the sunny brochures and websites of universities and training institutes – all green meadows, pensive smiles and integrated ethnicities, a little embellishment to a ruthless and philistine pragmatism comes via noticeable lip service paid to self-discovery, self-development and self-proclaimed love of diversity.

This brings to mind another association: the linking of philosophy, from Aristotle onwards, with wonder. All philosophy starts in wonder – how cute – until Nietzsche comes along and spoils the fun by saying that philosophy starts in *fear*. The grassy meadows and the wondrous contemplation – in psychology and psychotherapy as in philosophy – cover up the real engine and the chief motivation that drive it all: profit for the corporations and for the centres of learning turned into businesses and entrepreneurial ventures. And if we pursue our unveiling, in Nietzschean fashion, what do we find at the heart of this blind humourless drive for profit? Fear, a tremendous fear of impermanence and futility. If we then ask the Nietzschean question: *who?* – What kind of person is thus driven – ruled by entirely reactive, uncreative forces? What kind of person is unable and unwilling to feel and be generous? Nietzsche has a name for this sort of person: *the last human*. I have offered my own, contingent version of the last human: *homo neoliberalis* (Bazzano, 2017a).

Fear and wonder

Homo neoliberalis goes to therapy in order to be reassured and sprinkle a touch of re-enchantment into little his/her fully dysfunctioning self, his/her thoroughly serviceable and mechanized existence. By talking to a fellow member of the same species for 50 minutes a week, he/she gets to bracket the digital confinement that glues him or her to a technological device. But there is some hope: the reawakened spark of wonder brought about by human communication may ignite fear. As with academic philosophy, the problem with academic psychology and the sort of psychotherapy that is taught at universities is that neither of them is frightening. For Nietzsche, what is lacking is, "*the* capacity to be frightened of what thought makes possible to us" (Strong, 2004, p. 199). This also implies that a reading of his thought that does not frighten us may well be a misreading. Could this possibly mean that if psychotherapy does not, on some level, frighten us, it cannot be of any real use to us? Fear, skilfully used for its transformative potential, can then become a guide in understanding ancient Greek culture and tragedy in particular. This is, admittedly, a stance that differs from the more fashionable mode of the Serenity Brigade, i.e. of those among philosophers and psychotherapists alike who are fond of praising the alleged imperturbability and serenity of antiquity in the way some of us wax lyrical about the presumed Eden of our gilded childhood. Of course, in order to seriously engage in philosophy one must first be "in the presence of a philosopher" (Strong, 2004, p. 204). Naive logic suggests that we would need to be in the presence of a psychotherapist as well as in a suitable setting in order for the experiment of psychotherapy to take place. But this setting would then be the very opposite of academic psychology, i.e., a place where the body of psychotherapy is weighed and measured before being placed into the coffin of fetishized knowledge.

There are, for Nietzsche, essentially *four lines of reasoning* that properly belong to the "philosophical voice" (Strong, 2004, p. 204), and any therapeutic orientation that claims to draw on the theory and practice of philosophy would do well to take notice.

a Philosophy is *destructive*; it is not its business to be positive, provide answers, and add a veneer of gravitas to the existing order. Its task is one of radical renewal of culture in the service of life itself – a stance that takes on religion *and* secularism, transcendentalism *and* scientism. Philosophy asks unsettling, untimely questions. Similarly, effective *care of psyche* (psycho-therapy) may need to move away from playing second fiddle to existing dominant ideologies and the demands of the market, and no longer lean on the unambiguous metaphysics of religion and/or the unspoken metaphysics of science.

b Philosophy occurs *in response to "the voice of another"* (Strong, 2004, p. 205, emphasis added). It is critique *and* appreciation (are they not one and the same? don't we engage and fight with what we love?) of existing philosophical voices, past and present, as well as in open dialogue, in honest and playful contest. This confronts head-on the cliques and petty politics of the more-congruent-than-thou variety and all those tribal, self-protective stances that plague our strange profession.

c Philosophy progresses *from fear to wonder*. Fright is the foundation; the affirmative response comes *after* the wakeup call brought about by a crisis. The latter is crucial in granting us a glimpse of the abyss or groundlessness. Awe is the common denominator in fear and wonder. A psychotherapy that shies away from the existential terror and the anxiety inherent in existence can only be skin-deep and will preclude access to true joy. This is the lesson Nietzsche learns from the Greek tragedians and the same dynamic, from terror to delight, can be an inspiration to the person, client or therapist, entering the psychotherapy domain.

d   Philosophy is another word for *authorship* – for finding one's own voice(s). Likewise, the therapeutic relationship is entirely instrumental to the above. We have lost sight of this primary task and enshrined intersubjectivity as the heart of the therapeutic endeavour instead. But the task of psychotherapy – if we are to use Nietzsche's parallel insights on philosophy – is to help the other become no less than a *genius of the heart.*

None of the above four reminders would be needed if we lived in a life-affirming culture. But this is not the case: Judaeo-Christian values, latent in secularism, have firmly established a non-culture based on the denigration of living-and-dying. It is for this reason that the philosopher has long ceased to be representative of a polity and has become instead an itinerant stranger who (given that both nation and culture were and are sold to vested interests) could not but conspire against nation and culture. The philosopher has earned the wholly justifiable mistrust of the indoctrinated flock, a fact that bears similarities with the suspicion that "priests of all religions" have always felt towards "innovative, inspired individuals in their midst" (Bazzano, 2006, p. 30). An uncannily similar mistrust, parcelled out in this case with a good dosage of anti-Semitism, was reserved at the dawn of the twentieth century for psychoanalysts and later (until the neoliberal/neopositivist colonization of psychology taking place since the 1980s) to psychotherapists.

A fierce dispute

Taking our clue from Nietzsche's general appraisal of Greek culture before its Socratic slide into rationalism (Nietzsche, 1872/2000), it may then be useful to be reminded of what philosophers and psychologists *can be* when living amidst a genuinely thriving culture rather than its pale surrogate. They are above all *physiologoi*, i.e. men and women of science, understood in this context as a discipline that requires: (a) a non-transcendental description of the world; (b) a good enough description of contingency and impermanence; (c) an appreciation of *agon* or conflict as inherent in human relating and existence (Strong, 2004). All three lead up to Dionysian wisdom. In contemplating them, it pains me to realize how all three, though effortlessly well-suited to the phenomenological project, have in reality been squandered in contemporary existential psychotherapy in favour of closeted transcendental narratives.

Taking on board Nietzsche's philosophical challenge means accepting as a given the fundamental agon envisioned by Plato in *Sophist* (White, 1991), which is a battle for the very soul of the philosophical (and psychotherapeutic) endeavour. It also means to stand firmly on the side of *becoming* against the entire canon of Western philosophy that has, from Plato onwards, posited the primacy of *being*. "It seems that there is something like a battle of gods and giants", Plato says; a fierce "dispute … over *being*" (ibid., p. 37).

Nietzsche's task – our task too, if we pluck up the courage to take on his legacy – is nothing less than *reversing* the outcome of this millennial battle and giving primacy to becoming. This would mean establishing the foundation of our philosophical thinking on Heraclitus rather than Plato. This would be our first task. After which, both notions of *being* and *becoming* eventually dissolve, once we become acquainted to be no longer attached to this fictitious duality.

Becoming, revisited

The task described above is not a task reserved for dangerous radicals and relativists on the fringes of psychotherapy; it is not solely the province of the philosophical counter-tradition. If one looks carefully, the primacy of becoming can be found hidden within the heart of the philosophical tradition too, though psychotherapy has been painfully slow in recognizing this. For instance, despite the unbridgeable gap separating him from Nietzsche, Hegel too, a prominent thinker *within* the tradition, is a disciple of Heraclitus. Like him, he greatly values *polemos* – the importance of struggle and conflict in human affairs – as well as becoming, the point of creative synthesis out of the impasse that gets us stuck in the opposition between the two abstractions of being and nothingness.

What does *becoming* mean in Nietzsche? Cox (1999) draws a twofold distinction. Becoming asserts, on the one hand, a *naturalistic* perspective on existence that counters all metaphysical apprehensions and strategies that forever posit "being, stasis, and eternity" in the background when describing the "ubiquity of change in the natural world" (ibid., p. 170). Becoming also portrays the bewildering array of perspectives that arise once we step into the river of life, in a world, that is, that "lacks a grounding essence" (ibid.). Both distinctions have tremendous value for psychotherapy, helping us to free our practice from the shackles of metaphysics and the fixation with the atomistic unity of the self.

A common view among those of us who are justly critical of a positivist stance is to think of becoming as the ineffable life beyond the reach of our senses and mental constructions. At times corroborated by the Wittgensteinian adagio *whereof one cannot speak, thereof one must be silent*, this position, appealing in a vaguely mystical way, represents a step back, a regression to Kant's noumenal sphere. It assumes a division between things as they appear and things in themselves, a division endorsed by early Husserl and several phenomenological therapists. Nietzsche's view of human experience as incarnate within a plural world of becoming cuts right through the above division. His loyalty to Heraclitus is unwavering, and presents us with a loving and aching immersion in a groundless world of multiplicities that does not require metaphysical justification and moral/religious redemption in order to be praised. In *Twilight of the Idols* (1888/1998), philosophers are berated for "their lack of a sense of history, their hatred of the very notion of becoming, their Egyptianism" (p. 18). Philosophers believe that praising anything has to mean de-historicizing it, eternalizing it and gazing at it in universalizing terms. The same applies to many psychotherapists today. History and becoming are yet to gain primacy in psychotherapy. So far, we are only acquainted with their semblance, for instance in notions of embodiment that either tilt towards reductive materialism by making of the body the final port of call or bestowing on it the idealized, subjective aura of the knowing soul.

It is for these reasons that Heraclitus, via Nietzsche's reading, becomes crucial to a re-visioning of psychotherapeutic practice. Heraclitus does away with the notion of being, salvaging philosophical practice from the errors of Parmenides and the Eleatics. This is an ongoing task, given that the error (of conceiving and speaking of 'being') was grandly resurrected by Heidegger and perpetuated by scores of existential/humanistic psychotherapists after him. Heraclitus alone (amidst a multitude of ancient worshippers of being) taught us to honour and trust the senses, and take on board their living testimony. He alone among the thinkers of antiquity saw being as empty fiction and affirmed *semblance*, a phenomenal world looked upon with disdain by thinkers who anticipated the systematized denigration of life at the hands of the Judaeo-Christian tradition. A weighty appreciation of Heraclitus is found in *Philosophy in the Tragic Age of the Greeks* (Nietzsche, 1962), a text unpublished in his lifetime, where Nietzsche's naturalism comes to the fore in his refutation of being in favour of the innocence of becoming. The latter is characterized as the affirmation of an artist's view of the world rather than a moralist's; it also confronts philosophical/religious notions of essence and substance.

Humane positivism

In person-centred therapy it is assumed – rightly, I think – that the person coming to therapy is in a state of *incongruence*. This is an interesting term of Latin origin that speaks of *non-meeting* and discrepancy, in this case between the entirety of one's organism and the self-concept, i.e. the notion one holds about oneself. It is also generally assumed – wrongly, I think – that 'successful' therapy means the coming together of organism and self-concept, "a process whereby [the person] becomes [the] organism – without self deception, without distortion" (Rogers, 1961, p. 111). Laudable as this is as an *aspiration* towards greater understanding and active acceptance of one's situatedness in the world, the claim that congruence can one day be realistically 'achieved' smacks of positivism, albeit of the rosier kind. An astute reframing of incongruence as inherent to human existence comes from Devang Vaidya (2016, p. 180):

> Firstly, incongruence is at the genesis of the self; self emerges out of a portion of the experiencing organism, therefore whilst it overlaps with the organism to some extent, it cannot do so entirely. Secondly, due to the inter-connectedness of the human organism with its surrounding environment, both congruence and incongruence are experience-specific and context bound. No person can be regarded as either congruent or incongruent for all times. Thirdly, with the infinite permutations of factors that constitute our phenomenal world, and with the certainty of death looming on the horizon of one's lifetime, "vulnerability and anxiousness" are ever-present to hand. Incongruence is thus an existential given.

The notion of incongruence can also be further problematized and redefined as *a state of being where reactive forces have gained the upper hand*. A person (or a society, a culture) is, without knowing it, ruled almost entirely by a fearful need for self-preservation, by *ressentiment* and passive aggression directed at those whom he or she perceives as having strength, creativity, health, and the ability to give and squander their resource out of sheer abundance. Incongruence can be conceived as reactivity in the sense of being incapable of aligning itself to *active* forces.

Vaidya is right in seeing incongruence as a given, but this is because within our 'no-culture', founded on the denial of tragic joy, organisms are ruled by a cluster of reactive forces. Kurt Goldstein (1939/1995) taught us that a sick organism naturally seeks self-preservation, whereas a healthy organism is naturally drawn to greater life. In self-preservation, there is an automatic shrinking of experience. 'Pathology' or incongruence can be then redefined as doomed attempts to achieve homeostasis, a neutral state where no stakes are made, no risks taken, and where no *pathos* (passion, intensity, as well as suffering) is allowed to go past the self's protective bubble. Pathology could then be defined as our fixation with an abstract and bloodless vision of normality, close perhaps to what Bollas (2011) calls 'normotic personality', present in those who are able to live "contentedly among material objects" and with a distinctive inability "to experience evolving subjective states" (p. 23), driven by a powerful desire to be and appear "normal" and where all semblances of an inner life with its inherent contradictions and difficulties is seemingly absent.

This type of personality can also be related to Joyce McDougall's (1980) notion of the *anti-analysand*, as well as to Helene Deutsch's fertile notion of the 'as-if' personality (Deutsch, 1942). Deutsch designated a particular form of mental distress: individuals who do not present at first any particular disorder or unusual behaviour, their "intellectual abilities appear[ing] unimpaired, emotional expressions … well ordered and appropriate" (cited in Russell, 2017, p. 302). These are socially adaptable, functioning people who nevertheless feel that 'something is wrong', although grasping what is wrong is very hard for both client and therapist.

Greater congruence can come to signify closer alignment with active rather than reactive forces. This state of being is never entirely achieved, nor has it ever been fully achieved. This is because, given the influence of two millennia of metaphysics and morality, human subjects are for Nietzsche essentially *reactive*. This is not pessimism on Nietzsche's part; a human animal, geared as it is to consciousness, knowledge, and the making sense of the vast natural and organismic life, is reactive *by necessity*. Our consciousness and ethics, our art, science and religion are designed to *react* to the felt text of nature. An active human in the process of transforming reactivity into activity, incongruence into congruence is neither a new human nor a person of tomorrow but a being at the very *edge* of the human, leaning towards what Nietzsche calls the *overhuman*. The jury is out as to whether the vision of the overhuman heralds an evolutionary leap. As I see it, this hypothesis is a little too neat and literal; it does not sit well with Nietzsche's nuanced style, with his subtlety and wit, or with his reluctance to provide final or programmatic statements.

The Apollonian is no picnic

Nietzsche is often alleged to have made a clear-cut dialectical distinction between an orgiastic and chthonic dimension (the Dionysian) and a light and orderly one (the Apollonian), but it is important to remember that the two forces (both present *in nature* hence in the psyche) coexist and influence one another. It is, for instance, the supposedly light and harmonious Apollo that in the second play of the Oresteian trilogy, *The Libation Bearers*, commands Orestes to avenge his father by killing his mother Clytemnestra and her lover Aegisthus. The jury is out as to whether Nietzsche overlooked, downplayed, or (as I am inclined to think) resolved in his mature writings this seeming contradiction by bringing forth a 'worked through' version of both the Dionysian and the Apollonian as an interplay of mutual forces. The tendency among scholars and psychologists has been towards oversimplification as much as sanitization, and while I wholeheartedly agree with those who point out that "the Dionysian is no picnic" (Paglia, 1991, p. 9), it must be said that the Apollonian is no picnic either. I would also add, adapting some insights from Massumi (1996), that it does not really matter to which plane of experience one appeals in the vain hope of finding consolation: "You get burned either way" (p. 227).

Apollo speaks through the Sybil without ornament or balm; the predictions and insights the god imparts via the oracle's frenzied speech are often harsh. Nietzsche may have missed this aspect of the Apollonian in favour of a more didactic representation. Perhaps, it has been suggested (Colli, 1975), he missed Apollo's inherent duplicity: he speaks harshly through the oracle while at the same time offering playful transfiguration through his favourite medium, art. There is harmony in the Apollonian, but it is a *conflicting harmony*, not the anodyne, pacified version of harmony we are accustomed to.

Apollo plays the lyre beautifully, but he also strikes his bow with lethal precision, both instruments made of the same material, the horns of the goat, sacred to Dionysus. Implicit in this dual nature is also perhaps a process of nonlinear transformation: art born out of fearless, frenzied speech. But also, crucially for the art of psychotherapy: wisdom and insight are born out of madness. This would imply the instituting of a craft that is not bent on sanitizing and controlling 'madness' but is instead able to learn from the threshold of its experience where it begins to speak and, in speaking, is painfully deciphered and interpreted. 'Interpretation' is necessary because, unless we romanticize 'madness', its message can, like Apollo's divination (alongside being a symptom of profound distress and acute suffering), be both hostile and lethal.

Plato does not mention Apollo in his dialogues, but he often refers to the Apollonian art of divination in *Timaeus* – a gift, he says, bestowed on folly rather than reason, a gift whose perception requires that our mind be obstructed by sleep or sickness. But a second person is needed, he insists, an interpreter able to discern a trace through the meandering reveries of the speaker, able to decipher through reason these wild visions so disjointedly communicated. This is the moment in the history of thought when the essential division is introduced between the frenzied oracle and the reasoning interpreter (Colli, 1975), with Plato's stance echoing and substantiating Empedocles', for whom the messages of the god were expression of an interiority that is concealed and obscure, and for that very reason *sacred*. Both disjointed speech and reasoned interpretation take place under Apollo's auspices.

It makes sense to conclude from the above that the practice of divination was sought after and greatly valued because it improved the social and political life of ancient Greece. Except that it didn't. As the plays of Aeschylus and Sophocles attest, complete faith in divination was one with utter blindness in the ethical and political life (Colli, 1975). Belief in fate is paradoxically married to lust for action bent on self-destruction. The two are intertwined and, within the Southern old chthonic worldview (strands of which survive within the new Athenian order), faith is not easily translatable into pragmatic mores of atonement and self-improvement that on Northern shores will, after lengthy gestation, give rise to Protestantism and its many epigones, psychotherapy included.

But 'care of the soul' cannot be made pliable to the moralistic demands of whatever ideology is predominant at any given time. Many rightly question the social and political validity of psychotherapy. Indeed, we have had *more* than 100 years of it and the world is getting even worse than Hillman and Ventura (1992) ever expected in the early 1990s, hence the cultivation of a robust scepticism in the role and purpose of one's own profession may be a desirable if overlooked virtue among psychotherapists.

Moreover, the old belief in fate is not incompatible with the arbitrariness of human deeds because belief in fate is at heart belief in capricious necessity rather than unmovable predictability; the gods may dictate stern rules to humans but they are themselves fanciful and unpredictable. Like the inorganic beings they often represent – river, thunder, wind – they embody, to human eyes, the conditions of freedom and lawlessness that an organic being tends to perceive as favourable conditions for playful discharge of their energies.

A brief history of the enigma

Within the old order, Apollo speaks through the enigma, i.e. allusively (*ainigma*, from *ainissesthai*, is 'to speak allusively'), one more indicator of his essential duplicity: a sign of artistry as well as cruelty. The Sphinx also reflects this duplicity: the ferocious animality in the haunches of a winged lion, the head of a woman; those who cannot answer her riddles perish and the only salvation (as with Oedipus, who answers correctly thus saving himself and the city of Thebes) is cleverness. At this stage enigma is still entwined with pathos. Answer to the riddle is a matter of life and death, not an exercise in cleverness; and for Nietzsche's beloved Heraclitus, *the enigma is key*. As we gradually move away from the chthonic worldview, the pathos of enigma begins to fade. In Plato's *Phaedrus* (Plato, 2005), the enigma still retains some import, albeit mystical, appearing when the object of thought is not expressed in words. By the fourth century, however, the pathos of enigma had wholly and truly vanished to make room for a society game, or used in education as mere 'mind training' and praised by Aristotle for the feats of similitude in rational discourse. Colli (1975) identifies three crucial phases the notion of enigma went through in ancient Greek culture: (a) the god Apollo inspires an oracular response and the interpreter translates the enigmatic pronouncements of the oracle into logos or rational discourse; (b) via the Sphinx, Apollo poses a dangerous enigma; (c) interpreters begin to compete for supremacy, each claiming the right interpretation. By this stage, the incisive and dangerous wisdom of the old chthonic world has given way to logical argument, dialectical reasoning and the cleverness normally associated with the philosophy of the Sophists, prelude to the discipline of rhetoric. With wisdom fading fast in the background, we first see the emergence of *love of* wisdom (philosophy) and this in turn becomes love of rhetorical knowledge and dialectical discourse. All pathos spent, the ruler in the Athenian agora by this point is discursive reason and Socrates its undisputed master. What still survives here is *agon*, the competitive spirit among rhetoricians, itself pale reflection of what is found in Homer, both in his epic poems but also in the anecdotal account of his death echoed in Heraclitus as well as Aristotle. According to this account, Homer died because he felt so disheartened for not being able to adequately respond to the following 'ordinary' riddle:

> Homer consulted the gods to know who were his parents and which was his homeland, and the god replied thus: "The island of Io is the homeland of your mother, and it will receive you when you are dead; but beware of the riddle of young men [...]"
>
> He reached Io. Here, seated on a rock, he saw some fishermen drawing near to the shore and he asked them if they had anything. Because they had not caught anything and had no fish, but were picking fleas off themselves, they answered him: "What we caught we threw away; what we didn't catch we carry with us", referring with a riddle to the fact that the fleas they had caught, they had killed and thrown away, and those they had not caught, they carried in their clothes. Homer, unable to solve the riddle, died of dejection.
>
> *(Aristotle, De Poetica, cited in Canestri, 2011, p. 49)*

For someone who, like Homer, enquires deeply within the nature of reality and the world, the inability to resolve an enigma can be deadly. The above example presents us with two implications. In the first, 'enigma' encompasses a wider, existential meaning. In this case, the 'solution' to a riddle is nothing less than the unlocking of a mystery, of something previously unknown or – which is perhaps its equivalent – the ability of the enquirer to live with/sustain the sheer mystery of existence and of his/her personal conundrum or *koan*. In the second instance, the death of the knowledgeable poet/scholar is more trivially the shame of not having been capable of upholding one's reputation as a clever person. In a more symbolic vein, and drawing on Heraclitus, the 'fleas' on the fishermen's clothes may represent the hidden and the unseen (Colli, 1975), and what the fishermen 'caught' are their perceptions of things. Not 'mere' perceptions; crucially, in Nietzsche's reading of Heraclitus, what is unique in this ancient thinker is the unwillingness to critique or degrade sensory perception and focus his investigation on the river of becoming rather than on the abstraction of being.

A musical ontology

Nietzsche wrote *The Birth of Tragedy* (1872/2000) aged 26, while on convalescent leave after a four-week experience, in September 1871, as a medical orderly on the western front lines of the Franco–Prussian war. There he had seen the dead being gathered from the fields, had gone with the convoy of the wounded and contracted diphtheria and dysentery. That first published work outlined for posterity a reading of ancient Greek culture that, scandalous at the time, is now the staple of academic knowledge. He famously distinguished between the *Dionysian* and the *Apollonian*. The horrific backdrop of war in which this idea was developed provides a necessary corrective to more simplistic dialectics that see the Dionysian as blissful revelry and the Apollonian as tranquil recollection. Blissful revelry is certainly part of the Dionysian, and so are the horror and the lust for destruction. Tranquil recollection is equally part of the Apollonian, and so are calculation, cold-blooded contest and the separation that gives birth to individuation. In an early draft, Nietzsche recounted how in the midst of the horror of the battlefield he strove to remain focused on his thoughts, and how lying together with the wounded soldiers in the freight car under a desolate night sky his thoughts drifted over the three abysses of tragedy – delusion, will, and despair.

In an early instance of what sadly became the common pattern of his creative life, the result of the publication of this ground-breaking work was a wounding rejection from the philosophical community and from his own mentor, Ritschl, as well as ejection from the Guild of Philologists. "My *Birth of Tragedy*", Nietzsche wrote in a letter to his friend Malwida von Meysen-Bug, "has made of me the most offensive philologist of the present day ... Everyone is of a mind to condemn me" (Nietzsche, 1969, p. 108). And in November of the same year, 1872, still holding a chair in philology at Basel University, he wrote to his then friend and mentor Richard Wagner:

> I have no students at all! ... The fact is, indeed, so easy to explain – I have suddenly acquired such a bad name in my field that our small university suffers from it! This agonizes me. A professor of classical philology at Bonn, whom I highly regard, has simply told his students that the book is sheer nonsense and is quite useless; a person who writes such things is dead to scholarship.
>
> *(Nietzsche, 1969, pp. 111–112)*

The style of *Birth of Tragedy* was judged too poetic, too polemical, and lacking in what we would today deem 'evidence-based' or 'scientifically detached' reasoning. More importantly, its insights were deemed unacceptable. Not only the scandalous notion that existence and the world are eternally justified as aesthetic phenomena, but also the disreputable idea that cruelty and horror are the bedrocks of sound cultural transformation (through ritualization and sublimation).

Nietzsche's philology mentor, Ritschl, was very late in responding to the publication of *The Birth of Tragedy* and Nietzsche had found this lack of early response intolerable. When the response finally came, it was devastating. Already in a letter to a colleague, Ritschl had lamented the fact that Nietzsche had squandered his methodological ability and scientific rigour by being too clever, too rhapsodic and even mystical.

Although both Kant's and Schopenhauer's influence is evident in the *language* Nietzsche uses throughout the book, partly relying on the terms set by Kant's opposition of noumenon and phenomenon as well as by Schopenhauer's metaphysics of will and representation, he does not merely reproduce them but introduces new *Dionysian* ideas. As a young writer who is still under their influence, however, he cloaks these new ideas in the old language.

Within a few years – particularly with the publication of *Human, all too Human* in 1878 (Nietzsche, 1984), his position on the matter will alter in favour of a more *naturalistic* view. Although at this early stage his insights surf on a distinctly late-Romantic wave of musical intensity, already in his preface to the second edition of *The Birth of Tragedy* we find, alongside critique, a greater appreciation of science, a stance that invites us to view the latter "under the optic of the artist, and art through the optic of science" (Nietzsche, 2000, p. 5).

The late-Romantic view belongs to a developmentally younger vision of the Dionysian (Bazzano, 2006), and it is clear from later advances in Nietzsche's writings – most notably in *The Gay Science* (Nietzsche, 1882/1974) – that "Dionysian" can also signify a naturalistic, anti-metaphysical ontology and epistemology. The received wisdom in Nietzschean scholarship roughly states that the Dionysian belongs wholly to his youthful enthusiasm and that his middle works are characterized by a more tranquil examination and detached psychological investigation. It is true that in his private pantheon psychology takes the place of art and that he ends up rejecting, at times with customary vehemence, some of the aesthetic and quasi-metaphysical statements present in *The Birth of Tragedy*. It is equally true that the idea of the Dionysian goes through an enriching progression (Bazzano, 2006) and that the expression 'Dionysian' continues to be used by Nietzsche in later years to designate his "naturalist and anti-metaphysical ontology" (Cox, 2006, p. 497), that is to say, a form of ontology that is distinctly *musical*.

This is due to the fact that music is very important to Nietzsche, with "remarks on the music of Beethoven, Bizet, Berlioz, Bach, Handel, Mozart, Schumann and others … sprinkled throughout" (Cox, 2006, p. 495) his work. If one took for a moment the liberty to substitute 'music' with 'reality' or 'the world' in the passage below from section 373 of *The Gay Science*, representing, among the three texts of his middle period, his "most mature philosophical position" (Ansell Pearson, 2006, p. 11), one could begin to get an inkling of what a musical ontology would sound like:

Assuming that one estimated the *value* of a piece of music according to how much of it could be counted, calculated, and expressed in formulas: how absurd would such a "scientific" estimation of music be! What would one have comprehended, understood, grasped of it? Nothing, really nothing of what is "music" in it!

(*Nietzsche, 1882/1974, p. 336*)

If Apollonian art relies on form and images (the solid poetry of sculpture and architecture being its privileged forms), Dionysian art falls back on music, an art without images. It is a simplistic dialectics that *opposes* the Dionysian to the Apollonian. It has been remarked (e.g., Cox, 2006) that the opposition is not even dialectical for it lacks an essential element of dialectics, sublation (Hegel's *Aufhebung*), a term simultaneously rendered as expansion, inclusion or synthesis. It is nevertheless justifiable, I think, to speak of different manifestations of Dionysus in Nietzsche:

> The early Dionysus is opposed, in the *Birth of Tragedy*, to Apollo: it is the Dionysus we know, the reveller, the God of the theatre, of madness and intoxication, of orgy and the dissolution of boundaries. The later Dionysus, still wild, still vibrant, is opposed, in *Ecce Homo*, to the Crucifix. He is *the God of passion sublimated*, as opposed to passion repressed. He is both Dionysus *and* Apollo. The power of the wild torrents of the soul has been harnessed, economized and put into service.
>
> (Bazzano, 2006, p. 142)

A tragedy is a 'goat song' (from *trago*, goat, and *ōidē*, song) – thus named because the prize in Athenian drama competition was a goat, and also because of its connection to satyrs, half-goat beings that were part of Dionysus's cortège. These are quite different from visions of the "idyllic shepherd of more modern times", a "man of the forest" that is "shamefully and timidly" portrayed by modern humanity as "a meek and mild flute-playing shepherd" (Nietzsche, 1872/2000, p. 47). Dedicated to Dionysus and infused with the after-effects and insights that follow what at the time Nietzsche saw as a fundamentally *untranslatable* Dionysian experience, the drama itself is possible only through Apollonian intervention:

> [W]e must understand Greek tragedy as the Dionysian chorus which again and again discharges itself in Apollonian world of images [...] Drama is the concrete Apollonian representation of Dionysian insights and effects and as a result a huge chasm separates it from epic.
>
> (Nietzsche, 1872/2000, p. 51)

What is essentially untranslatable (and necessitates Apollonian mediation via the artistic and literary forms presented by the tragedies of Sophocles and Aeschylus) is the tragic core of existence, the unbearable intensity of forces shaping the chaotic/creative movement of living-and-dying. These forces are not unreachable because supposedly akin to Kant's *noumenon* (a 'thing in itself' only indirectly perceived by our senses) or Schopenhauer's *will* (the foundational being of the world in relation to which the latter is representation). They may be instead compared to the sun: while it is *not* transcendent, its extraordinary intensity is nevertheless unbearable to our naked human eye. This is where Nietzsche's tragic perspective begins to emerge – a radical move within philosophy as well as a natural development from Kant and then Schopenhauer. Nietzsche's treatment of the Kantian opposition between appearance and thing-in-itself is "twice removed from Kant" (Cox, 2006, p. 499). The first, shrewd detachment from Kant was found in Schopenhauer, for whom the thing-in-itself is not an unknowable mediated by thought ... but one that can be experienced directly and physically (John Mackessy, personal communication). Schopenhauer *adopts* the Kantian dichotomy but in ways which are "peculiarly un-Kantian" (Cox, 2006, p. 499).

> [T]he thing in itself is known immediately in so far as it appears as [one's] own body, and only mediately in so far as it is objectified in the other objects of perception.
>
> *(Schopenhauer, 1966, p. 19)*

Schopenhauer succeeds in naturalizing Kant's distinction, but his formulation remains metaphysical because he accepts the general terms set by Kant, agreeing to placing the thing-in-itself "outside of space and time" (Cox, 2006, p. 499). This lingering metaphysical trace is obliterated by Nietzsche that sees Dionysian and Apollonian energies as *immanent* to life and the world.

The intensity of the Dionysian is both life-giving and life-destroying. It is life–death and death–life. Although Dionysian artists and philosophers acknowledge that this intensity is not directly accessible into the meaning-making, myth-creating human domain, they are nonetheless willing to affirm it and become, as it were, complicit with its power. The tragic view – some would say tragic pessimism – that emerges from Nietzsche's Dionysian perspective is thus transformed into a life-affirming stance that is far greater than the dominant rosy progressivism the West inherited from rational Socratic dialectic and its later expression, Hegelian dialectic.

Virtual and Dionysian

We also find in this stance full acknowledgement of the existence (alongside the domain of *actual*, observable 'subjects' and 'objects') of what Deleuze (2006) calls the *virtual*: the entire "flux of pre-individual, impersonal differences ... forces and affects that constitute these subjects and objects while also preceding and exceeding them" (Cox, 2006, p. 505). While it is true that both belong to the same plane (as there is only one plane according to Nietzsche, the plane of immanence), the latter are not available to empirical scrutiny. For instance, "geological pressures and movements, genetic codes and flows, relations of power and desire" (ibid.): none of these are accessible to consciousness. Acknowledging this is crucial to any psychotherapeutic orientation and practice keen to sustain some degree of intellectual honesty whilst steering well clear of two common pitfalls: transcendentalism and positivism. For these are, all things considered, two sides of the same coin, as they both claim capture of the virtual and the Dionysian (albeit through different idioms).

At its inception, psychoanalysis had come up with a formidable notion that helped somewhat find a way out of this historically recurring impasse: the *unconscious*. But the trajectory of this idea has been, at the very least, bumpy: it went from reification and sanctification (via royal roads, neutral highways and intersubjective dual carriageways) to progressive dilution ('making the unconscious conscious') and eventual evaporation ('there is no such thing as the unconscious; it is a matter of time until all of it will present itself to awareness').

Correlated notions and parallel ideas that in other theoretical approaches used to indicate the limitation of empirical knowledge and that recognized the essentially unknowable domain of experience – for instance the notion of *organism* in humanistic psychology (Rogers, 1961; Goldstein, 1939/1995; Perls, 1973) – have been similarly co-opted in recent years to serve either the neopositivist zeitgeist or to be inscribed within marginal transcendentalist narratives.

The polarization in psychotherapeutic discourse between positivist and transcendental narratives overlooks what is central in a Nietzsche-inspired perspective: the plane of immanence where both Apollonian and Dionysian forces are at play. The plane of immanence is a "variegated domain populated by forces in tension" (Cox, 2006, p. 505). It actualizes or brings forth "distinct entities through temporary condensations and contractions of forces and materials" (ibid.). Their seeming solidity and resilience provide us with an "illusion of transcendence" (Deleuze & Guattari, 1994, p. 80).

The almost exact equivalent is found in Nietzsche's thought: moments of crystallization in the dynamic flux of becoming give us the illusion of a static being. This particular point represents a crossroads to how we understand psychotherapy practice: by falling for the illusion and abstraction of *being* – no matter how historically, contextually and/or relationally determined our definition of being may be – we move fatally away from *life* and its rich ambiguity. In section 373 of book V of *The Gay Science*, Nietzsche writes:

> [S]o many materialistic natural scientists rest content nowadays [with] the faith in a world that is supposed to have its equivalent and its measure in human thought and human valuations – a "world of truth" that can be mastered completely and forever with the aid of our square little reason. What? Do we really want to permit existence to be degraded for us like this – reduced to a mere exercise for a calculator and an indoor diversion for mathematicians? Above all, one should not wish to divest existence of its *rich ambiguity*: that is a dictate of good taste, gentlemen, the taste of reverence for everything that lies beyond your horizon [...]
>
> A "scientific" interpretation of the world ... might therefore still be one of the *most stupid* of all possible understandings of the world, meaning that it would be one of the poorest in meaning.
>
> *(Nietzsche, 1882/1974, p. 335)*

Distinct and obscure

For Nietzsche there is no contradiction between unity and multiplicity. We find in his writings both affirmation of unity *and* plurality, the presence of a substratum that is both one *and* constituted by a vibrant interface of passions, affects, and forces. In *Beyond Good and Evil*, he writes:

Granted that nothing is "given" as real except our world of desires and passions, that we can rise or sink to no other "reality" than the reality of our drives — for thinking is only the relationship of these drives to one another —: is it not permitted to make the experiment and ask the question whether this which is given does not *suffice* for an understanding even of the so-called mechanical (or "material") world? [...]

Granted ... that one succeeded in explaining our entire instinctual life as the developments and ramifications on *one* basic form of will ...; granted that one could trace all organic functions back to this will to power ... — one would have acquired the right to define *all* efficient force unequivocally as: *will to power*. The world seen from within, the world described and defined according to its "intelligible character" — it would be "will to power" and nothing else.

(Nietzsche, 1886/1978, pp. 48–49)

Deleuze, like Nietzsche a philosopher of immanence, will corroborate and articulate this point further with his own formulation of *substantive multiplicity* (1990), perceiving essential accord between the one and the many as the constitutive element of immanence. Substance is *one* and differentiated at the same time.

What is crucial to our discussion here is that, for Nietzsche, this differential play of forces, tensions, and affects comes *before* their apparent crystallization as objects and subjects of our ordinary perception. Even what we conceive of as *thinking* is nothing but the "relationship of these drives to one another" (Nietzsche, 1886/1978, p. 48). We ourselves (our cherished, fenced-in, relatively individuated selves and identities) are but transient shimmers from the Dionysian blaze. Ensnared as it might be in the late-Romantic, semi-metaphysical language of its day, Nietzsche is nevertheless saying something radically new. As with all great innovators, the breadth and scope of his insights takes a while to dawn on us, partly because of the fact that an innovative writer or artist in question is bound to the *spoken speech*, a received Grammar of words, gestures and perceptions which perpetuate, despite their alleged impartiality, the vegetative lives of long taken-down deities and other fictive entities. Both God and the 'I' are, after all, functions of Grammar.

It is important that in the necessary passage from the Dionysian to the Apollonian (or, in Deleuze's language, to the passage from the virtual to the actual) some of the profound ambiguity and even obscurity of the former is retained. In psychoanalytic language: the unconscious does not and cannot become fully conscious; this is the hubristic illusion of reductionism, of positivism old and new. For Deleuze, the virtual is both *distinct* and *obscure* (Deleuze, 1994, Cox, 2006).

A rationalist in the audience

The creative dance of Dionysian and Apollonian forces that Nietzsche describes in *The Birth of Tragedy* succeeds in radically *re-expressing* the pre-classical period of the ancient Greek world for us. It superimposes, against the anodyne cardboard fantasies of arcadia that were all the rage, three-dimensional, flesh and blood images of true vitality out of which the fierce and tender imagination of the great tragedians was born. The pre-classical age of Aeschylus and Sophocles that Nietzsche is fond of re-describing for the modern mind is the expression of a world implanted in myth.

Already with the dramas of Euripides and the philosophizing of Socrates this world enters its twilight and irremediable end. Both Euripides and Socrates challenge myth with the idea of "the world as rational order" where "there is nothing to fear, provided we take reason for our guide" (Vattimo, 2005, p. 169). This is the beginning of decadence which in a culture at various times in history often signals the waning of the life force.

There may be interesting parallels here with the recent shift towards rationalism in psychotherapy, a shift possibly brought about by the pervading influence of neopositivism and the dictates of the market. It looks admittedly far-fetched to suggest, as I have consistently done for some time (Bazzano, 2006, 2013b), a link between the advent of Socratic philosophy in ancient Greece and the current takeover of rationalist narratives in psychotherapy. What is common to both moments in history is a profound mistrust, in the culture as a whole, in the intelligence of the emotions and the passions, a fear to be taken over by them and a clinging to reason as the last resort.

According to Nietzsche (1872/2000), Euripides envisioned, when writing and staging his dramas, a critical, rational observer in the audience – the type epitomized by Socrates – who would draw a moral from the story, turning it into an edifying parable useful for the spiritual and ethical advance of the Athenian citizens. Euripides wrote with this spectator in mind, which is why, unlike the tragedies of Sophocles and Aeschylus, his dramas are already imbued with an aspiration to instruct and educate. What Nietzsche does not say, but can be inferred from his account, is that with Euripidean dramas a new element enters the scene: the spectator. Until that moment, the staging of a drama had no *spectators* but instead *participants* to a mythic and religious event consecrated to the god Dionysus. Participants partake of the luscious body and wild, cruel spirit and boundless heart of Dionysus, the One who is dismembered and disseminated in the Many: the masked actors, the chorus, the audience that, reassembled, become One again. The 'learning' ensuing from this *unio mystica* is of a different kind than the one gained through Socratic dialogue. It is visceral: being swept by the sheer force of raging passions blasting through the staged drama, being deeply affected to the point of loss of self and in the process finding that self transfigured. For the duration of the ritual, the participant accesses the core of *lifedeath* and the conundrum of human existence within it. She accesses it by identification. Lifedeath becomes her. The Apollonian appendix to this unorthodox learning consists in recognizing and accepting in oneself the powers of creation, the power of poetic imagination and, finally, *will to power* – in Nietzsche's idiom, akin, among other things, to the instinct of freedom.

For a while, Nietzsche sincerely believed that a renaissance of this pre-classical, pre-Euripidean culture would be possible through the medium of art and of Wagner's music in particular. Wagner and his circle had genuinely provided him for a short while with a renewed faith in the power of heart. Soon enough, this faith waned; his heart sank once he experienced first-hand the gathering of moneyed cultured philistines that was Wagner's Bayreuth festival, a sort of Glyndebourne for the bourgeois elites in search of "intense cathartic (Brecht would say 'gastronomic') emotions" (Vattimo, 2005, p. 172). He accurately predicted how Wagnerism would sooner or later give way to half-baked Christian metaphysics – which promptly happened with *Parsifal*.

Nietzsche's profound disappointment and subsequent break with Wagner signalled an important turn in his philosophical trajectory. Art, so crucial for him in providing a glimpse of the intensity and power of nature, no longer offered a reliable way out of decadence. This shift in Nietzsche's thought is poignant when one considers that, at heart, he thought life without music to be an error (Nietzsche, 1888/1998). But it is because of this shift that he turned to psychology, which he redefined as "queen of the sciences" and as "the road to the fundamental problems" (Nietzsche, 1886/1978, p. 23).

What remains valid for him in *The Birth of Tragedy*, later reiterated in his *Attempt at Self-criticism*, his introduction to the new edition of the book, is the pessimism of strength, a proclivity to appreciate the chasm at the heart of existence as well as its profound ambiguity – existence, whose original face is like that of Medusa. It is this view of the Ancient Greek world, rather than the alleged 'serenity' attributed to it by classic humanism, that remains constant throughout his work and is central to our understanding of Nietzsche's psychology.

2

LOVE AND THE UNCONTESTED LIFE

Lawless

Michael, a client in his late twenties, was visibly distraught when he came in on that Tuesday afternoon after a three-week gap in our sessions. It took him awhile to collect himself. Eventually he said after a long sigh: "we are, well ... basically breaking up." A few days before, his girlfriend Claire had asked him, 'seemingly out of the blue', whether he had ever touched a woman inappropriately or without her permission. A pause, then he added: 'no, her question wasn't exactly out of the blue.' They were having a conversation on the Me Too movement against sexual assault and harassment. Both of them had been impacted by the avalanche of revelations and allegations all over the newspapers and social media. From a general discussion on gender and sexuality, the conversation had at some point taken a sharp turn towards personal matters, including their relationship.

It was then that the question had sprung up. Michael was surprised. He hadn't liked the inquisitorial ring he thought he had detected in the question and at first brushed it off. They were silent for awhile, him busy searching his mind, she looking at him intently. He thought he had to be honest with her. She was his best friend, his beloved companion. He started recounting something that had happened six years before when he and his friends went to a lot of parties, drank and smoked weed. He had woken up early one morning after one of these parties. Everybody was still asleep, including his friend Laura. He looked at her and slowly ran his hand across her back and down to her legs. He then had the sense that he was doing something wrong and stopped. Laura remained asleep throughout. In previous sessions, I had seen worry, sadness, anger, joy in turn clouding and lighting up Michael's face. But the anguished look he had at this time was new to me. He felt deeply ashamed. Claire had at first responded calmly, the conversation had moved on. But the next day she confronted him, saying that she could no longer trust him, that they needed to rethink their relationship. A 'trial' period ensued, during which they took some space and only met occasionally, and during which Michael felt ill at ease, unable to reconcile his view of himself up until recently with the notion of a 'potential or actual abuser' that he saw emerging from the conversations with Claire.

For my part, I did what I could to 'walk along' with him, exploring some of the layers of feelings, the different thoughts and emotions that came up during our subsequent sessions. It was more difficult to suspend my different perception on the matter, a difference ascribable perhaps to the generational gap and transcultural differences. My concern was that by seemingly chastising himself, and by readily accepting his girlfriend's disapproval, he would come to isolate a vital part of himself that, while in need of refinement, was inextricably close to his core. I based my reasoning on the strength of our seven months of work together, as well as on the general assumption that waging war against oneself rarely results in greater self-acceptance and freedom.

There is ample room in Nietzsche's psychological constructions for a *contested* life. He greatly values the sort of creative conflict within the psyche that gives birth to new, more supple and agile versions of ourselves that are better equipped to encounter the vagaries of experience. Yet the premise for the creative psychic conflict he invites us to cultivate is *play*, a stance that is hardly ever allowed expression in a climate that, bruised by violence, harassment, and widespread misogyny, becomes dominated by sharply defined and seemingly indispensable notions of right and wrong. The recent resurgence of feminism and the overall reassessment of gender politics that from October 2017 followed the exposure of cases of sexual misconduct, harassment and abuse of power on a wide scale helped bring into sharp relief, among other things, the unmistakable presence of a certain type of man. He is at heart insecure, plagued by a sense of inferiority, hopeless at conversation, unable to listen or show genuine interest in others – someone who, however, feels entitled, given his privileged status, his wealth and power, to simply bypass what he perceives as pointless niceties and engage freely in locker room banter. It would be a mistake to see these pantomimes of power as true power, and obvious displays of powerlessness as strength. Here Nietzsche's views chime with those expressed by Hannah Arendt (1970), pithily summarized by Jacqueline Rose: "it is illegitimate and/or waning power that turns most readily to violence" (Rose, 2018, p. 3). What seemed apparent in relation to my client Michael – a thoughtful, receptive and deeply empathic young man – is the emergence of a paralyzing dread of his own thoughts and desires paired to a will to curb his sexuality – something that, as psychotherapy literature long taught us, "is *lawless* or it is nothing, not least because of its rootedness in our unconscious lives, where all sexual certainties come to grief" (ibid., p. 6, emphasis added).

Women's anger against harassment is presently widespread and wholly justified; the actions of these 'powerful' men are despicable, violent, and criminal. They are also insufferably *idiotic* and, it could be said, at the opposite pole of what Kierkegaard (1843/1992) had to say in a section of his *Either-Or* titled "The Seducer's Diary", a partly ironic representation of German Romanticism.

Johannes, the seducer in question, is the brooding aesthete whose main enjoyment derives not from seduction itself but from the emotional intricacies and sensual complexities the process entails. His genuine desire is for creating situations that will spawn inspiring reverberations in his own mind, with the sensuous world providing the raw material for his aesthetic designs. For Johannes, seduction is a sophisticated art whose ultimate aim is not conquest but heightened aesthetic experience. This is still manipulative, yet different somewhat from the pathetic coarseness of the infamous 'coasting coach' practices rife in Hollywood and elsewhere. The latter are of course not merely pathetic but potentially dangerous in the extreme, as Dayna Tortorici (2017, n.p.) explains:

> Combine male fragility with white fragility and the perennial fear of falling, and you end up with something lethal, potentially. Plenty of men make it through life just fine, but a wealthy white man with a stockpile of arms and a persecution complex is a truly terrifying figure.

As with my client Michael, however, we also face a situation which is shared by many young men like him. They want to do 'the right thing', but find the sedimentation of primeval, anti-sexual guilt handed down by their (often Christian) upbringing cemented by what they confusedly perceive as an attack on them *as men*. My sessions with Michael ended shortly after Michael and Claire's breakup. They had taken him, he said, to a significant point in his exploration. Despite the confusion, he managed to maintain an appreciation, a sense of openness and vulnerability in relation to sexuality which are essential to a redefinition of power.

Nietzsche's thought has been hastily associated in the course of history with a coarsely understood, 'masculine' power that forgets two of the fundamental attributes of his notion of power: (a) true power is not power *over* others (for Nietzsche this is a sign of weakness); (b) power implies active *cultivation of vulnerability* – it is the power to be receptive to the tremendous beauty and terror of the world.

A failure of desire

Kierkegaard does not endorse the seducer's actions but presents them didactically, showing their inherent vacuity and selfishness. He also believes that discarding the aesthetic dimension altogether in favour of ethics and religion means losing the qualities of poetry and imagination, of irony and subtlety, replacing them with a stern, legalistic ethics and with a thoroughly prosaic reading of religion. For this reason aesthetics are, in mock-Hegelian fashion, *sublated*, i.e., both rescinded and preserved within a 'higher' synthesis, namely an aesthetic reading of religion itself. This makes of Kierkegaard, alongside a handful of others (Hafiz, William Blake, and Leonard Cohen come to mind) a rare poet of religion. Within his synthesis, love and philosophy, desire and wisdom are grasped as belonging to the same domain.

Something very similar happens with Nietzsche. In the first words of his preface to one of his middle works, *Beyond Good and Evil* (1886/1978), he compares truth to a woman, likening philosophers – "when they have been dogmatists" – to inept lovers and would-be seducers with "little understanding of women [given their] clumsy importunity ... and improper means" (p. 13) for winning their favours. This passage has been interpreted as misogynistic, yet in the light of our current discussion the above quote can help deepen our understanding. The ineptitude of coarse males could be usefully related to the equally contemptible stance of dogmatist philosophers who approach 'truth' with a distinctive lack of tact and insight, and who are perhaps a little too eager to unveil it. Whether one thinks that the metaphor of truth as woman is acceptable or, as some say, contemptible (e.g. Williams, 1993), Nietzsche's twofold aim here is to discredit a style of thought that has clouded our entire perception of life.

With its discrediting and unmasking of religious and moral values and prejudices, one could be forgiven for seeing at first glance Nietzsche's enterprise as reductionist, or even cynical. Such reading would fail to take into account, however, how central and far-reaching affirmation of life is in Nietzsche's work. His critique of nihilism is at heart a broad critique of what is inimical to life. His array of images, metaphors and symbols all deplore the lack of creative friction and the atmosphere of spiritual slumber that are by-products of nihilism. At times, these images present "the problem of nihilism [as] a *failure of desire*, the flickering out of some erotic flame" (Pippin, 2006a, p. 4, emphasis added). The core of Nietzsche's argument in these texts appears to be the need to re-establish a vital link between *thought* and an intensity of *affect*, the latter often, though not exclusively, expressing itself in human experience through some powerful erotic pull.

Desire and diversion

For the seer and priestess Diotima of Mantinea, who makes a significant appearance in Socrates' account of love in the *Symposium* (Plato, 1951), philosophy is a more elevated form of sexual desire. On this initial point Nietzsche is in broad agreement, seeing the philosophical drive not merely as an attempt to lessen the suffering that comes with being in existence, but as an endeavour aimed at making life better. Diotima then tells us that love and desire of a beautiful body is desire for eternal possession of the good, and depicts love as love of immortality that alone can make up for the loss of beauty we witness with old age and decay. This eternalism Nietzsche finds clumsy. As he sees it, it offers inane spiritual consolation to pacify our insecurity, much in the same way as insecure lovers continually demand that the flame be rekindled, in the hope that their mutual insistent pledges of unending love will alone keep it from being snuffed out at the first breeze. Diotima's path of ascent – sublimating eros in the name of abstract beauty, truth and goodness – is for Nietzsche a *diversion* from what eros can achieve when, moved by its impetus, we allow for risk and uncertainty. The wish to divert the life force towards purposes considered higher than life reveals an underlying attitude of disdain and perhaps fear of life. Anticipating by some 400 years the Christian rhetoric of hope and the afterlife, the Platonic view conjures up, in Robert Pippin's words, an "erotic anticipation of wholeness and completeness" (2006a, p. 18), projected onto a spiritual realm where we can momentarily park our dread of instability and our resentment against time.

As he did elsewhere in comparing favourably aspects of Nietzsche's and Hegel's thought, Pippin (2006b) problematizes the anti-Platonism *de rigueur* in so much Nietzschean scholarship, suggesting oblique and daring similarities between Nietzsche and Plato, despite the radically different directions of their respective philosophies. His disparaging of Platonic Ideas and ideals notwithstanding, there is in Nietzsche acknowledgment of the usefulness of some of our human attachment to ideals. He sees their cultivation functional, if not in the (vain) pursuit of truth and virtue, at least in the cultivation of "artists as [the] highest ranks" (Nietzsche, 1886/1978, p. 67) among religious people. Spirituality and religiosity become not only bearable but stimulating when cultivation of their intoxicated ideals is used to nourish the work of artists. Platonism and mysticism become useful if they allow us to turn the imagination not towards consolatory homilies but in the direction of the urgent and exhilarating task of creating an art, a philosophy (and in our case, a psychotherapy) of the future.

The crucial difference is that these ideals are not inscribed within pre-existing, allegedly eternal templates, but are instead motivated by the desire to *experiment, tempt* and *attempt* – a play of words, in Nietzsche's writings, aligning philosophical/psychological attempt (*Versuch*) to erotic temptation (*Versuchung*). Risk, danger, and uncertainty are at the core of what animates the psychologists and philosophers of the future: they are *those who attempt*.

Great, again

What makes a person 'great'? Is it generosity, honesty, humility? Or is it perhaps that vague attribute – virtue? These questions may sound strange at a time when the notion of 'greatness' is being usurped by populist pledges to make this or that country 'great again'. Posing them may nevertheless be useful when introducing a vital aspect of Nietzsche's thought. For Nietzsche, none of the attributes listed above would make a person great. From Goethe, a writer he admired unreservedly, he borrowed the notion that the one thing that makes a person great is *not shying away from a direct encounter with powerful forces* (forces of *nature* as much as forces of *destiny*) which Goethe (1808/1949) called 'daemonic'.

> This principle, which seemed to step in between all other principles … I named Daemonic, after the example of the ancients, and of those who had become aware of something similar.
>
> (*p. 682*)

For Nietzsche, a person is great when she is capable of allowing her desires "free play and scope" and because of the power "that knows how to press these magnificent monsters into service" (Nietzsche, 1968, p. 521). A person is great when he or she is able to discern, embrace and dance with 'the passions', the term disparagingly used for centuries by theologians and philosophers alike to brand compelling feelings and desires. But this is only one half of the task at hand. The other half is to press the passions – these magnificent monsters – into service: Nietzsche's dictum invites us to be both daring *and* creative, i.e. firstly by not shying away from experiencing their full force, and secondly by handling them imaginatively.

We need daring if we are to take on the passions with equanimity and succeed in mitigating the stultifying grip that two millennia of moral and religious injunctions are still having on our lives. This stance alone is already very different from merely giving in, now and then, to bouts of risk and rage, of despondency and pleasure – only to be beaten down by remorse next day and perhaps seek counselling in the hope of restoring an imaginary static balance called 'mental health'. What we may need instead is encouragement in appreciating the intrinsic intelligence of emotions. Here Nietzsche anticipates neo-stoic thinkers who redescribe the ancient Greeks' notion of *eudaimonía,* or human flourishing, *in terms of* rather than *against* the emotions, creating the basis for what Martha Nussbaum calls "eudaimonism of emotions" (2001, p. 53).

Creativity is also needed, alongside daring, if we want to avoid being overwhelmed by the sheer power of the passions and succeed, as Nietzsche suggests, in pressing them into service. This is very different from the platitudes of 'trusting your inner feelings', 'following your heart', and 'going with the flow'. It calls for an active role on our part, not in terms of affect-control (or even 'affect-regulation') but in terms of *artistry*. Our creative intervention is necessary. This is because acknowledgment of the inherent intelligence of powerful emotions goes hand in hand with the recognition that they can also weigh us down with their "stupidity" (Nietzsche, 1888/1998, p. 21). If we know how to dance with them, they can also "marry the spirit, 'spiritualise' themselves" (ibid.). Accepting the emergence of powerful emotions in their various manifestations (in their acumen as in their folly); declaring ourselves ready to play and toil with them by moulding their formless intensity into a distinct living sculpture; being moulded by them in return – all these are acts of *friendship*. This stance represents a clean break from liturgical, straitlaced demonization, from the misguided war on the 'passions', and our hubristic attempt to eradicate them:

> In the ... Sermon on the Mount ... it is said ... with reference to sexuality, "if thine eye offend thee, pluck it out": fortunately no Christian acts according to this precept. Destroying the passions and desires merely in order to avoid their stupidity and the disagreeable consequences of their stupidity seems to us nowadays to be itself simply an acute form of stupidity. We no longer marvel at the dentists who pull out teeth to stop them hurting.
>
> *(Nietzsche, 1888/1998, p. 21)*

Nietzsche does not advocate eradication or censure, but 'spiritualization'. This alchemic process becomes possible once we are able to play freely with these magnificent monsters, rather than chastising them as sinful or abnormal. More than *alchemy*, this is more akin to *gardening*:

> One can ... cultivate the shoots of anger, pity, curiosity, vanity as productively and profitably as a beautiful fruit tree on a trellis; one can do it with the good or bad taste of a gardener and, as it were, in the French or English or Dutch or Chinese fashion; one can also let nature rule and only attend to a little embellishment and tidying up here and there; one can, finally, without paying any attention to them all, let the plants grow up and fight their fight out among themselves – indeed, one can take delight in such a wilderness, and desire precisely this delight, though it gives one some trouble, too. All this we are at liberty to do: but how many know we are at liberty to do it?
>
> *(Nietzsche, 1881/1997, p. 225)*

An anecdotal Zen story tells of a spiritual apprentice engaged in the task, assigned to him by a teacher, of attending to the temple's garden. For a whole year, the student works vigorously maintaining the garden utterly spotless. Then one day the teacher comes to appraise the work. To the student's dismay, he walks about looking annoyed and all of a sudden begins to shake a few trees wildly, until hundreds of leaves scatter on the immaculate path. Now visibly happy, the teacher says: 'That's a *lot* better; now the garden looks more alive.'

Do we conceive of our being as something to be retrieved in its innocence and, as something that can be accessed only *after* all the weeds and dead leaves are cleared? Do we think of ourselves independently of our passions, of the turmoil and contradictions of life? Or do we rather imagine our existence *in terms of* these passions?

The uncontested life is unliveable

> Every talent must unfold itself in fighting.
>
> *(Nietzsche, 1872/2006b, p. 98)*

It is problematic, however, to envisage the spiritualization of passions as a conscious process of sublimation activated by a self-existing, unified construct called 'I'. The latter is itself a compound of different forces and tendencies – not so much the locus where these components convene as the forces themselves being what constitutes it. One useful example may be anger, and its link to hatred. There is a difference between the two. Anger in all its gradations – from irritation to rage – is a fire. It rises up; it inflames us, more or less fleetingly. It is at heart innocent – a wave in the living stream. Hatred is different: it pays no heed to the life stream. The dedicated hater fastens her obstinate investment onto a person who, under her gaze, is turned to stone and removed from the living current. The real or unreal offence one has suffered sets the final verdict – on the person in question, as much as on one's relation to them. An intriguing definition of hatred sees it as *perverse intimacy* (Løgstrup, 1997). When I hate someone, I implicitly admit my inferiority in relation to that person. We hate those who would defeat us if we were to openly challenge them in an open, honourable conflict (Bazzano, 2012a). Nietzsche has interesting things to say about open conflict. Refusing to fight is for him an unnatural act, a by-product of warped Christian morality; acknowledging and honouring the competitive spirit, finding creative ways to expiate and spiritualize murderous tendencies is for him a prerequisite for any noble culture.

Nietzsche has been an inspiration throughout my life and close to being a mentor, however strange that may sound. I never really had a mentor. With a handful of exceptions, teachers and more experienced colleagues often felt threatened by my inquisitiveness and did not recognize the respect implicit in my doubting and questioning. But I never bothered questioning the teaching of someone whom I did not respect. If I spend time and energy building a critique, it is because I consider it worth the effort. Honest disagreement and a stance of honourable combat are, however, deeply unfashionable. During my five years as book review editor of a humanistic psychology journal, I noticed how, if asked, reviewers would invariably refuse to write a piece on a book which they did not like. They were only happy to write appreciative reviews. What this 'positive' stance fails to consider is how much careful and constructive thinking can go into thoughtful criticism. I have no means of knowing whether this chumminess and timidity are particular to the society and the therapy circles I find myself in, or whether this is a more widespread phenomenon. Either way, it is the very opposite of Nietzsche's vibrant, polemical stance that actively cultivates *a thirst for worthy enemies*.

Nietzsche's stance of open, honourable conflict, in itself a reflection of a truly agonistic ethos encouraging pervasive ('inner' as well as 'outer') competitive interaction is central to his work. It goes hand in hand with the "overcoming" of the "subject of morality" (Acampora, 2006, p. 326), that is to say, of the human self as we know it. Contest – whether in sport, art or education – provides us, in Nietzsche's view, with a regulating and motivating structure. As he wrote in 1872 in his brilliant short piece *Homer's Contest*, this is true both individually and collectively. The goal of agonistic learning was, for Athenians, "the well-being of the whole" (Nietzsche, 1872/2006b, p. 182). Unlike modern ambition, agonistic ambition in Athens was neither openended nor limitless. Artfully tempered by a larger vision, aspirations were closer and simpler to achieve; the result was greater freedom. "Modern man, on the other hand" – Nietzsche tells us – "is crossed everywhere by infinity, like swift-footed Achilles in the parable of Zeno of Elea: infinity impedes him; he cannot even overtake the tortoise" (ibid.).

In his *Apology*, an account of his teacher's argument during the trial, Plato has Socrates utter in passing what later became one of his most celebrated dictums: *ho de anexetastos bios ou biotos anthropoi*, usually rendered as "the unexamined life is not worth living" (Plato, 2011, p. 16). This pronouncement, enshrined in psychology primers old and new, dutifully intoned for generations by many a psychologist-sage, made of the 'examined' life the avowed noble purpose of the entire therapeutic endeavour. The rendering of *anexetastos* as 'unexamined' is correct.

But there is another, equally correct translation of *anexetastos* that is perhaps truer to its context. At this particular point in the argument, before a jury of 500 Athenians who accuse him of snubbing the conventional gods and misleading the youth, Socrates tells them: "Some of you will say: Yes, Socrates, but cannot you hold your tongue, and then you may go to a foreign city, and no one will interfere with you?" (Plato, 2011, p. 16). But holding my tongue, he adds, would mean disobeying the gods, and the same goes for conversing of virtue and other things "about which you hear me examining myself and others". This kind of conversation, he goes on to say, is "the greatest good of man, and … the unexamined life is not worth living" (ibid.).

Does Socrates really mean 'examining'? *Exetazo* in current Greek (a word linked to *anexetastos*) still means giving a school exam. Except that Socrates was no school teacher, but a gadfly: he challenged his interlocutors; he did so mercilessly, even disturbingly. The main thrust of his argument at this point in the *Apology* is that he simply cannot politely hold his tongue and exile himself to another city. Polite obeisance to social mores and the philosophical endeavour do not, in his view, go hand in hand. He simply cannot lead an *uncontested* life; rightly or wrongly, he made it his mission to *contest* the life of those who run after illusions. In the same sentence, the Greek *ou biotos anthropoi*, 'not liveable for a human being', is usually rendered as 'not *worth* living': the difference may be subtle but it is not slight. Worth (or value) here is an afterthought. What is more pressing is that for the Socrates of the *Apology* it is impossible to live an uncontested life; such a life would be unliveable, it would be the existence of a living dead. After all, he was perceived by the Athenians as a destroyer (Spiegelberg, 1964).

In this sense, *the uncontested life is unliveable* may then be another legitimate translation of the famous dictum. For Socrates (as for Nietzsche) a life without creative inner strife is uninhabitable. Equally so is a society which, out of a compulsive need to obey and conform, fails to honour contest in human affairs. This kind of society would merely make up a *civilization* but not a *culture*.

Fully living

Even when understood within Freud's congenially gloomy frame of restoring ordinary unhappiness, the more or less explicit aim in therapy is to assist a person in leading a more complete existence: to become *fully living*, a term I like better than the celebrated *fully functioning*, and one that is openly linked to the ancient notion of *eudaimonía* or flourishing. To make of a fully lived existence the desirable aim of therapy implies that a human life has intrinsic value, that it is not treasured merely as means for something else.

From its inception, and despite the ongoing pressure to conform to conventional narratives, psychotherapy has been at odds with utilitarianism and its ramifications in those Northern European countries where it first developed. Even today, despite successful attempts to bend therapy to the needs of consumerism and an ideology of happiness, the therapeutic endeavour across different orientations thankfully retains a thread of anti-utilitarianism.

A focus on a person's flourishing is itself at odds with the notion of happiness now prevalent: the latter is at heart utilitarian, and understands gratification as the goal of human actions; it ignores the wider array of meanings eudaimonía held for the ancients (Austin, 1970), as well as the value that action itself has over and above outcome. For instance, the pursuit of social justice is, for Aristotle, worthy in itself, and not because directed towards a state of final collective equilibrium and individual contentment. Apart from being intriguingly at variance with contemporary notions of 'happiness', the ancient notion of eudaimonía remains captivating for another reason: it is inextricably linked to the emotions, to the point where it is legitimate, even at a time when Hellenic thought has been arguably dominated by rationalism, to speak of a eudaimonism of emotions (Nussbaum, 2001). This seems contradictory at first: how can human flourishing, characteristically related by ancient philosophy to imperturbability (*ataraxía*), be affiliated to human emotions, a domain normally perceived as unruly? The reasons are complex. According to Martha Nussbaum (2001), ancient (Aristotelian) eudaimonism overestimated the presence of harmony within human designs, something that became outmoded and unthinkable with the advent, 300 years after Aristotle's death, of Christianity and the Christian chastising of emotions and 'passions'.

Emotions are conventionally understood as subjective, as ways to look at the world from an individual perspective. The one exception to the rule is *wonder*. This emotion presents the following important characteristics: (a) it is mostly projected onto an object and is only marginally alert to the person's own plans; (b) it is closely linked to grief; and (c) it is an important factor in the development of a child's ability to feel compassion and affection (Nussbaum, 2001).

In the first instance, we experience *rapture*, i.e. we are, as the word suggests, seized, kidnapped. We are *seduced*, i.e. drawn away from our personal projects. We temporarily cease, Nietzsche would say, to inhabit our imaginary interior life of spiders that live within their carefully constructed web, catching now and then external objects engulfed within our self-created constructs. Similarly, when experiencing grief, we are jolted into the painful awfulness/awesomeness of existence.

I remember gazing at my father's dead body when everyone else had finally left the small room in the morgue on that day in April 13 years ago. I experienced a strange combination of pity, numbness and perplexity. The face I had known was irremediably changed; the afternoon itself had morphed into a white cave; the thoughts in my head felt like a faint stream of inanities, running on empty, avoiding zooming in on this implacable simplicity. And during a brief spell several years ago working in palliative care as part of my training, I had a whiff of this very same strange feeling again, and heard often from seasoned practitioners of the implausible yet evident pairing of grief and wonder. A milder version of the above is what Benjamin (1997), after Baudelaire's *Á Une Passante*, referred to as *love at last sight* – the fleeting, accidental encounters taking place in the stream of crowds in big cities: wonder and loss in the blink of an eye before the (archetypal and phenomenal) apparition vanishes down the escalator of a Metro or Subway station.

Thirdly, if secure attachment has for the most part been established, paired with an ability to play with transitional objects, the child develops a strong curiosity about the world as well as a capacity to imagine and, in particular, the ability "to imagine the suffering of the good object" (Nussbaum, 2001, p. 213). Simply put, curiosity and wonder greatly aid imaginative empathy. "Wonder" – Nussbaum writes – "as non-eudaimonistic as an emotion can be, helps move distant objects within the circle of a person's scheme of ends" (ibid., p. 55).

In praise of forgetfulness

Unlike anger, whose fire is pure, hatred is *simulation*. When I hate, I refuse to own up to my helplessness. Instead, I project it onto the other and in this way maintain a peculiar proximity with my opponent. If anger is sudden *fire*, hatred is patiently distilled *poison*. The latter requires the harnessing to perfection of the art of *voluntary* memory, the ability to fasten one's memory onto a particular event in the past.

At odds with the customary view, forgetfulness – "active forgetfulness" (Nietzsche, 1887/1996, p. 38) – becomes a virtue. Nietzsche's view in this regard is unusual among philosophers and psychologists alike. To see forgetfulness in a positive light is a near taboo. Memory is at the heart of how we understand education; loss of memory, as in conditions such as Alzheimer's disease, has obvious devastating effects. But what is normally overlooked is how helpful forgetfulness can be. Nietzsche reminds us of this. Personal identity, and even the identity of a nation (Bazzano, 2012a), depend on the carefully constructed work of memory, without which the magnitude of life's flux would be overwhelming, for it would threaten our sense of self and along with it the meaning we attach to activity itself:

> A person who did not possess the power of forgetting at all and who was thus condemned to see everywhere a state of becoming: such a person would no longer believe in her own being.
>
> *(Nietzsche, 1874/1983, p. 62, translation modified)*

Forgetfulness is also a cure for an excessive sense of history; it is indispensable if we are to act without being incapacitated by historical self-consciousness. As we shall see, the *deed* is for Nietzsche more important than the *doer* and *expression* more decisive than *intentionality* in beginning to fathom who we are. To some extent, this means relaxing our internal system of 'mindful' self-surveillance and consenting instead to spontaneity, taking for granted that most of our everyday activities will imply a degree of unfairness or blemish that would not stand to high-minded or straitlaced scrutiny.

A prodigious memory

A burning hatred had dominated Joe's life for more than two years. He hated his sibling, and this hatred had paralyzed his life. He felt he only properly lived when away on holiday, away from his constant torment. Something his brother had done upset him deeply, but over eight months of therapy he just could not bring himself to say what it was, even though time and again he nearly did. Because of this, he felt isolated from his family. Refusing to speak to his brother had created ripples in the family and even cut him off from close friends. He often said that it was not acceptable to feel hatred and that he should be 'rational' about it. Were he to give in to this potent emotion, Joe feared he would either 'go mad' or do something he would later regret. Many times he considered confronting his brother, but was frightened that his fury and rage could explode and that he would end up killing him. Through therapy, Joe wanted to reach a state of 'serenity and understanding' and find a more satisfying answer to the one offered by his religious faith and morality. What he asked of me, more or less unambiguously, was that I provide confirmation of his vital need to subjugate his hatred. He resisted any hint and invitation on my part to access the reality of his present experience; instead, he wanted me to provide him with 'tools' for achieving imperturbability. This was corroborated by him knowing about my involvement with Zen, a practice that in the popular imagination is hopelessly confused with a postcard idyll of other-worldly tranquillity.

I never go out of my way to deliberately frustrate my clients, even though I have come to accept that some situations may require a touch of that. But in this case, the fact that I was not responding like the 'Buddhist therapist' he so wanted me to be, was more than enough to irritate Joe. Soon his irritation became rage, a new outlet for the bottled-up cold hatred he felt for his brother. This was a potential turning point in our work, despite the unpleasantness of being at the receiving end of his anger. However, because I did not meet his increasingly erratic demands (meeting for a three-hour session instead of an hour; meeting three times a week instead of once; meeting fortnightly instead of weekly and so forth), he ended therapy with a long letter in which he went to some lengths to explain why I was no good. I remember to this day my work with him as one of the most difficult and wearisome experiences I have ever had as a therapist.

The letter was meticulous; it charted in painstaking details and chronological order what I had said during our sessions, highlighting context, texture, the content he had brought up and in relation to which I had in his view failed to respond. I am in the habit, most of the time, of jotting down shorthand notes highlighting content, interventions and process. But Joe's precision utterly defeated me. He had made a mental note of every conversation and wrote everything down, more or less consciously building his case for the final showdown. Joe's prodigious ability to memorize was matched only by his assiduous cultivation of his prodigious memory – a fundamental requisite in a person animated by what Nietzsche calls the spirit of revenge.

Beautiful souls

Proust, at heart a Platonist, is at first glance as far removed from Nietzsche as one can imagine. The temptation of a comparison between the two writers is often strong, but the main reason I want to briefly refer to Proust here is not because of philosophical affinities with Nietzsche, but because his shrewd analysis of powerful emotions can aid our understanding of Nietzsche's 'magnificent monsters'.

At the root of strong emotions, Proust sees love – erotic love in particular. In his case, erotic love also alerts him to the presence of an invisible life beyond the flux of phenomena. This manifests at first as the life of those who become objects of our longing and desire, and it presents him with "that prolongation, that possible multiplication of oneself" (Proust, 2016, p. 407). A fleeting but unmistakable glance from one of the young cyclists passing by makes Marcel aware of "an inaccessible, unknown world in which the idea of what I was could certainly never enter or find a place" (ibid., p. 406). Love, a longing beyond description, is a primordial pull that wants *union* – whether in the grip of pain or in the ecstasy of desire. It has been said, particularly within the humanistic tradition, that the practice of therapy is itself a form of love, close perhaps to two of its several manifestations: (a) *philia*, which is akin to the friendliness and benevolence arising out of shared mutual endeavour; and, even more markedly, (b) *agape*, or divine love. This position conveniently bypasses the inherent subversion of *eros* and ignores the complexities of human interaction, including the latent presence of hatred within love's fold and projecting a neo-Christian view of the therapist as the beautiful soul (Bazzano, 2018c).

For Otto Rank, "the therapist can be neither an instrument of love, which would make the patient more dependent, nor of education, which attempts to alter the individual, and so would inhibit the positive will by arousing the counter-will" (Raskin, 1948, n.p.). This stance is instructive and significantly at odds with two positions found in contemporary therapy. The vision of the therapist as an instrument of love is all the rage in sections of humanistic psychology. The therapist as educator is an equally pervasive stance found across the theoretical spectrum – especially in psychoanalytic psychotherapy, cognitive behavioural therapy (CBT) and mindfulness-inspired approaches. Both stances focus on the therapist rather than the client and implicitly rob the latter of her inherent ability to self-direct.

Lying dormant at the root of all other emotions, erotic love triggers for Proust upheavals of thought. One moment, he says, the mind resembles a flat plane; then suddenly a mountain range thrusts itself into view, mountains sculpted and swollen into various combinations: Rage, Envy, Jealousy, Hate, Pride, and Love. The notion that erotic love might constitute the basis for all emotions can provide the practitioner with a healthy antidote to the wave of sentimentality that has taken hold of some sections of psychotherapy. I borrow my definition of sentimentality from Martha Nussbaum (2001): sentimentality is *thinking about sentiment* (and building a notion around it) *rather than simply feeling it*. Quantitative, data-ridden research measuring love and depth of relating is thus, at least according to the above definition, sentimental. A good depiction of sentimentality comes from Tolstoy, who writes of those Russian ladies who wept at the theatre and were utterly oblivious of their coachman sitting outside in the freezing cold (Nussbaum, 2001).

By sentimentalizing the therapeutic encounter and emphasizing moments of deep relating, depth and love, we end up anaesthetizing eros itself, who (like hate) is a *daimon*, i.e., a 'force' entirely *outside* the parameters of Platonism and Christianity. To say that love is a daimon implies above all that love is *without ascent*. We need not hark back to the pre-Socratic or Dionysian rites to have a taste of that.

Great literature is full of these examples. Heathcliff in *Wuthering Heights* is a manifestation of a love so profound that it is "total exposure of self to other from which [the other] shrinks in fear and shame" (Nussbaum, 2001, p. 604). This love is *outside* the sphere of self-protective control and calculation. Heathcliff derides the domesticated 'love' which Cathy's husband Linton gives her as planting an oak in a flower pot.

The existential psychoanalyst Rollo May came up with the formidable notion of the *daimonic* (May, 1969). He understood it as the reconciliation of the imaginative and the dialectic/rational domains as exemplified in the figure of Socrates. But with Socrates the descent towards the tyranny of reason and pre-Christian virtue had irremediably set in. In this context, Merleau-Ponty's work gives greater scope and range to human reflexivity beyond the domain of logic; it expands "our conception of the possibilities of scientific explanation" (Merleau-Ponty, 1968, p. 3); it "plunges into the world instead of surveying it" (Merleau-Ponty, 1968, p. 38); it descends toward it without imposing "upon the world in advance the conditions for our control over it" (ibid.).

It has always been the case that philosophers had to wear the mask of the contemplative priest, for their vocation was suspect. The same is perhaps becoming true of those psychotherapists who are fast filling the gap of moral arbiters and spiritual guides rather than provide a much-needed space for the exploration of what perhaps cannot be said and experienced anywhere else. I am talking of a therapeutic practice free of the notion of redemption, one that understands love without ascent – a notion of love outside the parameters of Platonism and Christianity.

It could be argued that the end result of Proust's trajectory is similar to Nietzsche's. Both are able to turn the anguish and suffering of existence into joy and active acceptance. But Proust's journey veers towards the eternal, particularly with regards to intimate relationships. For him, the lover who makes us suffer is appearance, a fragment that reflects, unbeknownst to her/him, the vivid, as-yet invisible Deity or Platonic Idea. As with Diotima, our task is for Proust to sidestep the lover and turn our gaze to the divine presence. The direction of our impossible longing is still external. Our vast longing finds solace in an equally vast presence that can harmonize it and contain it. This movement upholds the loving, 'devotional' element – it is a form of surrender. The link with the divinity and/or the Idea redeems not only the longing but also the lover and the beloved. The result – via the powerful media of art and literature – is redemption of the phenomenal world, a movement that turns the anguish of our uncertain existence into delight. Proust's movement is one of *ascent* – Platonic to the core yet undeniably compelling.

For Nietzsche, on the other hand, the world is not in need of redemption. The movement he incites us to pursue is one of descent: the world does not need Platonic Ideas or the presence of deities. Humans need not avert their gaze from immanent reality and direct it towards the heavens. We would do better to focus on the living joy and pain of organismic life. Here too, however, the outcome is uncannily similar to the one suggested by Proust when he appears to fathom, in Nussbaum's reading, that it would be only "when a human being becomes a plant that she can be loved without hatred" (Nussbaum, 2001, p. 514). Whether fragment of the divine or inhabitant of organismic reality, the human is decentred from separate existence and in both cases revealed through art rather than through life itself. Or at least, in Nietzsche's case, through a life that is never 'life itself' but instead an act of artistic (self-)creation. This is an ascent of sort, even a form of transcendence, but a transcendence that no longer looms or hangs over us, but one that we alone can (and are compelled to) express – through incarnate existence, creative expression and a creative will, whose activation can be seen as one of the aims of psychotherapy.

Truth, love and all that jazz

Can love be fully realized in everyday interactions? Given our human neediness, compulsively biased vision, and self-absorption? Given our inescapable enmeshment in habit and routine, our persistent envy, our refined means of self-disguise and self-reassurance? Given our "oscillation between anguish and deadness" (Nussbaum, 2001, p. 514)?

Within that heap of verbal notions and pragmatic plans we call life, Proust tells us, we cannot realize either genuine objective insight or unselfishness. Love's true ascent and the actualization of life can only happen through art. Some of Nietzsche's interpreters (e.g. Nehamas, 1990) have said the same thing in relation to Nietzsche: life's true purpose is realized through literature. A work of art or a novel may help us decipher what is bound to remain concealed in the hustle and bustle of daily living. It is indecorous, Nietzsche tells us tongue-in-cheek, to *unveil* truth. Not only indecorous but arrogant, with arrogance being the main itch behind a therapist's (and client's?) need to arrive at a 'truth' that one imagines lying there, pure and unadulterated, behind the facade of what one sees, hears, smells, and touches.

It may be equally arrogant to speak of the therapeutic encounter and of psychotherapy in general in terms of love. There is an implicit naiveté in this stance that ignores first of all love's shadow: hate. To speak of therapy in terms of truth and love is to *literalize* it, forgetting that the domain of therapy is at heart symbolic, representational, a dimension *parallel* to the real, a space that reminds us of the theatre and that, like the theatre, can be effective in fostering transformation. Like art and the theatre, therapy allows us a glimpse into our existence – to what purpose? This very much depends on the sensibilities at play. One possible direction is *transcendence*, in the wider sense of the term: finding the thread of meaning (obfuscated by habit and self-concealment) *outside* the everyday. Another path open to the therapeutic endeavour is *immanence*, again in the wider sense: discovering the absence of hidden meaning and bringing forth the creative will.

The stance I am advocating here is not rooted in intersubjectivity or in avowedly relational or dialogical forms of therapy, i.e., in forms of therapy that have, in my view, turned the relational dimension into a veritable dogma. For Nietzsche – as for Proust – we cannot escape our essential solitude, and the pain this recognition engenders is the raw material for the creative act, both in the gifted artist and in the life of the individual who, by undergoing therapy, may find her creative will. Congruent echoes of this stance found their way into contemporary psychotherapy via the work of the most gifted of Freud's pupils, Otto Rank (1978). The creative will is also the space of true giving, which is in turn the often forgotten manifestation of what Nietzsche calls *will to power*.

It is important to realize, however, that true giving belongs to the symbolic domains of art and literature, as well as to the 'transferential' domain of therapy and the fictional domain of theatre. In the everyday, we are "doomed by our jealous projects" and what we often see is "some aspect of our own needs and wishes" (Nussbaum, 2005, p. 514).

What kind of hatred is psychotherapy?

There are entire sections in Proust's *In Search of Lost Time* – I am thinking of *The Prisoner*, *The Fugitive*, as well as *Sodom and Gomorrah* – which present an unsettling view of human emotions and human sexuality. These sections are usually overlooked, glossed over, neglected or held at tranquillizing distance. Worst of all, they are often 'integrated' and seen as the narrator's obligatory rite of passage and temporary dark exploration through the fallen world of social pretence, lying, cheating and fretful desire – all within a reassuring and edifying spiritual quest with wisdom and virtue as its final aims. This interpretation of Proust's magnum opus is "misleading and absurd" (Bowie, 1987, p. 47), for what Proust effectively suggests in these easily overlooked passages is outrageous. His novel refuses to be systematized, and it is difficult to translate its prickly insights into a set of comforting certainties. Rorty (1989) made us aware of the fluid speculative possibilities open to Proust's novel and to its psychological riches. First of all, a good work of fiction is free of those onerous metaphysical claims that are inevitable in philosophical works. Secondly, *La Recherche* is a lot more than an exhaustive work of fiction. It is, in the words of Malcolm Bowie, a fictional kernel surrounded by a commentary; this commentary requires of us the same sort of credence as a work of aesthetics or moral philosophy (Bowie, 1987, p. 47).

Interwoven in the story, Proust is asking us to consider difficult questions. In *The Prisoner*, the narrator is painstakingly and obsessively driven by jealousy, here portrayed as a form of compulsive intellectual investigation, parallel, in its methodologies, to the analytical procedures undertaken by philosophers of science, metaphysicians and, yes, psychologists.

What Proust is telling us is that rigorous modalities of inquiry employed by science (both the inductive and the hypothetico-deductive method) are akin to spontaneous impulses of a mind under conditions of torment. Let me state it in plain English: Proust is effectively asking: 'What kind of jealousy is science?' If one adapts this rather scandalous remark to our context, one could legitimately to ask: 'What kind of hatred is psychotherapy?' Before we hurriedly come to the conclusion that the above question is far-fetched, let us go back to Nietzsche.

'Ressentiment' and the spirit of revenge

For Nietzsche's *Zarathustra*, the literary character who heralds the vision of the *overman*, there is only one (hypothetical) kind of redemption: transforming every 'it was' into an 'I wanted it thus', that is to say, *to redeem the past by willing it retroactively*. This is, of course, impossible. It is precisely from this impossibility that the *spirit of revenge* is born. What is the spirit of revenge? It is our deep aversion to time and its ineluctability; our antipathy to its inexorable and elusive progress – towards change, impermanence and death. How does the human will react? It 'discovers' cause and effect in the flux of becoming; it searches (and finds, or believes to have found) the *origin*, the bedrock; it assigns *responsibility* and *culpability*. The instinct of revenge has dominated metaphysics, religion, science, psychology, history. Above all, it has ruled over our 2,000 years of Christianity and Christian morality.

For Nietzsche, *every search for a foundation is a form of resentment*. To the customary objection that religion at least teaches gratitude, the answer is: gratitude is simply the *flipside* of revenge. Even the *will to truth* (i.e. philosophy) is animated by *ressentiment*.

But what does *ressentiment* really mean? Here is Deleuze:

> "Ressentiment" is a vengeful, petty-minded state of being that does not so much want what others have (although that is partly it), as wanting others to not have what they have ... Nietzsche sees ressentiment as the core of Christian and Judaic thought and consequently the central facet of western thought ... the desire to live a pious existence and thereby position oneself to judge others, apportion blame, and determine responsibility.
>
> *(2006, p. 34)*

The term, which can be broadly translated as 'resentment', is fundamental in Nietzsche. It is one with what he often calls the *instinct* (or spirit) *of revenge* and constitutes for him the very foundation of our way of thinking and of conceiving science (hence psychology) and religion.

A gateway to affect

An important stage in a Nietzsche-inspired investigation applied to psychotherapy would imply taking a different, unbiased look at emotions, including those powerful emotions that are normally perceived as a potential threat to the stability of the self. Such an investigation would implicitly suspend or even discard two positions that have been fundamental in the construction of psychology as we know it. The first, influenced by the ancient philosophical tradition, is based on the hypothesis that emotions are essentially ordered and harmonious; this stance perceives a close link between emotions and human flourishing. The second position, particularly with the advent of Christianity, casts a suspicious eye on emotions; it chastises them as unmanageable and capable of leading humans into temptation. Our task is to acknowledge the worth and cunning of both views before respectfully casting them aside.

There is of course a link between human flourishing and emotions as held by ancient eudaimonism. It is true that emotions can aid us in the pursuit of flourishing; it is also true that they are, from the subject's perspective, unruly. In this resides their latent value: they are connected to intensity and *affect*, to what the self necessarily ends up translating as individualized, singular emotion or feeling. To this neutral intensity of affect Nietzsche gives a name borrowed from myth: Dionysus. The perceived disorderliness of strong passions alerts us to a greater degree of intensity, to the neutral dimension of affect that we must contend with in constructive and affirming ways, if we are to keep our vitality as humans. This has to mean refraining from drawing unhealthy barriers against the life force – from what we essentially are – and welcome emotions as a gateway to affect. It is never entirely possible to access 'pure' affect. The relationship is necessarily mediated, but in Nietzsche one finds a crucial difference: the subject welcomes this intensity, learns from it in the same way as a devotee of Dionysus receives the god's presence. We also do not project onto the god our human dream of imperturbability, serenity or *ataraxía* (philosophy's error), nor do we shun his exuberant way of being (the error of morality).

Approaching emotions in this way prompts us to ask a fundamental Nietzschean question: *Which one?* That is to say: What particular force, or cluster of forces, is being represented by this particular, emerging emotion? And what does its emergence signify for one's self? What can be learned, explored, assimilated by this creative encounter? What lessons can be drawn? Taking this step is the therapeutic act par excellence. It requires willingness to suspend one's judgements and suppositions, not only about who one is (an entity? a soul? a cluster of forces?), but also about the emergent phenomenon gleaming at the threshold of consciousness, the powerful emotion that enlivens, entices or disturbs us at this particular moment in our existence. One practitioner who investigated this area of therapeutic endeavour with an explicit link to Nietzsche's work is Rollo May (1969), who formulated the notion of the *daimonic*.

Of the devil's party

May (1969) described the daimonic as "any natural function which has the power to take over the whole person" as well as "a fundamental, *archetypal* function of human experience – an *existential* reality" (p. 123, emphases added). He did not elaborate, but the second statement is surprising, even though it is not entirely clear whether May himself grasped the full import of his assertion. In any case, the psychotherapy world did not take any notice at all. Yet the statement brings together two 'domains' normally kept separate, the archetypal and the existential/phenomenological. Despite the odd exception, most of us think of archetypes in the Platonic mode, i.e. as transcendent, apart from the phenomenal world, rather than immanent i.e. manifesting in our everyday reality and visible particularly when our perception is sharpened – when semblance becomes, so to speak, *apparition*: angels at the bus stop, the devil disguised as a ticket collector.

To be *overwhelmed* by the daimonic, May intimates, throws the door open to psychosis; to suppress the daimonic leads us to *apathy*, the absence of *pathos* – of active suffering, of passion as well as 'pathology'. May's undeniable merit was to draw attention to this area of experience and to suggest that therapy may well be the only place left where the daimonic can be safely explored. The latter suggestion, uttered in the late 1960s when *Love and Will* was published (May, 1969), now sounds positively archaic, even quaint, in a cultural landscape arguably dominated by the need to anaesthetize psyche and experience. This is because the dominant, self-consciously 'non-ideological' ideology of our times, neoliberalism, conceives the human organism as unpredictable, not pliable to the demands of capital and of cybernetic techno-sentience (Land, 2011) in relation to which we are secondary, replaceable appendages – *things*, essentially, serving the smooth-running of the machine. Equally compelling is his opposing of the daimonic to conscience, which May sees as a social artefact linked to contingent mores and to the power of the superego.

Thus conceived, the daimonic belongs to "the power of *nature* rather than the superego, and is *beyond good and evil*" (May, 1969, p. 124, emphases added). This juncture in May's argument is crucial in relating to Nietzsche's thought and in making it useful to psychotherapy. This is also the place where, unfortunately, May's argument veers in an altogether different direction. "Aristotle" – he writes – "comes closest to 'taming' the daimon in his concept of eudaimonistic ethics" (ibid., p. 124). He then relates Aristotle's eudaimonism with our modern "state of *integration* of potentialities" (May, 1969, p. 125). From an intrinsically *plural* force of nature, the daimonic becomes *singular*, beginning to resemble Socrates' internal oracle. It is also assumed that Aristotle's view of psyche (essentially harmonious) is both accurate and applicable to modern humanity. May's error, as I see it, is to have conceived the daimonic in *rationalist* and even positivist terms, as something that, as he puts it, "needs to be directed and channelled" by "human conscious-ness" (ibid., p. 126). Human consciousness is, in Nietzsche's terms, a mere symp-tom, a *reactive* force, i.e. a force that is essentially *subordinate* to the superior organismic body, a force that must be reminded at all times "of its necessary modesty" (Deleuze, 2004, p. 36). May's formulation, on the other hand, anticipates the stance of contemporary mainstream psychotherapy: "Consciousness" – May writes – "can integrate the daimonic, make it personal" (May, 1969, p. 126). This he sees as the very purpose of psychotherapy.

But this makes of psychotherapy a *reactive* enterprise, that is to say, an endeavour aimed at making the unconscious conscious. Arguably, this was not always the case, nor does this stance apply to all its current manifestations. The early days of Freud's psychoanalysis were characterized by the 'discovery' of the unconscious. In my understanding, this discovery did not particularly aim at unearthing as much as tracing, mapping out an organismic and psychic area that clearly demarcated the borders of the conscious, acting both as an antidote to hubristic consciousness and as a warning to the hubris of the human subject. But very few of the early analysts remained loyal to this ethos; Otto Rank was one of the few remarkable exceptions.

Freud himself arguably proceeded along more positivist lines. As for contemporary psychoanalysis and psychodynamic psychotherapy, the increasingly common inclination seems to even question the very existence of an unconscious.

A royal road to tedium

"What keeps the theory of the daimonic" – May asks – "from leading to anarchism?" (May, 1969, p. 155). He does not define 'anarchism' but in the next passage, when linking it to "individual arrogance", it is clear that the term is used colloquially, as in mayhem and disarray. Yet anarchism can also be understood affirmatively, particularly in relation to the daimonic, as absence and/or active refusal of the enforced "*arché* or prototype" (Bazzano, 2012b, p. 139) that posits the centrality of a self as well as the centrality of consciousness. Far from being a nihilistic position, this rejection invites a more rigorous evaluation of the dominant forces at play in the psyche at any given time. In this case, the blow to rudimentary narcissism ('we, the good people') experienced with the upsurge of natural daimonic forces is not deflected towards the craftier narcissism of the righteous ('we who conquered chaos through conscious effort, prayer, or therapy'), but is transmuted into a more mature affirmation of the inherent multiplicity and complexity of human experience.

This stance is arguably needed now more than ever, in an era that, as T.J. Clark has it, not only inherited the "undeadness" of bourgeois society (Clark, 2016, p. 17), but succeeded egregiously in universalizing it, with chronic apathy and ennui being the end results of the originary royal road to tedium, 'psychological adjustment'. Without a doubt the daimonic, or a version of it, was fully acknowledged by Freud who wrote of the powers that can take hold of us. For that insight he was regaled by the European elite, particularly in France, with rabid anti-Semitic prejudice thrown at his newly born art of psychoanalysis which they saw as 'irrationalism' and a concerted assault on venerated Cartesian 'rationalism'.

A well-known story dating back to the early days of psychoanalysis tells of an American woman who, during a lecture by Ernest Jones on dreams and the unconscious, objected that Jones could only speak for Austrians; in her case, as with her fellow Americans, all dreams were positive and altruistic (Rose, 2011). The abiding fear is that 'chaos' may well be part of what we are – a fear that, unacknowledged, famously engenders unsavoury projections. This fear is in turn aligned to a view of chaos that is greatly influenced by the Judaeo-Christian tradition. Nietzsche's view of chaos draws from the ancient Greeks, and is radically different from the above and for that reason invaluable to our discussion. For him, "the total character of the world is in all eternity chaos, in the sense not of a lack of necessity but of a lack of order, arrangement, form, beauty, wisdom and whatever other names there are for aesthetic anthropomorphism (Nietzsche, 1882/1974, p. 168).

His view is at sharp variance with the Judaeo-Christian tradition and, arguably, also with popular science's accounts. For Nietzsche, chaos amounts to the origin of the creative potential, which is where our investigation will take us next.

3

FABLES OF IDENTITY

A coalition of affects

> Alas! Albertine was several people in one.
>
> (Proust, 1923/1996, p. 384)

Nietzsche is consistently full of praise for the work of the eighteenth-century Jesuit priest, polymath and diplomat Boscovich. The latter's *Theory of Natural Philosophy* (1763/2015) had a considerable influence on his thought (Stack, 1983), an influence that perhaps has not been fully recognized, given that it was central in Nietzsche's formulation of the two notions of *will to power* and the *eternal recurrence*. Boscovich's writings also encouraged Nietzsche to articulate a shrewd analysis of human subjectivity. "Boscovich" – Nietzsche says – "taught us to abjure belief in the last thing on earth that 'stood firm' – belief in 'substance', in 'matter', in the earth-residuum and particle atom" (1886/1978, p. 25). We must go even further, he adds: we must "declare war on the atomistic need" which, just like that other, more celebrated, metaphysical need, goes on living where we'd least expect it:

> One must also first of all finish off that other and more fateful atomism which Christianity has taught best and longest, the *soul atomism*.
>
> (ibid.)

Nietzsche is determined to take apart this view of the soul as indissoluble atom or eternal monad. He sees this as a continuation of similar developments that in the natural sciences have critiqued the notion of indivisible matter. At the same time, his is not a facile secularism, for it does not exclude the soul hypothesis but prompts him to bring forth new arresting descriptions: he writes of the "'mortal soul' and of the 'soul as multiplicity of the subject'; he speaks of 'soul as social structure of the drives and emotions"' (Nietzsche, 1886/1978, p. 25). As a "new psychologist", he feels "condemned himself to inventing (*finden*) the new – and, who knows? – perhaps to discovering (*erfinden*) it" (ibid., p. 26).

What we call 'self' is for Nietzsche *irreducible multiplicity*, crystallized into seeming unity not by an unconditional, pre-given nature, but by a particular disposition that organizes and selects various micro-dispositions of different nature, identified as drives (*Triebe*), desires (*Begierding*), instincts (*Instinkte*), powers (*Mächte*), forces (*Kräfte*), impulses (*Reize*), passions (*Leidenschaften*), feelings (*Gefühlen*), affects (*Affekte*), and pathos (*Pathos*). All of these are becomings, actions – primary in relation to the doer. If we had to choose one of them as approximating a 'ground', the preference would go to affects. This is not because they represent the 'ground of being', but because they are the ones who interpret and evaluate:

> What is the meaning of the act of evaluation itself? Does it point back or down to another, metaphysical world? ... In short: where did it originate? Or did it not "originate"?
>
> Answer: moral evaluation is an *exegesis*, a way of interpreting. The exegesis itself is a symptom of certain physiological conditions, likewise of a particular spiritual level of prevalent judgments: Who interprets? – Our affects.
>
> *(Nietzsche, 1968, p. 148)*

Does it follow that affects are to be seen as primal? Do they constitute a new, perhaps more appealing metaphysical basis than the atomistic soul hypothesis? They could be construed as such if one were to think of them as unified entities, instead of how Nietzsche conceives them, i.e., as an organic version of the force-points posited by Boscovich as alternative to the unit of the atom (Cox, 1999). On a micro-level, Boscovich saw these basic units as dynamic, differential centres within a force field, as temporary dams – more akin to nodal accretions of force than intrinsic entities (Gillispie, 1960). On a macro-level, affects within us are tendencies or *becomings* rather than *beings*. They are not 'things' but, as Nietzsche writes,

> dynamic quanta, in a relation of tension to all other dynamic quanta: their essence lies in their relation to all other quanta, in their "effect" upon the same. The will to power is not a being, not a becoming, but a *pathos* – the most elemental fact from which a becoming and effecting first emerge.
>
> *(Nietzsche, 1968, p. 339)*

Love, hatred and fear are not things but dynamic quanta. They are not isolated, but clustered as well as relational, in the sense of the "pulling and pushing of the organism in one direction or another" (Cox, 1999, p. 128). This gives us another insight into what Nietzsche means by *perspective*, namely "a coalition of affects" (Nietzsche, 1968, p. 348), with some prevailing and being dependable on the organization of other clusters of affects that would otherwise be in disarray. The body itself is, in this sense, a political structure, with the individual self an assemblage, an aggregate of no fewer than two levels, 'body' and 'soul', seen by Nietzsche in a continuum with varying degrees of intensity and durability – from the more changeable to the less changeable. Although essential for the notion of a self, the body is not the final ground, but itself *interpretation*, in the broad Nietzschean sense of extended genealogical struggle and evaluation. As he writes in his later work, "the essence of a thing is only an opinion about the 'thing'", adding:

> One may not ask: "who then interprets?" for the interpretation itself is a form of the will to power, exists (but not as a "being" but as a process, a becoming) as an affect.
>
> The origin of "things" is wholly the work of that which imagines, thinks, wills, feels. The concept "thing" itself just as much as all its qualities.- Even "the subject" is such a created entity, a "thing" like all others: a simplification with the object of defining the force which posits, invents, thinks, as distinct from all individual positing, inventing, thinking as such.
>
> *(Nietzsche, 1968, pp. 301–302)*

Self-examination is the starting point in this path of discovery, provided self-examination is itself cleansed of the "narcissism of self-improvement [and] the … trap of interiority as atonement" (Bazzano, 2012a, p. 95). For Nietzsche, the path of discovery goes way beyond introspection, reflection and even 'reflexivity'. It is a path as yet un-trodden and, as such, potentially dangerous and exhilarating, involving excursions in *time* and *space*. Going in search of lost time, Proust's narrator hopes to find an essential self, a quest that is at heart resistance against death. What he finds instead are myriad selves. No Cartesian *cogito* is discovered, nor any sign of Kant's unity of apperception. As the quest intensifies, a sense of loss begins to emerge for the many selves that he once was. Proust's narrator believes a true self will emerge someday from the wreckage of a fragmented individuality, while Nietzsche's own response is noticeably different: he delights in an active acceptance of fragmentation, and his delight is less a mark of temperament than the result of discipline and training. For Nietzsche, we must resist the strong pull of wanting to construct a 'deep' or 'authentic' self out of sensory involuntary memory. He sees this as a superstition derived from the need to fathom the existence of a doer behind the imaginary screen of a deed and, as he points out in his early writings, by our desire for "the pleasant life-preserving consequences of truth" (Nietzsche, 1871/1979, p. 81).

Like Argus, the hundred-eyed giant of Greek mythology, we must trace and intuit the complex genealogy of our multi-layered subjectivity from many different angles and perspectives. These time excursions are akin to gaining *a sense of history*; the past goes on stirring within us in myriad waves, Nietzsche writes in a passage from his *Assorted Opinions and Maxims*:

> [W]e ourselves are, indeed nothing but that which at every moment we experience of this continued flowing. It may even be said that here too, when

we desire to descend into the river of what seems to be our own most intimate and personal being, there applies the dictum of Heraclitus: we cannot
step into the same river twice.

(Nietzsche, 1887/1996, p. 268)

Undertaking this path also involves forays into space, i.e. *travel* – both literal *and*
metaphorical:

> To understand history we have to *travel*, as the father of history Herodotus travelled,
> to other nations – for these are only earlier stages of culture grown firm upon which
> we can *take a stand* – to the so-called savage and semi-savage peoples, and especially
> where humans have taken off the garb of Europe or have not yet put it on. But there
> exists a *subtler* art and object of travel which does not always require us to move from
> place to place or to traverse thousands of miles. The last three centuries very prob-
> ably still continue to live on, in all their cultural colours and cultural refractions, *close
> beside us*: they want only to be discovered. In many families, indeed in individual
> human beings, the strata still lie neatly and clearly one on top of the other.
>
> *(ibid., translation modified)*

Could psychotherapy be the place for these explorations in space and time?

Fables of identity

> The human body is composed of a great many individuals of different natures, each
> of which is highly composite.
>
> *(Spinoza, 1677/1996, p. 44)*

At the heart of the misguided yet ingenious idea of the self is our inveterate belief in
causality, a legacy of the philosophical and religious tradition as much as of language:
the idea that there is an 'I' (cause) behind a deed (effect), a point Nietzsche explores
in a section of *The Gay Science*:

> Cause and effect: such a duality probably never exists; in truth we are confronted
> by a continuum out of which we isolate a couple of pieces, just as we perceive
> motion only as isolated points and then infer it without ever actually seeing it.
> The suddenness with which many effects stand out misleads us; actually, it is
> sudden only for us. In this moment of suddenness there is an infinite number of
> processes that elude us. An intellect that could see cause and effect as a continuum
> and a flux and not, as we do, in terms of arbitrary division and dismemberment,
> would repudiate the concept of cause and effect and deny all conditionality.
>
> *(Nietzsche, 1974/1882, p. 173)*

The difficulty in perceiving the fluidity of existence is increased by our necessary
use of grammar that ultimately engenders the functional, descriptive 'I' on which

the lofty notions of God and soul are based. Nietzsche reminds us that 'I' is *Wirkendes Wort*, word in action, a functional tool signalling a quantum of will and action:

> A quantum of force is just such a quantum of drive, will, action, in fact it is nothing but this driving, willing and acting, and only the seduction of language (and the fundamental errors of reason petrified within it), which construes and misconstrues all actions as conditional upon an agency, a "subject", can make it appear otherwise. And just as the common people separate lightning from its flash and takes the latter to be a *deed*, something performed by a subject, which is called lightning, popular morality separates strength from the manifestations of strength, as though there were an indifferent substratum behind the strong person which had the *freedom* to manifest strength or not. But there is no such substratum; there is no "being" behind the deed, its effect and what becomes of it; "the doer" is invented as an afterthought, – the doing is everything.
>
> *(Nietzsche, 1887/1996, pp. 25–26)*

On the basis of this ancient fable called 'I', humans have projected notions of 'being' onto life and the world. Our simple psychological error, i.e., our belief in the 'inner life', founded on causality, has blighted our understanding of ourselves and the world we inhabit. Our psychotherapeutic and philosophical task must then be twofold: unmasking the self; unmasking the world. One implies the other. Our so-called inner world must be seen through as a "parasitical (non-)entity" (Large, 2001, p. 166), and its corroboration understood as another error resulting from our mistaken view that distinguishes between the doer and the deed. This mistaken view is then projected onto the distinction – common to the entire religious, philosophical and psychological tradition – between the *real* world and the *apparent* world. The 'inner world', this fundamental lie that tells us of a doer behind the deed, is as compelling as it is pervasive. If it is impossible to free oneself from its grip, this is because it is continually reinforced in three ways (Large, 2001, ibid.):

a   Through *socialization*. Consciousness and language originate in our *"need for communication"* (Nietzsche, 1882/1974, p. 298) as is our need to bolster the notion of 'me' as a stable, permanent self in an unstable, impermanent world.

b   Through *philosophical prejudice* – Descartes' *cogito*, fossilized into dogma and proliferated into many 'dead ringers' variations, from Kant's 'unity of apperception' to Husserl's 'transcendental ego' and Heidegger's *Dasein*.

c   Through our relatively *short human lifespan* that "misleads us to many an erroneous assertion about [human] qualities" (Nietzsche, 1878/1984, p. 45), promoting the illusion of an unchangeable human personality. "If a man eighty thousand years old were conceivable", Nietzsche suggests, "his character would in fact be absolutely variable, so that little by little an abundance of different individuals would develop" (ibid.).

Stations of the Cross

For some, Nietzsche's rebuttal of bourgeois Christian morality is prelude to a more severe morality (Solomon, 1989, pp. 105–121). Others have written of hospitality and xenophilia (love of the foreigner, of the stranger, and the *other*) as a higher ethics (Levinas, 1998; Løgstrup, 1997; Derrida & Dufourmantelle, 2000), or radical ethics (Bazzano, 2012a). It is possible to align psychotherapeutic practice with higher or radical ethics, considering that inspiration here comes from phenomenology and post-phenomenology, two disciplines that inform humanistic and psychodynamic practice.

The immediate contribution Nietzsche makes to this domain is at an intrapsychic level. The problem with practising psychotherapy within a moral (and moralistic) frame is that this perspective tends to regard freer and more imaginative impulses as detrimental to the common good and that it consequently projects them on to individuals who are judged as immoral and wrong. Bourgeois and Christian morality turn humans into the only animals in existence capable of turning against their own nature. The reaction we are accustomed to sets the 'rebel' against social conformity and the pieties of the silent majority. The example of Johnny 'anti-Christ' Rotten who two decades later morphed into John 'English Country Butter' Lydon, proud advertiser of conventional homilies, is enlightening in this regard. The rebel is counterpart of social conventionality, part and parcel of the very same configuration. Nietzsche often appeals to rebellious youth in search of an identity. But if his philosophy strongly resists the utilitarian edification of society, it also opposes the notion of the individual. *Neither society nor the individual can be the final centre of ethical decision.* This does not rest with society, because society is an institutional aggregate that works in favour of reactive forces. It does not rest with the individual, because there is not such a thing as an individual. What Nietzsche presents us with is an image of the self that is radically different from what we have inherited through the centuries: not individual but *dividual*. This lack of unity in a person was first revealed by morality itself: "In morality, man treats himself not as an 'individuum' but as a 'dividuum'" (Nietzsche, 1878/1984, p. 54). In Nietzsche's psychology, the fundamentally divided, fragmented nature of the self does not require integration. The overhuman, or beyond human (*Übermensch*) signals an opening, a breakthrough and a refusal to settle with a unitary notion of the subject.

The prospect of a 'demise' of the human subject may sound destructive; in fact, it opens the exploration to greater fluidity. Given that the overhuman represents an opening, a point of rupture, it is not really possible to utilize it for the building of a 'new human model'. Some humanistic and dialectical interpretations (Bloch, 1995; May, 1969; Adorno, 1970), though impressive, still rely on affirmative statements that turn a process of liberation *from* the self into a project of liberation *of* the self. They reconcile the subject with nature or history and end up substantiating it. Instead of "dis-subjecting" (Vattimo, 2005, p. 164), we find instead a process of appropriation of experience on behalf of the subject. What is central to this area of Nietzschean investigation is that the notion of the self derives from a neurosis whose name is morality; as a product of a neurosis, *the subject itself is a form of neurosis*. The intrinsic neurosis of the self is evident in its comic assertions in favour of oneness, unity, and solidity, in its avowed intention to suffer gladly the burdens of conscience and responsibility. It is no surprise that this kind of human self desperately needs God as the "helper necessary for the realization of the moral miracle that is asked of him/her" (Vattimo, 2005, p. 164).

At this juncture, psychotherapy may help a person or a group negotiate a path out of the dead end of morality. A new path opens up, away from the presumed solidity and oneness of the Cartesian self and the beaten tracks represented by various 'ways of the Cross'. This is no endorsement of immorality but incitement to greater intellectual integrity – and light-heartedness. Nietzsche's dislike of morality is motivated by a desire to puncture its rigid claims on human experience and expression. He invites us to live with a greater acceptance of multiplicity. Can we do without our personal Manichean tales of damnation and salvation and without its secular equivalents? Can we do without our black and white tales of integration and fragmentation, recovery and addiction, growth and non-growth, congruence and incongruence, mindfulness and mindlessness? It is a cliché to say that a certain degree of acceptance of those aspects that we find difficult or unacceptable in ourselves is often the first step towards healing and a fuller, more meaningful existence. But can non-growth, incongruence, fragmentation, addiction, dependence, mindlessness and so forth be instrumental in showing us our intrinsic multiplicity? Stepping into that threshold is one of the many ways of seeing into the multiple realities of our nature and experience.

The kneejerk reaction, conditioned by centuries of religion and morality, and corroborated by a century of psychotherapy, is to reach out instead for the solid notion of a unified self that is a reflection of God in a hall of mirrors where God is in turn the reflection of the self. The other, more difficult movement, is to renounce the props and rafts of traditional morality, religion and psychology and actively encourage the dissolution of the self – to see through the self's multiplicity and ultimate insubstantiality.

Love of music

Like Pascal before him, Kierkegaard spawned a poetic resistance to the double-headed tyranny of reason and morality that characterize the philosophical and religious tradition in the West. Yet both thinkers are thoroughly ensnared inside the net of interiority. Interiority is a spider, and neither Pascal nor Kierkegaard, for all the irresistible beauty and intensity of their trajectory, ever break free of its metaphysical ruse but erect their philosophy on its basis. Both of them require all the facets of the interiority drama: "anguish, wailing, guilt, [and] all the forms of dissatisfaction" (Deleuze, 1962/2006, p. 34). Nietzsche moves one step ahead. Not content with presenting an opposition to morality and reason, his work invalidates the primary prejudice, the atomistic notion of the self. This brings about a wholly different style and a different course of action, both thoroughly disengaged from Christianity. Famously, Pascal proposes a wager, while Nietzsche's Zarathustra tells us that he loves those who are embarrassed when the dice fall in their favour, for they do not want to win, but perish.

'*Without the Christian faith*', Pascal thought, 'you, no less than nature and history, will become for yourselves *un monstre et un chaos*'. This prophecy we have fulfilled, after the feeble-optimistic eighteenth century had prettified and rationalized man
(Nietzsche, 1968, pp. 51–52)

Kierkegaard invites those of us who dare to take a leap and follow the knight of faith in leaving aside the mores and conformities of our tribe, while Nietzsche, distrustful of any tyrannically stern god, will be moved only by a deity whose very presence will make him want to dance: "Nietzsche's thought is not about betting but *playing*; not leaping but *dancing*" (Deleuze, 1962/2006, p. 34). While Pascal bets, Nietzsche plays; while Kierkegaard leaps, Nietzsche dances.

It is the bad player who bets and above all it is the buffoon who leaps, who thinks that leaping means dancing, overcoming, going beyond.
(Deleuze, 1962/2006, p. 34)

What kind of person bets *in order to win*? A bad player, a scheming player, one who works out the odds and is focused only on one thing: being successful, being *saved*. And who is a good player? One who plays for the sake of playing. What redeems Casanova or Don Juan, assuming they are in need of redemption? The discovery that, unlike the banal 'playboy', he is deeply *affected* by the women he loves, that his search is "the search for conquest without possession", that his loving "give[s] up all thought of possession ... [and] overcome[s] anal fixation, the need to hoard money" (Kristeva, 1987, p. 196). Don Juan, particularly in Mozart's incarnation as Don Giovanni, exudes "the pure jouissance of a conqueror ... but a conqueror who knows he has no object, who does not want one, who loves neither triumph or glory in themselves, but the passing of both – the eternal return, infinitely so" (ibid., p. 193). Don Giovanni is a *musical soul*, one that is devoid of interiority: he "is a multiplicity, a polyphony ... the harmonization of the multiple" (ibid.). Why is it that multiplicity is virtually unheard of in psychology? Could this be because psychotherapists and psychologists have shown, from Freud onwards, very little love of music?

A vital field

Music played a key role in Nietzsche's life; what he revered most was the power of musical improvisation. He was a pianist and a composer, and during those youthful years when he rapturously embraced Wagner's music, what he most appreciated in it was the presence of unbroken melodies. What he liked even more was improvising on the piano – surrendering to a melody emerging seemingly out of nowhere and with no clearly defined end. And if the musical raptures experienced by the young Nietzsche tended to lead him, in true Wagnerian/Schopenhauerian fashion, out of the perceived dread of everyday reality, in the long run the wave-like motion of musical improvisation will give him a template for affirmation and re-enchantment of the very same reality.

Musical improvisation is one of the keys for approaching Nietzsche's thought and getting closer to a compositional stance that blends melody with logic, using the varied tempos of rapture, aphoristic synthesis and ironic fugues to interrupt, disrupt, and enrich logical reason. Improvisation is experimentation, and experimentation is directly linked to experience. Nietzsche's philosophy is above all experiment (Russell, 2017), as well as attempt/temptation (Bazzano, 2006). And if any one of us is able today, against the trend, to even think of *psychotherapy as experiment*, then Nietzsche's writings will provide a treasure trove for them.

Musical creation is also the place where "bold strategies" (Smith, 2017) are enacted, as Wadada Leo Smith says in relation to the music of Thelonious Monk: "an illustration of silence, not as a moment of absence … but as a vital field" (ibid.). Within this vital field, Cartesian self and individual body lose their edges, are consumed; they register (boldly *and* deferentially) a different order of belonging: experiencing? And what would be a good example of a non-musical, non-experimental, non-experiential human domain? The answer comes, once again, through art, in this case, the theatre.

It's a (Tes)man's world

Among the innovations introduced by a new, modern-dress production of Ibsen's classic play *Hedda Gabler* (Van Hove, 2016), one of the most striking was the way it recast the protagonist's husband, Tesman: not as the stuffy gentleman of more classic depictions but as a young academic with an American accent who bounces impudently on the stage snapping his fingers and slapping his thigh, seemingly on the verge of a step-dancing routine, to the rhythm of abstruse Latinate quotations. I half expected him to do an impromptu PowerPoint presentation or regale the audience with a 15-minute, wisdom-while-u-wait TED talk, delivered with monotonous exactitude whilst stroking his hipster's beard.

Eagerly expecting a professorship he does not deserve, and with his transparently narcissistic self doted on by his beloved aunt, he is despised by his bored, anguished wife Hedda. This characterization was a stroke of genius, reflecting a state of affairs that many will recognize in the world of contemporary psychotherapy. With a mercurial role reversal and invisible swapping of masks worthy of the most subtle Apollonian drama, the conservative academic of today does look like a hipster – nay, *is* a hipster. Walking and talking like a savvy post-punk, he injects a near-lethal dose of morphine into the ailing body of psychotherapy as we speak. He presents us with a gaudy barrage of data on a giant screen showing how, via a series of expedient techniques, the unconscious will be made conscious, the therapist's empathic attunement will be duly measured and – wait for this – the human condition in general will be properly explained, its anguish dispelled, its fleeting delights prolonged and enhanced.

In this neopositivist hall of mirrors, it is perhaps the more rigorous practitioners who begin to look positively archaic – as inexorably doomed (and Byronic) as Lovborg, Hedda Gabler's ex-lover, a man who, unlike her academic husband, possesses true brilliance, and whose masterpiece she will destroy. In the brave new world of neopositivist psychology, Lovborg therapists look picturesque: they might insist on notions such as transference, empathic attunement, edge of awareness, free association, felt sense, embodiment, attachment, congruence. They may speak of emancipation, hanker for meaning, clamour for deep psychological transformation without ever realizing that the tune has changed, that what 'people' want is a measurable sum of 'happiness', a proven token of 'wellness' and, above all, *security* – rather than any risky and knotty venture such as 'becoming oneself', 'actualizing' or, God forbid, chancing one's way into the dark waters of the unconscious.

For Nietzsche, nihilism is at heart *denigration of life*; it is the triumph of the ascetic ideal that has contempt for life, seeing it as imperfect, transient and sinful, and which finds corollaries in the myth of objective, desensitized knowledge owned by the scholar and the academic. In the broadest sense, the character of Tesman represents, in Nietzsche's terms, the psychological model for our age, if it is true that we have now reached what he saw as the inevitable outcome of nihilism: the advent of the *last human* – a person devoid of passion and involvement, lacking vision, seeking only security, comfort and a stupefied 'happiness'. Whether cloaking her language in secularist, religious or agnostic language, this being is unable to see beyond work as her only hope of redemption. At this general level, the bleakness and inherent despair of nihilism is soothed by data, diverted by scholarly knowledge and beautified by computer graphics. Transposed onto the world of therapy, the contrast between Lovborg and Tesman represents the irreconcilability of psychotherapy and academic psychology. Despite the fact that every effort was made in recent years to reduce the former to a set of teachable skills, predominantly aimed at social adjustment, the two disciplines belong to a fundamentally different order of discourse. Psychotherapy potentially belongs to the domain of *culture*; academic psychology is largely an enterprise of *acculturation* a.k.a. indoctrination (Bazzano, 2017a). It is safe to say that by the time a living, breathing practice enters academia, it becomes embalmed.

There are interesting parallels here with philosophy, particularly in relation to how Nietzsche (1886/1978) understood the *role* of philosophers: not as labourers whose task is to perpetuate an inert set of harmless doctrines but as *experimenters*, whose sensibility is attuned to the future. Philosophy in Nietzsche's sense is an ongoing experiment – a series of repeated attempts/temptations for which no suitable environment has been created yet. For him – as for Schopenhauer – universities are not suitable for hosting the wild plant of philosophy. Similarly, psychotherapy is founded on experiencing rather than on conventional notions of knowledge (Russell, 2017). It too looks to the future, in a vision that naturally expands the psychotherapeutic venture outside the walls of academia and into the wider world.

The lunacy of nationality

Towards the end of therapy, my client Ahmed made plans to leave the UK. Brexit (the UK's referendum vote to leave the European Union) had been the last straw. A bright thirty-something from Algeria, he had built a career in the creative area of banking, one that allows him to employ his natural talent for mathematics. To a degree, our weekly meetings helped him, I think, steer a difficult balance that brought him some respite and the clarity needed to act. The turning point came after the referendum, the culmination of a long process. He had been aware for a while of uncomfortable feelings and emotions that had come up since the move to London, brought about by his affluent neighbours' gracious indifference after years of him living there, by the courteous interrogations he felt subjected to at the school parents' meetings, and by the probing question, 'Where are you from?', reserved for anyone whose accent or complexion is different. Add, twice a day, the swarming assaults at train carriages, the aggressiveness of commuters shoving their way in, fighting for that corner where they can inter their monadic being in the cultural delights of the *Evening Standard*, and it was no surprise that Ahmed had had enough. 'Let's move to France': his wife agrees. The kids are excited. Not that he harbours illusions about France's *fraternité*, with all the brouhaha about *burkini* and the mounting secularist intolerance. For another thing that annoys Ahmed is being routinely asked to come up with assertions about Islam, the religion of his upbringing he feels connected to, but not as a badge of tribal identity.

This last point became central. His reluctance to view identity in these terms raised two questions: (a) Why do we view identity solely in terms of *membership*? (b) What happened to identity as radical uniqueness, something one finds ('finding one's voice') – something that demands temporary exile from one's tribe of origin?

Other clients too voiced their dismay after Brexit. Europeans among them felt the ugly xenophobic undertones. My British clients were discomfited by what they saw as the narrowing of the horizon, the claustrophobic nausea they felt of being aboard a ship of little islanders captained by Livid Nigels in Mr Kipling blazer and Dyed-blond Chancers waving the Union Jack on a City bike. Before it gained currency, the term 'Brexit' sounded jarring to me. There is no exit in Brexit but closure, vainglorious enclosure, self-confinement within a brittle notion of identity that believes itself encircled by swarming migrants at its borders, and contaminated by multi-culturalism in its midst. These sentiments belong to a brutal legacy that sees "a homogenous country [as] more peaceful and stable" (Robinson, 2012, p. 25), a legacy that plays on a misguided metaphor borrowed from genealogy, according to which a homogenous stone is more solid than a heterogeneous one.

I am no fan of the EU, especially after what they did to Greece. The 'good European' of today supports austerity and casts a suspicious glance on outsiders. But there is another meaning to the phrase 'good European', if one thinks of Europe as the font of modern Western culture – understood, with Said (2001), to be "the work of exiles, émigrés, refugees" (p. 173).

Becoming free of national identity carries its own risks, particularly if it entails leaving behind the philosophical and religious tradition and with it, the hubristic dream of noble humanity. Yet this project is also exhilarating; this is what I aim to explore in the next chapter.

4

AGAINST HUMANISM

How to be a philistine

Nietzsche's admiration for pre-Socratic Greek culture is consistent throughout his oeuvre, even though tone and emphasis fluctuate considerably – from the musical ecstasies of his Wagnerian youth, through the light-footed scepticism of the middle period, to the weightier pronouncements of his later work. But his is no run-of-the-mill love of antiquity. For all their variations and deviations, the key note in all of Nietzsche's writings on the Greeks remains one and the same. It can be described as dissolution of the notion of 'humanity' and of the idealization of 'humankind' that is so dear to the humanist-classical tradition – from Erasmus to von Humboldt and Winkelman down to the present day including, it must be said, large sections of psychology and psychotherapy.

For Nietzsche, that tradition is the very foundation of philistinism. A philistine may be coarse as well as cultured, and it is the latter that cheerfully embodies a particular *Philisterdasein*, a stylishly idiotic way of being in the world, a 'Socratized' existence: optimistic, moralized and thoroughly rationalized – what gave birth, according to Nietzsche, to the modern culture we still inhabit today. Against this mollifying picture, Nietzsche presents us with a mode of thinking and being whose background is myth rather than logos; he invites us to perceive the human as existing on a precarious balance over the abyss, "always on the verge of being subdued by annihilating and barbaric instincts" (Masini, 1978, p. 43).[1] An artist, philosopher or psychologist that is aware of this will conceive of humankind solely in terms of *nature*:

> If we speak of *humanity*, it is on the basic assumption that it should be that which *separates* it from nature and is its mark of distinction. But in reality there is no such separation: "natural" characteristics and those called specifically "human" have grown together inextricably. The human, in its highest, finest powers, is all nature and carries nature in itself. Those human capacities which

are terrible and are viewed as inhuman are perhaps, indeed the fertile soil from which alone all humanity, in feelings, deeds and works, can grow.

(Nietzsche, 1872/2006b, p. 95, translation modified)

It is not so easy to defuse Nietzsche's dynamite thought and bend it to the needs of humanism, though many have tried. His view of the human establishes an altogether different rapport with nature and the animal, and widens the exploration to the enigma of the nonhuman as well as the threshold of the overhuman. The very idea of nature inherited from the classical tradition is radically altered; it is no longer seen "as though it were a proof of the goodness and protection of a God" (Nietzsche, 1887/1996, p. 134). As for "one's own experiences", these can no longer be explained "as pious people have for long enough explained them, as if everything were predetermined, everything a sign, everything designed for the redemption of the soul" (ibid., p. 135).

How would the above translate into psychotherapeutic practice? The nonhuman and the overhuman imply for Nietzsche a movement towards a threshold; this movement is excessive, both in the sense of being intense and in excess. Is paving the way for the overhuman the same as 'actualization'? And – here comes the difficult, anti-humanist as much as 'anti-democratic' question – are we *all* capable of doing that? What does it take to make that plunge towards the threshold of human experience – to embrace, in Nietzsche's words, "the psychology of the orgiastic as an overflowing feeling of life and strength" (Nietzsche, 2006, p. 485)? What kind of psychology (and psychotherapy) would care for and encourage a vital need to say "yes to life, even in its strangest and hardest problems" (ibid.)?

> *This* is what I call Dionysian; this is what I sensed as the bridge to the psychology of the *tragic* poet. Not freeing oneself from terror and pity, not purging oneself of a dangerous emotion through its vehement discharge – such was Aristotle's understanding of it – but, over and above terror and pity, *being oneself* the eternal joy of becoming – that joy which also encompasses the *joy of destruction* ...
>
> *(ibid.)*

What psychology (and psychotherapy) would support this profoundly *soulful* need to go beyond self-preservation and find actualization through expenditure and generosity? Certainly not an over-regulated psychotherapy whose every move, formula and procedure is geared towards the maintenance of a philistine culture motivated by the pursuit of happiness.

Becoming-free-for-death

The last human is Nietzsche's term for the type of human he saw slowly coming into being at the end of the nineteenth century. This is someone who only cares for his/her survival; someone whose main concerns are adaptation and conformity; someone whose only desire is to be happy. Lest we think he was referring to some imaginary being: he was talking about you and me. *We* are the last humans, Socrates' farthest children. You and me and he and she: we, the true nihilists, the last signposts of Platonism and Christianity. We are the ones who use psychotherapy not in order to explore the limits of human experience – its breadth and depth – or to cultivate a vulnerability that opens us up to the intensity, horror and beauty of the world, but so that, our hurts briefly wrapped, we can go gently into that good night via our desks and our TVs, our careful loves, our plotted routes.

Haven't we done well? We have unassumingly fulfilled the nihilist destiny of a millenarian culture by revamping its fundamental *decadence* with an evidence-based modernist and post-modernist veneer. Decadence is the need to justify the silver river of life through religion, morality and science. The last human embodies the secularized version of the Christian notion of happiness, and it was conceived at the same time as the notion of the overhuman. The two are intimately connected: the former, attached to his pieties and securities, rejects the possibility of greater experience because of its inherent dangers – above all, the danger of discovering both multiplicity and ultimate insubstantiality at the core of an alleged unitary 'being'. As Nietzsche's last humans, all we want is to live as long as possible, moderately enjoying our small virtues and vices, our little joys and sorrows. But "this is no true love of life; [this] very moderation is a mark of ignominy" (Masini, 1978, p. 231).

The first step out of this happy little trap we may find ourselves in is to begin cultivating a healthy disenchantment from the beautifully designed interior of our self-construct. Disenchantment is crucial, for this is where our pilgrimage towards self-overcoming (*Selbstüberwindung*) begins. The route Nietzsche dares us to take is not one that leads to a cathartic overcoming of the world, for he invites us to love the world and also to *create* a world – a Dionysian *topos* whose landscape we traverse with tentative, energized steps. The ensuing intensification of experiencing makes us keenly aware of the ever-present abyss and danger we are implicated in the minute we actively affirm (rather than submit to) our being in the world. We are in this way primed to become 'one who goes over' (*Hinübergehender*), stepping right into the bewildering chaos and magnificent beauty of the world. Going over is both overcoming (self-overcoming) and overturning: not so much being-towards-death as becoming-free-for-death.

Modern depths

There is a twist in the tail. We, the last humans, so entrenched in our stability, in our assumed gift for living in a tidy here and now where history (as we are told by a host of trendy historians) either comes to an end or its carcass is giddily exhumed to the mummified glories of lost empires – are now to face what Nietzsche calls *the untimely*. This is Nietzsche's sharp, "eccentric critique of humanism" (Masini, 1978, p. 45) that shatters the homely dream of human universality promoted by a cortege of ersatz priests and beautiful souls who legislate on right and wrong, on 'being' and virtue, and whose ranks are now supplemented by a movable squad of therapists adding *mental health* to the venerable list of pieties. The twist in the tail is that for Nietzsche the untimely is contained *within* modernity. This is another way of saying that modernity is "more profound than it seems to those who venerate it as optimistic progress and moral harmony" (Masini, 1978, p. 45). Modernity is also more profound than it appears in the descriptions of those who berate it as a sure symptom of fallenness and inauthenticity. Modernity (and post-modernity) is neither the higher rung in the ever-ascending stairway to progress, nor is it a fall from the presumed serenity of antiquity. Nietzsche is neither your average peddler of evolutionary growth nor is he a cheap merchant of doom. Modernity is for him incessant reflection of a reinterpretation of antiquity. Any attempt to gain real historical sense ushers in an image and a locus greatly treasured by Nietzsche: the *labyrinth*.

For Nietzsche the labyrinth – with its elaborate combination of paths and passages where it is hard to find one's way out, represents in architecture a more accurate reflection of the configurations of soul or psyche. But it is hard to resist the consolations of classical architecture and its insinuations of scientific rationality, purposeful logos and divine providence. Elevating the labyrinth to chosen architectural form would be disturbing; it would mean admitting to the diminishing of the human subject and the emergence of play, of mask-wearing – not fakery but artful creation. Acknowledging both is too confusing to minds and bodies trained in the Platonic/Christian ways of life-denigration. Perhaps it is too much for us to bear, this prospect of upholding, alongside our will to truth, our equally powerful *will to artifice*. The risk is too high: a "tragic risk, like the one incurred by Kierkegaard" (Masini, 1978, p. 47), who gets to this day chastised by literalists for presenting a deeply experimental aporia that is closer to art and poetry than to the clunky dictates of institutionalized religion and institutionalized psychotherapy.

Nietzsche's labyrinth does not imply acceptance of the received 'archetypal' meanings of the maze. If it did, he would have merely anticipated the neo-Platonism of Jung. His evocation of the labyrinth does not fit snugly with the archetype, for in Nietzsche's case the image, even though powerfully evocative, is a form of novel and daring experimentation that "tears off the protective sheath from the myth and subverts it" (Masini, 1978, p. 47), translating it into the "forgotten and inconsolable voice of modernity itself" (ibid.). Evoking an image from antiquity (the maze and its inevitable correlatives: the Minotaur, Ariadne's thread …) is useful in exploding the snug sobriety of classical and neo-classical architecture and the alleged unity and rationality of psyche. A moment later, Nietzsche tells us that the maze resides, unseen and unacknowledged, at the heart of modernity; that the archetype is a living manifestation of a phenomenal reality that we are too timid to acknowledge. He transgresses on both fronts, mischievously leaving no chance for others to erect on the ground of his philosophy either an archetypal or a modernist psychology.

A storehouse of discarded deities

Nietzsche's radical, 'honest' atheism is a landmark within the remarkable trajectory of European thought and one that was achieved with great difficulty, via the tortuous route of Schopenhauer's thoroughgoing secularism and despite the latter's penchant for Christian nihilism (Masini, 1978). This achievement has largely been lost, supplanted by docile sub-Darwinian 'atheism' and post-Hegelian historicism – both nurtured under the long shadow of a dead God. Despite its avowed adherence to experience and observation, psychotherapy is prone to follow an arc of its own, dimly aware of other developments. For that reason, it can often become the storehouse of discarded deities. In order to implement any of Nietzsche's insights, a lot of catching up and sieving through is needed first; a long process of rummaging through the exhausted ontologies and the second-hand metaphysics – both religious and secular – psychotherapy has come to rely upon. On the whole, the world of psychotherapy still believes in 'God', even if only implicitly. The three-letter word may not be mentioned (we are, after all psychologists and scientists), but we go out of our way to manufacture a wide collection of shadows, surrogates and substitutes of God. We give them new names: collective unconscious, formative tendency, presence, 'Being'. We attribute a purpose to existence, benevolent designs to the passage of time, and apply a cosmos to chaos. We construct a narrative with a beginning, middle and end. We also earnestly believe in that other wonderful fiction: human nature.

We may help clients rewrite their story, substituting a faulty narrative with a meaningful script. Here too, God's shadows turn up in our aid, well disguised in secular garments: growth, development, integration, self-actualization, mental health, individuation and so forth. I have lamented elsewhere (Bazzano, 2013c) the conspicuous absence of even a sprinkle of Hegel's *Phenomenology of Spirit* in psychotherapy curricula, which may partly explain not only our profession's meagre consideration for contingency, but also our penchant for shallow universalism alongside our bypassing of *conflict*.

Paradoxically, Hegel's arguably less beneficial teachings have been absorbed to a fault. For instance, his ability, as Nietzsche hints in *The Gay Science*, to convince us at last of the divine nature of existence via that sort of magical sixth sense, the *historical sense*. To Hegel (and partly to Darwin) we owe the attribution of a persuasive gloss of intentional design to existence, an offshoot of which is the belief in the 'formative tendency' found in the writings of some humanistic practitioners (e.g., Rogers, 1980). Far from being an expression of post-modern relativism, the very same critique presented here can be found at the inception of humanistic thought. For Feuerbach (who was saying this already in 1841), Hegel was guilty of having *rehabilitated* Christianity through his rush reconciliation of religion and atheism, philosophy and theology. Feuerbach brought back to the human domain those qualities and prerogatives that are traditionally attributed to God. Up to a point, Nietzsche did something similar; he too affirmed humanity as thoroughly as he dismissed the deity. But he went much further: alongside the human notion of God, his atheism also *undermines the human*. Crucially, this movement does not shut the door on the sacred, but opens a route to "new and as yet unexplored possibilities of the 'sacred'" (Masini, 1978, p. 161).

Contemporary psychotherapy is doing the exact opposite. In some quarters, it vainly attempts to resuscitate God's carcass by transplanting transcendental narratives into human experience. In others, it will shrink its scope and range within the narrow confines of cognitivism, neuroscientism, quantifiable data and algorithms.

In Nietzschean terms, these are smug routes to short-lived consolations; means to avoid the very real impact that the death of God (i.e., the coming apart of any law, the disintegration of values) is having on us. His invitation is to acknowledge nihilism and confront the wasteland it discloses before our very eyes. While Feuerbach resorts to reason and the humanistic tradition followed suit, Nietzsche sees the *power of the human* as the power of a "'mythical animal' that is … being newly fecundated via the disposal of the moral God, the God-judge, understood as metaphysical boundary" (Masini, 1978, p. 162).

Shadows of God

> *The Human dies also* (finished is the belief in the substitution of humanity for God, the belief in the Human-God who would replace God-the-Human) … Nihilism must go all the way, to the end of itself, in the human being who wants to perish, the last human.
> *(Deleuze, 2004, p. 74)*

A tremendous possibility of actualization is open to us, Nietzsche is effectively saying, only once we arrive at the necessary collapse of our illusions. This is the welcome end of our pride as a species indulgently positioned by theology as the crown of creation. It is also the necessary demise of the bourgeois ideal that goes on adorning and revamping to this day its bubble of exclusive tastes and worthy beliefs, surviving trends, co-opting counter-traditional narratives and hiding what, with Nietzsche's help, can be seen through as quintessential mediocrity. In the long run, this entails the end of anthropocentrism, a genuine shift towards a meaningful ecology away from climate change denial, but also from the inveterate narcissism of environmentally conscious *belles âmes*. In the short run, this has to mean the demise of the happiness industry that has invaded psychotherapy over the last couple of decades turning it from exciting experiment into normative methodology for the preservation of the psychological, spiritual, and political status quo. Instead of actualization, the mental health industry has strengthened *der letze Mensch*, the last human – a being who is only interested in 'happiness' and no longer has time, energy or courage for exploration, experimentation, discovery.

The above stance, however densely disguised and secularized, is but a remnant of monotheistic theology. This is hardly controversial or even novel; the close link between anthropology and theology had been made explicit already by Feuerbach: anthropology harbours a more or less 'hidden' theological narrative within itself, while theology is marred by the fundamental anthropological prejudice of the separate human self. Add to this the blow to the alleged scientific objectivity of the anthropologist given by decolonization, and the appeal to anthropology doesn't have a leg to stand on. And yet this essential critique of anthropology *is* controversial *and* novel, given that anthropology is still regarded as "a more appropriate analogy" for therapeutic work than Freud's "archaeological 'digs'" and given that "the expertise of the anthropologist" is deemed to provide fertile inspiration for therapeutic work (Spinelli, 2007, p. 141).

The instinct of revenge is at the heart of monotheistic theology, and consequently at the heart of anthropology. Our belief in God is one with our belief in the human (the latter engendering our belief in the self and in 'universal' human values, which are often the values of empire and/or dominant cultures). They feed on each other: monotheistic prejudice informs psychology, and psychological prejudice informs monotheism. They place an entity, respectively 'God' and 'self', at the centre of a plural world of becoming.

At least polytheism, through its vast array of divine and semi-divine beings, allowed for the possibility of a parallel affirmation of multiplicity within the psyche. But faith in one God also gave us faith in a *normative* God, and a consequent doctrine of a singular human type whose epigone is the last human: contemporary women and men whose hope is that therapy will get them back to their cherished seat in the traffic jam.

To negate God is easy, especially in societies where secularism is the norm. In that sense, the humanist project exemplified by Feuerbach has succeeded. But this is not enough for Nietzsche; he invites us to let go of religious *predicates* as well and liberate the sacred from the grip of theology. Here he anticipates not only post-metaphysical thought but also what has come to be known as post-secularism (Barber, 2014) or the post-secular turn (Braidotti, 2008). Beyond the conventional understanding of the latter as return of those repressed religious postulates which contemporary culture failed to exceed or re-express, post-secularism problematizes the facile polarization of religion vs. secularism.

What matters to Nietzsche is not the human but the creative process itself, the mytho-poetic power residing in the human that has been waning since the advent of a historical rationalism bent on linear, positivist notions of progress. Realizing the mytho-poetic power of the human is a scandalous process of de-humanization. It means privileging the (*animal*) *psyche* over the human itself. Nietzsche no longer regards the human as the 'historical' humanity hitherto conceived via the Platonic and Christian (nihilist) trajectory, nor as universal humanity seen "in the simplicity of its aspirations (happiness)" (Masini, 1978, p. 164). What matters to him is the natural power that traverses the human flesh and gives flesh to the dream, to dream-think, weaving ever-new, intricate and compelling tales, concocting stimulants of all kinds – art, science and religion among them.

For classical humanism and its various appendixes (on whose tenets much of the ethos and ideology of contemporary psychotherapy arguably relies), appreciation of the human is concurrent with an overcoming of conventional religion. For Fink (2003), "the murder of God liberates man by uncovering the creative powers of human existence" (p. 143). He sees Nietzsche's radical critique of religion (as well as morality and philosophy) as an apologia of the human. What is more difficult to accept is that this is only a first step; the next step Nietzsche invites us to take is accepting that *the human too must perish* alongside our God or gods. What perish alongside the human are also those particularities and subjective individualities that limit the scope and breadth of the individuation process to the limits inherent in individuation. This is a welcome death; it gives birth to a world of *dividuations* or, in Deleuze's words, "impersonal individuations" and "pre-individual singularities" (Deleuze, 2004, p. 137) – the mythopoetic name for it being the very same as that of a god – *Dionysus*. This presents us with a truly surprising turn, often overlooked: from the radical secularism and light-hearted scepticism of his middle works, a vista suddenly opens onto an immanent spirituality. This opening is horizontal; it does not ascend towards the divine but branches out in rhizomatic, promiscuous embrace with the world; it is *loaded* with the world, "even animals" (Rimbaud, 1871/1986, p. 12)

Zarathustra, the prophet who announces these strange glad tidings – the death of God and the death of the human – also perishes. What is being heralded instead? The *Übermensch*, Nietzsche tells us, or the *over*human. Not the superhuman, or even the fashionable post-human. Not a new utopia or a new model for humanity. Not the "self-actualized" person (Maslow, 1962, p. 25) or the "persons of tomorrow" (Rogers, 1980, p. 351). Not even, perhaps, that most Nietzschean of simulacra: the *mask*. Instead, the overhuman points towards what stands *over* the habitual human diagram: a threshold, an outside, a point of crisis, danger and opportunity that does not resolve into a new model.

Therapy without prejudice

To speak after Nietzsche of humans as mythical (and myth-creating) animals is no friendly nudge to transcendence but re-expression of the thoroughgoing materialism that is at the heart of his investigation. Unlike pop songs and pop psychology, philosophical ideas travel slowly; it has taken a little more than half a century and the emergence of Deleuze's radical empiricism (Deleuze, 2004) to even begin to grasp what Nietzsche's 'materialism' communicates and entails besides the simplistic atheism that it is commonly alleged to represent. We now know that it points at an *anti-metaphysical affirmation of reality as multiplicity of forces*. As such, it categorically refuses to be reduced to unity – not only the unity of God and His creation (or its secular versions, e.g. interdependence, universal relatedness and intersubjectivity). It also refutes the so-called primacy of conscience in its various manifestations – social, historical and individual. Active refusal to link materialism with social and historical conscience means that (sadly for some of us) Nietzsche's philosophical adventure cannot be easily harnessed to the project of dialectical materialism (Masini, 1978). True, Nietzsche draws on both materialism and dialectics, but he does so in order to overthrow the 'text' of metaphysics by disrupting its grammar and write in a different text, the *transvaluation of all values* – a task performed through a process of infinite interpretation.

Equally, his refusal to link materialism with an individual, secularized conscience facilitates the emergence of a psychology that is free of moralizing guilt – something that ought to be of interest to the practising psychotherapist. Not only is moralizing guilt for Nietzsche one of the long shadows cast by religion; he believes that, as a science, a coherent psychology must be free of all prejudices, first of all religious prejudices.

Here an important distinction is necessary: ethics – understood as more than mere obeisance to societal rules – must be the backbone of the psychotherapeutic profession if the latter is to exist at all, whereas "psychology should not be moralistic" as "it is the pride of psychologists to deny this weakness in their science" (Rank, 1978/ 1929, p. 14). Otto Rank, that most coherent of Nietzschean psychologists, drew a superbly useful distinction between psychology and therapy:

> Therapy can never be without prejudice for it sets out from the standpoint that something should be otherwise than it is, no matter how one may formulate it. Psychology, on the contrary, should describe what it is, how it is, and, where possible, explain why it must be so. These two diametrically opposed principles, Janus-headed psychoanalysis has necessarily mixed up and the lack of insight into this condition as well as a later denial has finally led to such confusion that now therapy is psychologically oriented and theory moralistically so instead of the reverse.
>
> *(Rank, 1978/1929, pp. 14–15)*

The investigative power and ingenious drive that goes into the formulation of theories in psychology – whether speculative, representational or imaginative – is at its best when left unencumbered by the burdens of societal, historical and individual conscience. This is not to deny the importance of the latter but only to emphasize the crucial need for a creative dimension of play that alone can advance the art within the science. Conscience – perhaps a more up-to-date term would be 'responsibility' – must undoubtedly play a role in therapy; but then the question remains as to what our aim is in therapy.

> To say it in one word, the aim is self-development; that is, the person is to develop herself into that which she is and not as in education and even in analytic therapy to be made into a good citizen, who accepts the general ideals without contradiction and has no will of her own.
>
> *(Rank, 1978/1929, p. 20, translation modified)*

A genuine understanding of the values of cooperation with others, of the importance of social and political responsibility, of what Adler called *Gemein-shaftsgefuhl* (Ansbacher & Ansbacher, 1964; Adler, 1964) – variously translated as communal feeling or social interest – has to be counted among one of the desirable outcomes of therapy, if not the most desirable. But if the weighty and worthy role of social responsibility *overrides* the creative investigation of psychology, if the latter is carried out solely as an appendix of an existing code of norms, the result will be a psychology that is simply expression of the dominant ideology. Rank's position, already at this stage removed from Freud's, is tangentially similar to a stance taken by Richard Rorty (1989), a thinker within the American pragmatist tradition of Dewey and James, who makes an important if controversial distinction between the unfettered creativity of "theorists" and the ethico-political demands required of us in the social sphere.

The etymology of *theoria* implies "taking a view of a large stretch of territory from a considerable distance", whether in the manner of metaphysicians, who try to climb above the plurality of the world and hope to determine from on high an "unexpected unity" (Rorty, 1989, p. 96), or in the mode of theorists such as Nietzsche who take pleasure in dismantling the all-too-neat edifice of metaphysics and in creating new narratives. The second mode, which for Rorty is the mode of the ironist theorist, is characterized by a playful and imaginative force.

From Rank we learn that this is not confined to artists, scientists and creative thinkers. It can be applied to every ordinary person's existence in relation to our capacity for greater congruence, individuation, and empathic imagination. In this sense then we can understand incongruence, neurosis or mental distress as instances of *failure in creativity*. It is our right to be allowed to think freely and imaginatively about our individual predicament without the straitjackets of morality and religion getting in the way. This is akin to – depending on which language we have been schooled in – finding one's voice, operating from one's internal locus of evaluation, becoming more individuated and, more generally, being unshackled from the introjected demands of the herd. But the freedom gained in this process is *not* individualism; what is revealed instead is the multiplicity of the self as well as its ultimate insubstantiality. As our fixed sense of identity is challenged in therapy, the outcome is not dissolution but greater flexibility, applicable within the socio-political sphere as solidarity, compassion and cooperation – qualities that will be all the more genuine when arising out of an internal rather than external locus. In this sense then, psychotherapy can potentially fulfil the central task of facilitating the above process in a boundaried and symbolic setting, provided the emphasis is not on intersubjective relating but on *authorship*, where the central questions are not dictated by the rules of familial attachment but focus instead on "how to create space for authorship to emerge" (Bazzano, 2017b, p. 87).

The instances of failure in creativity discussed above may be compared with falling short of finding one's own voice and not attempting to complete "the birth of individuality" (Rank, 1978, p. 11). As unfashionable as this may sound at a time when notions of intersubjectivity rule unchallenged, this "has to do … with a *conflictual separation* of the individual from the mass, undertaken and continued at every step of development into the new" (ibid., emphasis added). It is, moreover, a necessary step if both psychology and psychotherapy are to be unshackled from the iron grip of religious as well as secularized moral nihilism that has ensnared them and that continues to taint their endeavour.

In praise of fragmentation

The majority of Nietzsche's vivid metaphors, from the eternal recurrence to will to power to *amor fati*, signal a point of rupture where the human gives way to the overhuman. What is lacking in his writings is a conclusive description of the overhuman. This deliberate choice on his part is refreshing as it does not allow us to turn it into a new humanist slogan. A few decades later, reflecting on the harrowing experience of totalitarianism and dystopia, de Beauvoir (1948) will write against ethical systems and in favour of ethical projects. By offering a set of certainties, an ethical system often delivers exploitation; conversely, the ethical project is encouragingly ambiguous, a work in progress that may open the path to greater emancipation. Could it be that in order to be more effective, humanism has to embrace anti-humanism? Could it be that to liberate the human means first and foremost to release it from the prejudice of the species? Humanism's first task then (and humanistic psychology's too), would entail working towards the dissolution of the subject we inherited from Christianity and bourgeois culture – that very self that normative psychotherapy strives to maintain and enhance. The dissolution of the subject is also prelude to the more general dissolution of "everything positive" and of "all forms" (Vattimo, 2005, p. 160) – first among them morality.

Nietzsche's critical assessment of morality is twofold: the first thing he emphasizes, against prevailing utilitarian claims, is that morality is *not* meant for the good of the person but for the preservation of societies and the status quo, even when it proves harmful to individuals. This notion of morality is akin to Hegel's *Sittlichkeit*, the 'ethical order' from *sittlich*, customary, from the stem *Sitte*, 'custom' or 'convention'. Morality is, in this sense, adherence to the introjected norms of social life, in particular to the interests of the dominant social and political group. The above position, and Nietzsche's oft-repeated derision of social groups as 'herds' justifies, at first glance, the habitual charge of 'individualism' levelled at his thought.

It is only when we look at the *second* movement of his critique of morality that we realize that there is more to it. This second movement has immediate links to psychotherapy and it is for that reason worth pausing over. Nietzsche does not place the individual one-sidedly against society. He is not a Romantic thinker who claims the grandeur of instincts and natural appeal of feelings and emotions against society's conditioned norms. He is not Rousseau or any of the humanistic psychologists who after Rousseau wax lyrical about subjectivity. For Nietzsche, the subject itself is not unified but fragmented. It is divided and ultimately insubstantial, hence it cannot claim the primacy of any of its features, be they emotions, reason, or conscience. The dominant role historically enjoyed by moral conscience is not justified because it fails to acknowledge that as individuals *we do not know what motivates our actions*. A common objection is that the person, endowed of free will, can choose morality over instinct. The point, however, is not that the person is not free but that the person *is not*. The person is only "a superficial play of perspectives, a hermeneutic appearance, nothing like what the metaphysical tradition took it for" (Vattimo, 2005, p. 161). This is the point where most secular humanists make a sharp U-turn. It is fine to avail oneself of Nietzsche, as long as the partially understood 'death of God' bolsters a superficial form of secularism; but if it implies the demise of the human self, humanists get worried – and with good reasons.

In 1887 Nietzsche asked: "What, strictly speaking, really defeated the Christian God?" (1887/1996, p. 134). He answers by quoting a passage published five years before in his *Gay Science*: What defeated the Christian God is Christian morality itself, alongside the increasing seriousness with which the concept of truthfulness was taken, the refinement of the Christian conscience in confession, translated and sublimated into the scientific conscience, into intellectual hygiene at all costs (Nietzsche, 1887/1996, p. 134).

"All great things" – he goes on to say – "are *the cause of their own destruction*, through an act of *self-cancellation*" (ibid., p. 135, emphasis added). If applied to philosophical systems in general, the statement uncannily anticipates one of the hallmarks of Derrida's deconstruction (Derrida, 1978). Self-cancellation is for Nietzsche the "law of life, the law of *necessary* self-overcoming" (Nietzsche, 1887/1996, p. 135); this is an irremediable process, no matter how eager one may be to preserve a system of thought or a religion. He continues:

> In this way, Christianity as dogma was destroyed by its own morality; we are standing at the threshold of *this* very event. After Christian truthfulness has drawn one conclusion after another, it finally draws its strongest conclusion, its conclusion against itself.
>
> *(ibid.)*

The same process he had previously observed, namely that excessive religiosity brings about the demise of God, he sees happening with morality. Thorough, conscientious introspection aimed at gaining moral hygiene reveals a fragmented self. It also exposes the lie of 'self-possession', the convenient belief that we know who we are and what the meaning of our actions is. At this point, psychotherapy can substitute morality by setting aside our cognitive and moral battles of subduing the passions in the name of reason and normative integration. It can do so by replacing its implicit moral rebuke with genuine *study of the self*, an activity whose originary meaning – *studium* – is closely linked to love and exploration.

In order to be relevant *and* effective, psychotherapy cannot function as mere surrogate morality. We would do well to resist the vanity of playing moral guide and the ambition to become functionaries and enforcers of dominant ideologies.

Start digging

We are, for Nietzsche, a plurality of (relational) affects, each of them with a particular point of view, each of them seeking dominance, hence in conflict. Even here, at this intrapsychic level, the Heraclitean *polemos* – war, conflict, strife as 'father of all things' – reigns supreme. But this is no random, free-for-all conflict; the important question Nietzsche poses to us is whether we can aid, guide, and arrange a particular type of conflict that would better assist the affirmation of active forces within our experience. I am not convinced that this is necessarily directed towards the "enhancement of the human type" (Acampora, 2004, p. 180), though it is inspiring, as well as valuable, to be able to even envision the concrete existence of women and men whose 'development' is no longer understood as being dependent on survival but on the creation of new values and new interpretations of reality. This thought experiment could effectively lead to conceive of human beings as "actively affect[ing] their organic development" (ibid.). Here we are only one small step from envisioning the birth of a new species – an ambivalent notion, to say the least. For if on the one hand this gives us permission to think freely and audaciously of *what can come into being* if and when the habituations that have so far constituted our species were to be supplanted by new ones, on the other hand we are perilously close to the dubious terrain of eugenics. There is little in Nietzsche that encourages the latter, despite the reckless ambiguity of some of his pronouncements. Deleuze's (1962/ 2006) emphasis on a decentred system of forces is helpful here, with his decisively non-Darwinian understanding of evolution occurring "in non-linear terms without fidelity to the distinctions of species and genus" (Ansell Pearson, 1997, p. 117).

This dilemma – central to psychotherapy, an art and a science founded after all on anthropology and, alas, bound by it – does not go away by sidestepping the human in favour of a neutral domain of forces. Let's ask the question in Nietzsche's language: Does *overcoming* – central to the overhuman – translate/transmute into an "overcoming being" (Acampora, 2004, p. 183), into someone who can embrace fate and say 'I willed it thus'? Or are we more realistically presented with a *pragmatic axiology*, i.e., a painstaking reorganization *of values* that digs a treacherous underground tunnel out of the prisons of morality, Christianity, and the nihilistic denigration of life perpetuated by all metaphysics?

There is no guarantee that we will succeed. And if we do manage our escape, we do not know what awaits us out of the prison. Unshackled from the spirit of revenge, we may be able to construct a greater, immanent meaning to existence. Free from the servile notions of adaptation, growth and development, we may be able to find in us the strength to mould our living flesh to poetic transmutations and create new interpretations. But a whole century has gone by since Nietzsche's death, and one of the things the twentieth century made abundantly clear, something articulated by de Beauvoir (1948) in her *Ethics of Ambiguity*, is that we should be wary of utopias – be they religious, humanist, or racist, be they inspired by the classless society, the Messiah's second coming, or the triumph of the Aryan race. It pains me to write what I just wrote, for I am certainly aware of where my sympathies lie, and also because I know first-hand the sorrow that comes with the burning of illusions. I too would like to believe, with Carl Rogers, in "the world of tomorrow, and the person of tomorrow" (Rogers, 1980, p. 339), but his optimistic predictions – on "the increased respect for and use of intuition" by an increasing number of individuals, on the experience of "altered states" through drugs and "psychological disciplines", on promising "paranormal phenomena", on the "growing interest in the spiritual and transcendent powers of the individual" (p. 344) – were made at the cusp of the 1980s, the very decade that ushered in a new, overpoweringly reactionary phenomenon that now reigns supreme: neoliberalism. Of course, it would not have been possible for Rogers to perceive then, let alone predict, the takeover of the humanities we witnessed ever since. Also, I hasten to say, my critique is not a dismissal tout court of buoyancy and confidence. But it is baffling to find that the notion of the persons of tomorrow is still being sponsored *today* as an article of faith at a time when it only succeeds in broadcasting the preciousness of one's beautiful soul.

Nietzsche's notion of the *overhuman* works as an antidote to the above. It helps us realize that we can refute mechanicism without falling into the trap of teleology. He outlines an uncertain, urgent route in between. While his notion speaks of transfiguration and transformation, it does not put forward yet another grand scheme of metaphysical reassurances and consolations. The above stance is as untimely now as it was when Nietzsche formulated it, given the renewed clamouring within contemporary thought for new certainties, as it is testified by a resurgence in popularity among progressive thinkers of figures like Saint Paul (Badiou, 2003), proverbial man of reactivity and bad conscience when compared to the active nobility of Jesus. At the same time, the aspiration to greater congruence, understood as closer alignment to active forces, is not only worthwhile but crucial to the renewal of culture.

Training

Culture thus understood would then be purposefully directed towards a point of rupture – an opening, a breakthrough. Training can mean two radically different things. For example, current psychotherapy training is for the most part an elaborate exercise in transmitting and apprehending the cognitive and behavioural elaborations of reactive forces. This intricate exercise takes place within institutions that are in turn almost entirely subjugated by reactive forces. This is not because trainers, trainees and administrators involved in this are particularly malevolent and/or mediocre, but because any endeavour aligned to psychology and psychotherapy is inherently *reactive*. As with other fields of science and the humanities, psychotherapy can be revitalized by alignment with active forces. The turning point in Nietzsche's project is when reactive forces can become active. This moment of turning, transformation, and becoming has no particular aim or end in sight. It is certainly "actualizing", but its creative, delightful subversiveness, its beauty and playfulness consist in the fact that it reflects a *transformative* rather than formative tendency (Rud, 2016). The space of training, the "educational" space, then becomes the playground of active forces, a place where we can learn to recognize and encourage active forces. This is not so much re-education but more a case of disporting oneself and *creating* oneself: a rewiring, a move away from the rationalistic, reactive, "Socratic" milieu of our educational settings towards greater incorporation of active forces.

Anti-education

The university in particular succeeds in keeping psychotherapy training in a state of refrigeration. The living body of the practice, its heart still beating, is kept safely under wraps for future reactivation. The words, phrases, and books once used to express a *culture* in the making are now dished out in bullet-pointed and Power-Point presentations that turn them into items of indoctrination. There is a rather poignant parallel here between psychotherapy and Nietzsche's thought: both are at heart experiments that, once transferred to academic settings, are forced to wear the pretence of quantifiable certainties.

The 'It' of the institution creates an aseptic space where notions of I-Thou are surreally imparted and absorbed in the neutral link of It-It. In large classrooms, in the newly built extensions of old venerable buildings, tutors repeat old homilies surrounded by glass and plastic.

In 1872, at the time of his rather high-minded love of the Greek tragedians, a 28-year-old Nietzsche delivered a series of lectures at the University of Basel titled *On the Future of our Educational Institutions*. He defended the values of antiquity against, among other things, what he saw as vulgar "journalism" and the tendency of academic institutions to manufacture "the servants of the day" (Nietzsche, 1872/2015a).

This is hardly a consolation, but it would seem that the neoliberal takeover of the humanities we witness today is only one of the many varied and concerted assaults on learning that went on long before – even long before Nietzsche. Stefan Collini (2017) charted some of this trajectory, pointing out how the (*active*) principle of free inquiry at the heart of higher education always had to contend with market-driven (*reactive*) forces. There are greater discrepancies in higher education between these two forces, one interested in culture (in its multiple, contradictory meanings), and the other pursuing economic gain and the political agendas of state and government. The difference is that reactive forces today are almost unanimous in privileging an ill-considered, philistine utilitarianism that places profit above all else and turns students into customers, teachers into shopkeepers, and institutions into businesses. For this reason, universities are, Collini argues, "doomed to be homes both to instrumentality on a large scale and to the critique of that instrumentality, in a tension or conflict that cannot be wholly resolved" (Collini, 2016).

Faced with such concerted assault on the humanities (psychotherapy training included), many of us are compelled to intervene in whole-hearted defence of the purity of research and the nobility of vocation – things that are in themselves questionable, for they generate *vocationalism*, namely "a focus on technical training [characterized by] the specialist's lack of intellectual openness" (Reitter, 2018, p. 30). This problem was lamented in Europe as far back as 1836, for example by the German progressive thinker and educator A. Diesterweg and some 30 years later by Nietzsche himself, for whom it is not "the triumph of systematic scholarship that sets the nineteenth century apart" but instead "the victory of systematic method over scholarship (cited in Reitter, 2018, p. 30).

Similarly, faced with today's mechanization of psychotherapeutic training, many of us feel obliged to fight a nostalgic battle in defence of the human (i.e., of a regressive rather than emancipatory discourse) and against the 'machine' – and in the process being wrongly perceived as mere 'Luddites'.

Going under

The overhuman announced by Zarathustra is not a messianic figure, i.e., one who is forever on the verge of appearing in the future. It symbolizes instead a necessary progression: the dissolution of the self as we know it. This is not a project or mission for the future but can happen this very moment. All it takes (though this is no small feat) is to shed our attachment to the human and the human self in particular, and open the gate to the overhuman. The *Übermensch* is neither 'superman' nor 'wonder woman' but the *over*human, a "depotentiated subject" (Vattimo, 2005, p. 165) who can dispose of the fictions of identity, unity and being, who can question the Cartesian self at its core, in a manner that will be echoed with a different language by Lacan (1994), for whom Descartes' approach is essentially directed "not towards science, but towards *its own certainty*" (p. 231).

To appreciate Nietzsche's subversion more fully: the destiny of humankind is for him not one of appropriation and linear progress but a *going under*, sinking. Our true condition is "to be someone who, continually and constitutively, is sinking" (Vattimo, 2005, p. 165). When applied to psychotherapy, the above statement may sound impracticable and even outrageous – going against all received ideas of what is right and proper. But if psycho-therapy is healing of *psyché*, of the Heraclitean 'soul', then the alleged cure must have at the top of the list the dissolution of the foremost neurosis that hinders it. And that neurosis is the self, in turn the offshoot of a secondary, all-pervasive neurosis: morality – and Judaeo-Christian morality in particular. Only if the self and its many shadows go under will there be any hope of healing.

All 'Being' and no play

The human must be overcome, Nietzsche famously says, in order to make space for the overhuman. This deceptively linear, allegedly evolutionistic proposition is open to myriad interpretations, all of them implied by Nietzsche – all of them valid to a degree. According to one of these, the human, restored through refined training and education to the animal-human continuum, becomes a myth-creating animal. The type of mythology announced is pre-dialectical or, more precisely, in the words of a Nietzschean scholar, a "destructive dialectics" (Colli, 1974, p. 47): agonistic, enigmatic, as well as, in twentieth-century parlance, deconstructive. It is linked to the Heraclitean ontology of *play* and *conflict* and at times described as "Dionysian cruelty" (Masini, 1978, p. 41) and as far removed from Hegelian dialectics and Gadamer's hermeneutics as can be.

Despite the protestations found in so many areas of humanistic therapy, interpretation is inevitable. Of course, the aspiration to suspend judgement and put aside our assumptions is not only commendable; it is *essential* if one values the ethics of hospitality (Bazzano, 2012a) – with its temporary "interruption of the self" (Derrida, 1999, p. 51) – and of our personal projects, upon which the psychotherapeutic endeavour must surely rest. At the same time, what we become aware of through the practice of *epoché* is the sheer volume of the assumptions we hold, as well as the near-impossibility of doing away with them. Coming to this realization is in any case preferable to either dogmatically believing that our assumptions are correct (a.k.a. *ignorance*) or that, having so cleverly bracketed them away, what we now perceive is naked and unadulterated reality (a.k.a. *arrogance*). The second stance is far more common than it is normally believed: almost everyone believes that there is something like 'pure experience' prior to 'knowledge'.

Interpretation is intrinsically woven into our perception of reality, as "we are constantly endeavouring to give meaning and order to our lives in the past, the present, and the future" (Auerbach, 1991, p. 549). As a result, our lives appear to us as necessarily distinct, unitary entities, even though they are constantly changing more or less radically, more or less rapidly, depending on the extent to which we are obliged, inclined, and able to assimilate the onrush of new experience. The essential difference is perhaps between a mode of interpretation that is invested in maintaining the abstraction of *being* – a relatively static and sub-stantial view of the world and ourselves within it – and one that recognizes and embraces the flow of *becoming* – the randomness and plurality of the world and the resultant multiplicity of the human consciousness reflecting it. A close expression of the latter has been achieved by modernist artists and writers. Psychotherapy appears to lag behind, and it will do so perhaps for as long as practitioners are unwilling to recognize that at its core psychotherapy is an art.

To speak of the self as a "flowing river of change" (Rogers, 1961, p. 122), as many have done, has now become a truism. Some of the painful nuances of this realization are, however, forgotten. Accepting the fluidity of the self is no mere speculation. It means abandoning aspects of our former self and our prior under-standing of past events. It brings about constant reappraisal, with the result being not always liberating but also veering towards disillusionment and anguish. Rebirths and renewals are always preceded by bereavements.

Existentialism embraced from the start the modern ontological condition of exile. It endeavoured to describe existence in the absence of a subject whose nature is groundless; it also promised to confront the philosophical tradition and its false hopes. It is legitimate to ask, however, whether mainstream existential therapy can still account for the above; whether, in the era of difference, it still gives voice to differ-ence. Whenever I speak of difference someone invariably asks: 'How do you know that you are different?' But this is not merely about feeling different from others. It relates, as in *Hamlet* (the first 'psychological' character in the history of drama), to time itself being out of joint; it has to do with an out-of-joint-ness with oneself, with the intrinsic eccentricity of being human, with our non-alignment of mind and body, and with the idiosyncratic nature of experience in general. The objection 'How do you know that you are different?' implies the following argument: in order to perceive myself as different, I must hold a notion of what is the norm or of what constitutes unity in relation to which my difference introduces a discordant note.

If one believes in the idea – popular across the majority of therapeutic orientations – of universal relatedness then, difference and rupture will be regarded as aspects of the fun-damental unity afforded by relatedness. My own understanding of the therapeutic encounter is that it requires the aspiration to momentarily suspend my own projects, passions and desires in the service of the other's (explicit or implicit) ethical request. So far, so predictable: the 'bracketing' of one's own assumptions and prejudices and even of therapeutic strategies is part of all sound therapeutic training. I suspect, however, that there is a little more to the practice of *epoché* than meets the eye. From its very inception, and judging from its own intricate genealogy, epoché has always been a lot more than bracketing, a little more demanding than setting aside a handful of conjectures that I might put back on at the end of the therapy hour. With its seeds in the living philosophy of Nagarjuna's Madhyamika School and its rendition into Western thought by Pyrrho and his sceptical school in Ancient Greece, epoché signalled from the start a much more fundamental 'suspension'. What is bracketed here is not just a handful of opinions, but the very roots of metaphysical thought: first, with Pyrrho, notions and beliefs that cannot be empirically shown and experientially perceived – such as ghosts, deities, the supernatural; and second, the belief in the independent existence of the human self (Nagarjuna). That these two sets of superstitions are inextricably linked we owe to Nietzsche, a 'sceptical' thinker who took scepticism to new heights.

What this means in relation to therapy is that it requires an active forgetting of 'Being' in the name of the concrete 'being' of the client sitting opposite. The real presence of the other is itself a breach, and this breach is not, as Gadamer has it, a "blow (*Stoss*) ... which thrusts itself upon us [and that] has to be accepted [given that] one must lose oneself in order to find oneself" (Behler, 1991, p. 154). *Interruption of the self* alone makes hospitality possible; this is ultimately an interruption of *Being* – we forfeit an abstraction inherited by two millennia of traditionalist thought in the name of *Life*. For those of us prepared to forget Being in the name of Life, Nietzsche provides formidable ammunition. For those of us keen to ground psychotherapy practice in the *organism* rather than in a set of moral, religious, and philosophical dictates, no other writer gives us as thorough a genealogical background and an exciting vision of possible futures.

For Gadamer, any form of disarray (in a text to be interpreted as in a dialogue between two people) is invariably absorbed and accepted. What keeps discontinuity at bay is an article of faith typical of the Heideggerian hermeneutic tradition that Gadamer popularized, namely a belief in the existence of a "non-present, removed totality" (Behler, 1991, p. 154). The remoteness of totality does not contradict its primary function as "underlying context" (ibid.), despite Habermas' later attempts to justify hermeneutics as presenting a 'softer' model of totality. A critique of the totalizing assumptions of hermeneutics is not a sign of relativism, as defenders of hermeneutics are bound to argue, but is grounded in two fundamental objections, already expressed by Derrida (1978). Firstly, the empirical endeavour of the subject is necessarily limited and perspectival. Secondly, we are at all times involved in a field where countless changes occur and where there is neither centre nor ground. These two objections open the investigation to the exhilarating domain of *play*, conspicuously absent in hermeneutics but central to Nietzsche – and eminently applicable to any inter-subjective human encounter as "a phase of play" (Derrida, 1978, p. 329).

Meaning itself – whether ascribed after the event or at the moment of perception – is for Derrida, who takes his cue from Nietzsche, "a *function* of play ... inscribed in a certain place in the configuration of a meaningless play" (ibid.). Play is here *antithetical to totality*. The latter is central in the construction of the hermeneutic edifice from Heidegger to Gadamer to current mainstream existential therapy.

Will to semblance

Even though existential phenomenology – particularly Merleau-Ponty's – continues to inform my own therapeutic practice, my position is ambivalent, as I find it increasingly hard to gloss over phenomenology's inherent prejudices. There are reasons why I have not abandoned it completely. Compared to an absurdly parochial therapy world, the phenomenological flock still forms a church that is broad enough to tolerate a handful of heretics in its midst. The history of existential phenomenology testifies this acceptance of genuine plurality, and I am naive enough to believe that it will one day open its fortress's gates to post-phenomenology (whose genesis is to be found in Nietzsche's writings), and even – wait for this – to the invaluable insights from Critical Theory – from Adorno to Benjamin to Butler. What would it be like, say, if orthodox existential phenomenological therapy were to suspend even for a short while its fascination with Heidegger's reactionary closeted theology in favour of Walter Benjamin's liberative political theology? For if one *must* dabble in theology, why not do it properly: make it angelic, messianic, bring on a future of revolutionary emancipation for body and soul alongside an intelligent critique of capitalism, instead of being narcotized by tedious accounts of a man in plus fours taking his constitutionals in the Black Forest.

Post-phenomenology and Critical Theory bear some of Nietzsche's more subversive insights and are both useful to therapeutic theory and practice. This is because they carry out a thoroughgoing critique of the religious and philosophical tradition, clearing the way for a renewed phenomenological investigation potentially devoid of more obvious prejudices and conformities. Yet the task at hand is hard, for existential phenomenology has always been good at co-opting more innovative accounts within its fold. It welcomed Nietzsche within its pantheon of supposedly pre-existential thinkers, succeeding in placing him, as Deleuze rightly says, "at the service of conformism" (2006, p. 1). Mercifully, the Nietzschean corpus proves even more refractory to the existential treatment than, say, Kierkegaard's. True, the latter has taken critique of the established order to formidable heights, to the *suspension* of the mores and customs of the herd in the name of a dangerous and seductive God. True, he is being promptly and punctually reprimanded by contemporary phenomenologists, his uncompromising stance chastised as "dangerous folly" (Spinelli, 2017, p. 288). Seen from a broadly 'Nietzschean' perspective, Kierkegaard, this great religious poet, can, however, still be seen as "ensnared in *ressentiment* … still [drawing his] strength from the ascetic ideal" (Deleuze, 2006, p. 34).

Because there exists, however tenuous, a link between Nietzsche's thought and existential phenomenology, the latter remains, despite its endemic penchant for compliance, open to the Nietzschean treatment and to a revisioning of phenomenological therapy as we know it. At the heart of this potential revisioning, there is in my view a necessary redirection of the therapeutic endeavour towards an *evaluation of natural forces at play*. Redressing the conventional topic of a 'search for meaning', Deleuze writes:

> We will never find the sense of something (of a human, a biological, or even a physical phenomenon) if we do not know the force which appropriates the thing, which exploits it, which takes possession of it or is expressed by it.
>
> (Deleuze, 1962/2006, p. 3)

Crucial to the above analysis is how one thinks of phenomena. We must begin to think of a phenomenon away from the notion of appearance, for this presupposes the existence of something behind the appearance. A phenomenon is also not an apparition but "a sign, a symptom which finds its meaning in an existing force" (Deleuze, 1962/2006, p. 3). Search for meaning (in a person's life, for instance, as in an event) cannot then be disengaged from its history, characterized by the progression of forces taking possession of it, as well as the co-existence of those forces competing for possession. *Agon* – conflict, struggle – is once again key. This multiple process of evaluation has little to do with current anodyne emphases on 'pluralism' in contemporary psychotherapeutic discourse. A section of *Genealogy of Morals* (Nietzsche, 1887/1996) makes this point abundantly clear. Here Nietzsche argues against the notions of final cause and "lawful aim" (p. 57) that often provide us with only one 'truthful' interpretation, and in its place presents "a more important principle" (ibid.) that recognizes that

> there is a world of difference between the reason for something coming into existence in the first place and the ultimate use to which it is put, its actual application and integration into a system of goals; that anything which exists, once it has somehow come into being, can be reinterpreted in the service of new intentions, repossessed, repeatedly modified to a new use by a power superior to it; that everything which happens in the organic world is part of a process of *overpowering, mastering*, and that, in turn, all overpowering and mastering is a reinterpretation, a manipulation, in the course of which the previous "meaning" and "aim" must necessarily be obscured or completely effaced.
>
> (Nietzsche, 1887/1996, pp. 57–58)

The above is a closer rendition of what a plurality of meanings and interpretations may begin to look like. Its effect is *hermeneutical disorientation* rather than mere 'tolerance of different views' exercised by a dominant, universalizing culture. There is a world of difference between the two. The 'pluralism' that is now fashionable in psychotherapy is egregiously exemplified in the aesthetic displayed in brochures and websites of most psychotherapy schools, institutes and universities: the logocentric, fossilized 'sacred' text of anodyne psychotherapeutic knowledge placed against pleasing images of 'diversity'. Photos of cheerful trainees on green lawns – black, Latino, WASP, Middle Eastern, gay men and women, young and not so young, all expressing wide-ranging heterogeneity – are there to decorate blurbs that spell out in attractive lingo the most crushingly homogenous content. The customer is of course free to choose the particular ambience and milieu that will determine the specific type of neopositivist, neoliberal indoctrination he or she will be imparted in the coming years of training. Cognitive behavioural therapy, psychodynamic, transpersonal, person-centred, emotion-focused, experiential, existential, phenomenological and so forth: a rich diversity of approaches – all cheerfully swaying to the same tune.

On the other hand, the hermeneutic multiplicity Nietzsche invites us to partake in, reminds us of the much-abused philosophical method of *empiricism*. Our neopositivist era may have neutered the latter to serialized, orderly barrages of 'evidence-based' data, but there is clearly a lot more to empiricism. It would be a pity to discard what is at heart one of the most valuable contributions of counter-traditional philosophy, namely: that a thing has many meanings, that "there are many things", and that something "can be seen as 'this and then that'" (Deleuze, 2006, p. 4). There is another, rather straightforward name for this: *interpretation*. This is *not* the interpretation that mediocre psychodynamic and psychoanalytic practice naively sees as getting to the 'bottom of things' or that dogmatic humanistic practitioners recoil from in sheepish horror. It is a far more subtle and, dare I say, sophisticated process. Interpretation is a difficult art and this is where Nietzsche's philosophy becomes invaluable to therapists. It is the fine weighing up of each event and its meaning, the assessment of "forces" that at any given time define the aspects of the event and its "relations" (Deleuze, 2006, p. 4).

In endeavouring to adapt Nietzsche's far-reaching ideas to therapy, it is not enough to passively subscribe to an existing therapeutic orientation that advertises authenticity and explicit allegiance to Nietzschean thought. We will have to start afresh. I have heard esteemed colleagues attribute to Nietzsche what in my view has very little to do with his writings: free will, authenticity, individualism. There is no free will in Nietzsche but instead difficult amalgamation of free will and determinism, seemingly incomprehensible to anyone schooled in Anglo-American logical thought. There is no defence of so-called 'authenticity' either, but a far more stimulating and exciting ethics (and aesthetic) of *inauthenticity*. There is, strictly speaking, no individualism or egoism either; there is no individual will in his 'will to power' (individualism being a wrong interpretation of will), nor is there power *over* another but power understood as generous expenditure. Is Nietzsche's thought too subtle for any therapeutic orientation? If one wants to apply Nietzsche's idea to therapy, the place to begin is *interpretation*, i.e. ascertaining what gives a person, an event, a 'thing' the force with which, as Deleuze says, "it has the most affinity" (1962/2006, p. 4). If one is so inclined, this can be described as seeking the *essence* of a person, event or 'thing' but in that case it would be important to uncouple the notion of essence from its transcendental meaning, from notions of sub-stance apart from its living presence within the innocence of becoming.

Rather than being anti-religion, anti-philosophy, anti-therapy or anti-psychiatry, the thing to do is to understand what kind of forces are at any given time taken hold of by a particular branch of learning or set of practices, and then see whether the balance can be re-established through creative struggle in favour of *active* rather than reactive forces. There are times when, stirred by these Nietzschean principles, I optimistically like to think that *any* institution, no matter how entrenched its structure, how frozen its practices, and how defensive its politics, is but another assemblage where, again, the balance can tilt in favour of expansive and experimental forces instead of being driven by a miserly desire for profit and obeisance to the narrow-minded guidelines of governments and corporate power. I am also painfully aware of the difficulty in sustaining this position, particularly when asked to do academic *karaoke*, i.e. repeating the lines written from a script that spell out with alarming certainty the articles of faith of this or that therapeutic orientation. Pursuing a mode of inquiry inspired by Nietzsche would on the other hand mean moving in the opposite direction – towards a dimension of *play* and *experimentation*.

What would it mean to redress the balance of a given situation in favour of active forces? The inspiration comes from Nietzsche's own way of applying this principle, and it involves the *mask*. Philosophers before him, whose thought was potentially disruptive to the vested interests and the rituals of civilized society, had to wear the mask of the religious person in order to be able to survive – for instance, not being burned at the stake as heretics. Because of this, philosophy historically adopted the role of herald of wisdom – provided the 'wisdom' in question was harmless and decorative. In later years, in order to survive, philosophers aped the alleged objectivity of the scientist – a fate that has befallen psychotherapists too. The triumph of analytic and logico-mathematical thought – presciently anticipating the rise of geekdom –made sure that philosophy went nowhere near the expansion of the possibilities of human experience. Both the religious person and the scientist are historically seen as trustworthy and safe by the status quo. This is because they share the ascetic ideal of remove from the 'risky', sensuous perception of the world. With their alleged moral uprightness and their love of objectivity, they exude reassuring distance from the passions, from the vagaries of subjectivity, and the uncertainty inbuilt in other types of investigations that are by nature more experimental. Both the philosopher and the psychotherapist inhabit a role that is potentially disruptive to social conformity and the political agenda of any ruling force. This is because the socio-political fabric is almost invariably dominated by reactive forces – forces whose raison d'être is self-preservation, which in turn fosters the maintenance of a status quo whose origins are in *ipseity*, i.e. "the superstitious belief in the self as an entity identical to itself" (Bazzano, 2012a, p. 12). The bourgeois values of possession and 'self-possession' are still the dominant ideals of civil society.

At their best, philosophy and psychotherapy disrupt these values, drawing attention to wounds, incongruities, and uncanny contradictions that open an unexpected wealth of exploration. This is why these two vocations are historically viewed with the same suspicion once destined to the *Kuenstler* of the middle ages (from which the German word for artist, *Künstler*, derives) describing both a craftsman or artist, as well as someone with no specific occupation, with a way of life outside the hierarchy of social and economic values, an outsider who would routinely arouse suspicion and even be perceived as evil. In his book on the work of the influential sociologist Marcel Mauss, Lévi-Strauss (1987) wrote of the inevitable existence within every culture and society, no matter how densely structured, of individuals who are placed outside its system. Rollo May (1969) relates the Kuenstler of the middle ages to the daimonic. Characterizing a philosopher or a therapist as somewhat closer to the daimonic may be too romantic a notion, a way to glamorize professions that are inevitably subjected to the greyness of the everyday, yet a look at the genealogy of both vocations raises interesting questions.

By wearing the masks of the wise, of the priest and the scientist, philosophers and psychotherapists adapt to a situation in order to be accepted and in order to survive. This is the first, protective task that putting on a mask accomplishes. There is also a second, equally important task the mask performs. A new emerging force must at first "borrow the features of the forces with which it struggles" (Deleuze, 1962/2006). In order to survive, a philosopher had to maintain a ridiculous disguise: he or she had to adopt the meditative air of the priest, with "the heart remote ... posthumous" (Nietzsche, 1887/1996, p. 88). To a certain degree, this can be appealing, even necessary; there are "conditions which are conducive to the highest spirituality" (ibid., p. 91); the ascetic/religious milieu is how philosophy itself learned to make its first tentative steps. By wearing the mask of religion and 'wisdom', however, philosophy started to believe in the mask itself:

> For a long time, *the ascetic ideal* has served the philosopher as a form in which to manifest himself, as a pre-condition of existence – he was obliged to *represent* it in order to be a philosopher, and he was obliged to *believe* in it in order to be able to represent it. The particular remoteness of the philosophers – with its negation of the world, its hostility to life, its scepticism towards the senses, its freedom from sensuality ... this is above all a consequence of the critical situation in which philosophy first emerged and managed to endure ... in so far as ... philosophy would not have been at all possible on earth without an ascetic shell and disguise, without an ascetic self-misunderstanding.
>
> *(Nietzsche, 1887/1996, pp. 94–95)*

The above is a necessary but difficult process, difficult in the sense that when philosophy begins to identify with religion, it forgets its own independent task. Something similar has happened, I believe, to contemporary therapists who have adopted the language and methodology of neopositivist, neoliberal psychology in the vain hope of dismantling the master's house by using the master's tools. At this point, the second important task of mask-wearing comes to the fore. It is our task to *conquer* a particular mask and then, like the philosopher in the task posed by Nietzsche, give it "a new sense which [in the case of philosophy] finally expresses its true anti-religious force" (Deleuze, 1962/2006, p. 5). In this second task, mask-wearing becomes trick and artifice, skill and artistry, qualities for which one needs courage and discipline. In Nietzsche's own words:

> Is there enough pride, daring, boldness, self-assurance, enough spiritual will, will to responsibility, *freedom of will* available today for the philosopher to be from now on really – *possible* on earth? ...
>
> *(1887/1996, p. 95)*

One could ask: Is there enough spiritual and political will today for the *psychotherapist* to exist? Too many times I hear colleagues argue in favour of the strategic use of this or that 'Trojan Horse': mindfulness, in the case of Dharma teaching and practice; academic psychology in the case of humanistic/existential/ psychodynamic ideas and practices. By definition, the Trojan Horse carries in its wooden belly the unexpected – something potentially disruptive to the status quo, but useful in the service of transformation. What often happens is that people inside the wooden horse become so pleasingly acquainted with its cosy interior and the soothing muzak that they forget to step out into the fresh air.

For Nietzsche, philosophy has to pierce through the various masks it has worn over the centuries and, through this process of unmasking, grasp its own essence. Wisdom too (*Sophia*, from which philosophy borrows its name) is a mask and has to be overcome or pierced through. To this active piercing through – mask after mask – Nietzsche gives the name of *interpretation*.

Philosophy is for Nietzsche still coming of age. Compared to it, psychotherapy is still in its infancy. For that reason alone, the latter's current infatuation with the shiny gadgetries of neopositivism, the soulless lingo of managerialism, and the crushing dullness of quantifiable data may be perhaps forgiven, provided we do not allow this new mask to solidify into our skin, bone and marrow but we learn instead what is there to learn (if anything) and continue the work of unmasking or interpretation in search of the *essence* of psychotherapy. Essence here is not understood in the abstract/transcendental meaning suggested by the etymology, i.e., the abstraction of being (*esse* = to be) perpetuated by centuries of idealist thought and the hegemony of the religious-philosophical tradition. Search for the essence means an investigation of *what kind of different forces* are at work in a particular object, in this case psychotherapy itself, bearing in mind that "the object itself is a force" (Deleuze, 1962/2006, p. 6). The essence of an object is then at all times *plural*: it is a composite of different forces at work. Should one still crave hermeneutics (a discipline that has, in my view, lost its way), it would be ideally oriented along *naturalistic* rather than *onto-theological* principles. Thus conceived, a hermeneutic practice will no longer be interested in the so-called 'truth' or in the so-called 'truth of being'. In its search for the essence, it will instead investigate what natural forces are at play, assessing whether the balance can be tilted in favour of *active* forces, i.e. of life-affirming, expansive and exploratory tendencies rather than *reactive* ones, i.e. life-denigrating tendencies whose chief aim is mere self-preservation. In Nietzsche's language, this is often presented as the polarity between health and sickness, a polarization he lived and suffered first-hand.

Pluralism, in Nietzsche's sense, always arises from this immersion in the organismic life of *physis* or nature, where one finds that "the being of a force is plural" and that "it would be absurd to think about a force as singular" (Deleuze, 1962/2006, p. 6).

This is also where Nietzsche breaks with Schopenhauer (a crucial point for those interested in linking Nietzsche to Freud's psychoanalysis), for whereas the will (much like Freud's *id*) is *unitary* in Schopenhauer, it is at all times *multiple* in Nietzsche. Even more significantly, while a unitary vision of the will as the prime motor of a 'fallen' or samsaric world brings about renunciation in Schopenhauer, a vision of the will as multiple eventually results in Nietzsche in the constant question "What does a [particular] will want?" (Deleuze, 1962/2006, p. 8). For Nietzsche, this question ends up eliciting an *affirmation of difference*, aligned to what he calls noble morality, antithetic to slave morality.

What is slave morality? Essentially, "the morality of utility" (Nietzsche, 1886/1978, p. 178). It is often ruled by *reactive* forces, has a "pessimistic mistrust of the entire [human] situation" (ibid.), and is characterized by a gregariousness born of cowardice rather than solidarity. On the other hand, noble morality is prevalently made up of *active* forces and the sheer pleasure of knowing oneself different. It "creates values" (Nietzsche, 1886/1978, p. 176); it has at its centre "the feeling of plenitude, of power which seeks to overflow, the happiness of high tension, the consciousness of a wealth which would like to give away and bestow" (ibid.). Despite what is commonly believed, there *is* compassion within Nietzsche's noble morality, "but not, or almost not, from pity, but more from an urge begotten by superfluity of power" (ibid.). It is a compassion born out of generosity rather than moral obligation. It is tempting to make of Nietzsche the champion of a self-styled and preposterous notion of imagined, egotistical 'nobility', and then proceed to extol or revile his writings accordingly. But his noble morality has little to do with those self-actualized, fully functioning, 'authentic' mini-gurus and ersatz priests out there, nor does it share an iota with the banal immorality of those who claim to have gone 'beyond good and evil'.

Above all, there are two traits, closely linked to one another, that characterize Nietzsche's 'noble person': (a) a move away from the "bad air! Bad air!" (Nietzsche, 1887/1996, p. 28) of *ressentiment* and the spirit of revenge that seek (moral) blame and are fixated on causation; and (b) a profound, un-gregarious appreciation of *difference*. The latter is not 'appreciation of uniqueness' of the kind favoured by the fashion industry *or* the psychotherapy industry alike. It is an incitement to evaluate and interpret the different forces that come to constitute our individuality. It also constitutes the basic outline of his profoundly *naturalist* philosophy.

Note

1 All translations from Masini, 1978 are by the author. There is no English translation of Masini's work at present.

5

HOMO NATURA

Elsewhere

One night, half way through writing this book, I dreamt I was a feral child. My name was Arthur Rimbaud. I was hiding in a dilapidated country barn, away from the foolishness and bigotry of neighbours and family. Barefoot, my clothes in tatters, now and then I would ensure the thick wooden door was tightly shut.

The dream left me puzzled and unsettled. I talked it through with a colleague. She thought it beautiful, and as a result my own perspective shifted: less focused on solitude, wildness, and hiding; more centred on the poetry that I knew would come from these. Then I remembered that some 40 years ago, when I first encountered Rimbaud's poetry, I instinctively associated it with Nietzsche's writings. The association persists to this day, despite the fact that I can now appreciate the difference between them. They were contemporaries and unaware of each other, and turned their back on their vocation, spending the protracted twilight of their lives with their gaze fixed on a remote elsewhere – Rimbaud in Africa, Nietzsche in Weimar. Both found the trail left by their shadow darkened still by a sacrificial choice (arms trafficking) and cynical manipulation (a Nazi sister). Both rose from the ashes of notoriety to surge above the limitations of their century. Both spoke eloquently of multiplicity. Both actively embraced intensity and the autonomous domain of affect; both championed just about everything that is condemned by religion and regulated by psychology. They embraced life fiercely, denouncing knowledge, religion and official literature as elaborate strategies to keep it at bay – as convoluted architectures ruled by fear.

Fear of life

Nietzsche's descriptions of the architectural metaphors of knowledge and culture, beautifully abridged by Sarah Kofman (1972/1993, pp. 59–80), provide invaluable material for psychotherapy. Whether understood as a progression or as each containing and implying the others, the following images are found in his writings: *beehive, tower, pyramid, columbarium,* and *spider's web.* Mainly intended as metaphors describing the trajectory of knowledge and culture, they are also, in my view, inextricably linked to how we ordinarily understand the relationship between the self and the world. To apprehend Nietzsche's contribution in this way is to see him as both physician of culture and psychologist of the individual psychic domain.

a The *beehive* of knowledge – where "*our* treasure is to be found" (Nietzsche, 1887/1996, p. 3) – represents the resolute and concerted activity of science. Used by Nietzsche to indicate the orderly organization of cultural/scientific ideas, it is still *instinctual*, and its beauty, though "not disinterested ... is symptomatic of ... neediness" (Kofman, 1972/1993, p. 62). In the same ways as bees build cells and fill them with nectar that has been gathered outside, so science builds an empty structure and crams it with the world. Being a *semiology* (system of signs) as well as a *mythology* (an extensive series of narratives), all science can do is attempt to describe the world. It does not and cannot *explain* it. Already with the beehive, only the first rung in this series of architectural images, we find a theme that will remain constant throughout successive stages. Having collected the nectar of experience from the external world, we too, "spiritual bees from birth, [have] our hearts set on one thing only – 'bringing something home'" (Nietzsche, 1887/1996, p. 3). We carefully preserve the treasure of experience gained in our forays into the external world within a remarkable, precarious structure. This is in many ways understandable and even legitimate. The problem arises once we gradually start believing that the descriptions gathered and classified within the edifice of knowledge – and within the cocoon of our self-construct – are not merely interesting attempts at describing the world but constitute its very essence. At the 'beehive stage', there are still signs of life: the link with the natural world is still tangible, the treasure gathered is still nourishing. This state of affairs soon changes, however, once the initial structure begins to morph into the next – the tower.

b The *tower*, or medieval fortress, boldly asserts itself as a stronghold of knowledge. Here the link to nature (as with instinct and intuition) slackens considerably. The tower's purpose is to *guard* the treasure of knowledge *against life itself.* Individually, "one must defend oneself against everything which affirms life, whether within, or outside of oneself" (Kofman, 1972/1993, p. 89). Collectively, the tower becomes a Tower of Babel: it knits an intricately artificial language whose aim is to turn living processes into an imaginary set of quantitative measurements. There is no doubt that this has helped the preservation of the human species; we found shelter and solace within this rigid, computable structure. But we also paid a high price, for it separated us from the living world. How can we become immune to the perceived dangers life poses for us? By *playing dead*, by being dead in life: "The rigidity of the construction mimics that of a skeleton; it is only by being always already dead in life that we can survive" (Kofman, 1972/1993, p. 66). The skeletal rigidity provides inspiration for building the next structure, the pyramid.

c   If some degree of uncertainty still lingered in the previous stages, parallel to a traceable, if dimmed, echo of life – the *pyramid* presents us with the certainty, hierarchy and perceived stability of a 'true' order, rational and reasonable, confidently set against a 'false' phenomenal world of varying impressions and unreliable appearances. Life itself is *entombed* within this structure, in exchange for the great achievement of fathoming a new "regulative" and "imperative" (Schrift, 1990, p. 89) conceptual world made up of sensory impressions that have been captured, killed and skinned. Once turned into mummies, they can now be more comfortably relied upon.

d   The move from the orderly and hierarchical mummification within the pyramid to the next architectural structure is but a brief step. Whilst the pyramid is still a noble tomb, where life, in some very impoverished form, is still at least conceivable, the Roman *columbarium* (a room or building with niches for funeral urns to be stored) preserves ashes of the dead, and can be compared, according to Nietzsche, to concepts in science, which are merely the dregs of metaphors. At this stage, all remnants or faint connections between life and the occupants of this structure have been cut off. The structure is no mere depository of concepts but ends up being *the very place we inhabit*. At the same time, Nietzsche is genuinely in awe of the genius of construction shown at every stage of this process. The building of several intricate temples and tombs of knowledge, and of complex concepts about ourselves – they all deserve our admiration. Even so, we would do well to remember that these structures rest on an illusory base, one which is "made out of the very material of those it has to shelter and protect" (Kofman, 1972/1993, p. 69). By the time all life has completely and irretrievably vanished from the picture, the last metamorphosis takes place.

e   If there was any doubt, up to this point, as to the profoundly reactive nature of this process, the emergence of *the spider's web* reveals the inherent destructiveness of the entire project of acquisition of knowledge and of the one-sided consolidation of the self-construct. The worthy industriousness of the bees results in, and perhaps even conceals, the harmfulness of the spider's web, a harmfulness which, one must remember, is not rooted in animosity but in "necessity" (Kofman, 1972/1993, p. 69). A spider's web on a sunny day, seen against the light, is a wondrous thing. It is easy to forget that the spider is also a vampire that sucks the blood of midges it has attracted into its nets, in the same way as the concept disfigures life, makes it pale and sad (ibid., p. 69). The act of converting the rich life of the world into an array of metaphysical narratives, whether 'religious' or 'scientific', is motivated by a nihilistic will. This is, in Sarah Kofman's wonderful turn of phrase, "a sign of a life which is afraid of life", a life that is anxious of "being seduced by sensuality because it would not be strong enough to bear its intoxication" (ibid., p. 72); a life that advocates objectivity and detachment from the senses because, despite a yearning for closer contact with the world, it is unable to endure it. Parallels with Freud's notion of the spider as symbol of castration, representing the phallic mother, are unavoidable and deeply resonant. It seems fitting to think of the enterprises of knowledge, science and metaphysics as elaborate schemes unconsciously aimed at enfeebling this uncertain and bountiful life to manageable and measurable levels.

Psychotherapy too, despite its revolutionary beginnings, is fast becoming another implement in the hands of an all-encompassing nihilistic project. This demonstrates the cunning of the latter's more recent incarnations, namely neoliberalism and its cultural appendix, neopositivism. That it does so while managing to repeat mantra-like the tenets of its once progressive endeavour can be seen, depending on one's sensibility, as ingenious, comical, or sad.

The great reason

Having followed the trajectory from beehive to spider's web, it is now tempting to fathom a Nietzsche-inspired philosophic-therapeutic project that advocates the undoing of all these layers of knowledge and metaphysics and the final unveiling of a natural substratum. Nietzsche seems to move in this direction when he hints at the "terrible basic text *homo natura*" (1886/1978, p. 143). The trajectory from beehive to spider's web succeeds in clarifying to what extent Western thought has been fuelled by a vampiric nihilist will, its exponents and advocates too becoming gradually lifeless.

> Don't you sense a long concealed vampire in the background who begins with the senses and in the end is left with, and leaves, mere bones, mere clatter?
>
> *(Nietzsche, 1882/1974, p. 333)*

There is much in his writing that seemingly reinforces some of the tenets of 'body-oriented' psychotherapies. It is only when one hears for the umpteenth time the body psychotherapist or supervisor asking 'Where do you feel that in your body?' that one begins to wonder whether this is just another tired formula among many. This type of routine question can even become problematic if the therapist/supervisor has not earned the trust of her client/supervisee, in which case it ceases to be exploration and becomes imposition. Naturalistic emphasis on bodily affects is a wonderful way forward towards a potentially rich exploration. The body is for Nietzsche the *great reason*, far more amazing a phenomenon than consciousness or spirit will ever be. However, this is *only the beginning* of the exploration. Arriving at a potentially more natural place where metaphysical constructs are seen for what they are is rewarding, yet the therapeutic endeavour is not a process of dis-covering or un-covering.

The very idea of truth as *unveiling* (for instance, of a false self giving way to a real self), so dear to some therapeutic orientations, is profoundly misleading, for it involves an imaginary opposition between appearance and reality – an opposition Nietzsche abolishes with a shrug. To be involved in a philosophical/therapeutic practice in Nietzsche's sense has nothing to do with discovery. Peeling off one mask does not take us to 'authenticity' but to another mask. Similarly, our journey from beehive to spider's web will certainly sharpen our understanding of how removed we have become from the text/texture of *homo natura*. This is itself a sign of strength, of our willingness to disrupt our cosy notions of truth. It may help us understand, feel and appreciate our neglected instinctual nature. But the journey cannot stop there. Nietzsche invites us to see that the instinctive and natural layer we come to is itself *interpretation*. The body itself (*life* itself) is not the ground of being but something that coincides with evaluation and whose aim is power. Is there a final port of call, an original text? Yes and no. There is *will to power*, but this is not an "ontological truth grasped by intuition [but] an unhypothetical hypothesis posited in the name of the method's 'demand for economy'" (Kofman, 1993, p. 94). Will to power is not the so-called truth of being but "a pure name [designating] every force which acts" (ibid., p. 95).

It is *an interpretation that knows itself to be an interpretation*; it presents itself as interpretation. It genealogically decodes all other interpretations not in terms of 'truth' and 'untruth' but as symptoms of sickness or health, of a play of natural forces which are either life-denying (reactive) or life-affirming (active). Nietzsche makes it clear that he is not describing an individual will, discerning and evaluating natural forces from an objective individualized stance, but instead the natural, 'neutral' process of interpretation:

> [T]here is no will, and consequently neither a strong nor a weak will. The multitude and disgregation of impulses and the lack of any systematic order among them result in a "weak will"; their coordination under a single predominant impulse results in a "strong will": in the first case it is the oscillation and the lack of gravity; in the latter, the precision and clarity of the direction.
> (*Nietzsche, 1968, pp. 28–29*)

Naked dance

Despite Heidegger's insistence that it should be seen as the truth of being, Nietzsche's notion of will to power is merely a symbolic name that, like life itself, takes several forms and different mythic and poetic guises, from Apollo to Dionysus to Oedipus. Will to power, in its endless process of interpretation and evaluation, symbolizes the protean nature of life. The nakedness of Dionysus is not the truth of being but the innocence of a life that is not turned against itself in condemnation. The naked body here is not 'truer' than the clothed one. To arrive at an embodied naked 'truth' can be as misleading as being caught in the layers of cloth woven by metaphysics and morality. The evaluative/interpretative choice is not between 'real' nakedness and 'false' wearing of clothes but between, on the one hand, "clothing woven by instinctive evaluations, which forms a perfect marriage with the contours of the body it clothes and thus reveals it", and, on the other hand, "a badly adapted clothing which travesties the person it covers" (Kofman, 1993, p. 98). The former is closer to a naturalistic reading of human experiencing that accepts its fundamental innocence. The latter, in its attempt to adorn and 'elevate' it, weighs it down with religious and mystical garments. The former affirms *life*; the latter manufactures *being*.

Poetic flight

Once in a while I am told that my writing and style of presentation are 'poetic'. This is usually meant as praise, though there are times, I feel, that this is a way of saying that I am not following the standards set by academia. Gaston Bachelard, a poetic philosopher of the highest calibre, wrote movingly and convincingly of Nietzsche as a poet. For him, "the poet [in Nietzsche] partly explains the thinker" (Bachelard, 1943/1988, p. 127). It is true that Nietzsche's imagination soars; that his metaphors and associations weave rich layers of meaning; that his writing has multiple styles, and that he switches the register expertly and unexpectedly. Yet it would be wrong to see Nietzsche 'only' as a poet, for this would mean neglecting a deeper engagement with his profound naturalism, something that he extends to our 'inner world', arguably the privileged domain of poetry:

> I maintain the phenomenality of the inner world, too: everything of which we become conscious is arranged, simplified, schematized, interpreted through and through – the actual process of inner "perception", the causal connection between thoughts, feelings, desires, between subject and object, are absolutely hidden from us – and are perhaps purely imaginary. The "apparent *inner* world" is governed by just the same forms and procedures as the "outer" world.
>
> *(Nietzsche, 1968, pp. 263–264)*

Naturalism and imaginative 'poetic' flight temper each other, with the latter out-witting the thoroughly metaphysical and oppressive injunction of having to find, as some would have it, a 'proper' language that will replace metaphysics (e.g. Fink, 1960/2003). Poetic language is one way of introducing ambiguity and refusing to settle with the prevailing accounts of organic life that go back to either biologism or spiritualism. In biologism, the body is "objectivised"; in spiritualism, it is "spirited away" (Blondel, 1991, p. 201). Nietzsche's response is twofold: (a) establishing a naturalistic primacy of the body; (b) refusing to settle with an empiricist notion of the body. Although Nietzsche's thought appears to swerve in the direction of Spinoza and his doctrine of *correspondence* – i.e., towards a monism that relies on a union *and* separation between body and spirit – his late writings tell another story:

> Nothing is more erroneous than to make of psychical and physical phenomena the two faces, the two revelations of one and the same substance. Nothing is explained thereby: the concept "substance" is perfectly useless as an explanation. Consciousness in a subsidiary role, almost indifferent, superfluous, perhaps destined to vanish and give way to a perfect automatism.
>
> *(Nietzsche, 1968, p. 283)*

Against the literalism of biologism and spiritualism, Nietzsche offers a set of metaphors that interpret physiology and its correlate/subordinate, 'consciousness', in the same way a philologist interprets a text. Far from asserting the body as foundational, the primacy he ascribes to it is a way to "guard ourselves against conceit" (Nietzsche, 1895/2007a, p. 15) – a way of placing humans alongside an animal-human bodily continuum that loosens the arrogant claim that conceives of humans as the "crown of creation" (ibid.).

A revolving door

The body could be compared to a revolving door between the wonderful chaos of the world and the sweeping simplifications of the intellect. The world is another term for the furthest reaches of multiplicity, for an infinite text that we can only begin to consider via the 'translation' of pure intensity – or neutral affect – into drives, instincts, feelings and emotions. This translation is a reduction, but one that is very different from the reduction made by the intellect. The intellect tends to translate the chaos of the world into *unity*; this oversimplification ends up neutering the experience the world. The body too inter-prets and simplifies the world but "only in order to pluralize it" (Blondel, 1991, p. 206), with the various affects comprising the uneven viewpoints of a game "in which they exist only in the plural" (ibid., p. 207). Thorough-going embodiment is a gateway to the plurality of affects, and a form of psychotherapy that calls itself embodied would need to take this into account. It is this detour via the body, i.e., via an intrinsic plurality of affects, that prompts Nietzsche to state that there are no facts, only interpretations.

The intention here is not to reduce the intellect to the body but "in presenting the body as a plurality of intellects, to reveal the radical nature of plurality" (Blondel, 1991, p. 207). His precursor here is Leibniz (1704/1982), a thinker whose ideas are rarely discussed in philosophy, let alone in psychotherapy, but one who had the "incomparable insight", Nietzsche (1882/1974) tells us,

> ... that consciousness is merely an *accidens* [accidental attribute] of experience and *not* its necessary and essential attribute; that, in other words, what we call consciousness constitutes only one state of our spiritual and psychic world (perhaps a pathological state) and *not by any means the whole of it*. The pro-fundity of this idea has not been exhausted to this day.
>
> *(p. 305)*

Reflecting on this fertile connection between Nietzsche and Leibniz in relation to the problem of consciousness, Blondel (1991) presents us with *four pointers* that can in my view be usefully adapted to psychotherapeutic practice, particularly, but not exclusively, to a type of practice that is keen on embodied experience:

a   The entire body is thought.
b   Conscious thought is only an *accidental* part of the body; it is more a relation (in Nietzsche's language, a *perspective*) than a 'thing'.
c   The body is real, not as substance but as "the movement and relation between forces" (Blondel, 1991, p. 208).
d   The difference between body-as-thought and conscious thought is not so much a distance between conscious and unconscious, but between simple and multiple.

Expanding on these four insights, Nietzsche adds an important twist, as well as a caveat. It would be wrong, he tells us, to think of "*intelligere*" (conscious thought) as "something conciliatory, just, and good – something that stands essentially opposed to the instincts" (1882/1974, p. 261). In fact, conscious thought is nothing but "a certain behaviour of the instincts towards one another" (ibid.).

Consciousness as a symptom

> All credibility, all good conscience, all evidence of truth come only from the senses.
> *(Nietzsche, 1886/1978, p. 82)*

Nietzsche is perhaps the first thinker who consistently gave primacy to the body over and above consciousness. In doing so, he outlined an altogether different route than the one pursued by the philosophical and psychological traditions. There are echoes here of another thinker who similarly advocated a different route for the sciences. For Spinoza (1677/1996), "the human mind does not know the human body itself, nor does it know that it exists, except through ideas of affections by which the body is affected" (p. 47). Counter-traditional thinkers like Spinoza, Nietzsche and Deleuze (among others) all tend to situate consciousness on a humbler position than the one normally granted by the tradition. For Nietzsche, consciousness is in a *servile* position in relation to the organism: it observes the body and the complexity of bodily affects, sending dispatches from the higher life of the body. Its relation to the body and the 'instincts', consciousness is an *aspect* of the instinctual life, one that is not particularly better, more moral, or even fairer:

> Just as the act of being born plays no part in the procedure and progress of heredity, so "being conscious" is in no decisive sense the opposite of the instinctive – most of the philosopher's conscious thinking is secretly directed and compelled into definite channels by his instincts.
> *(Nietzsche, 1886/1978, p. 17)*

Attempts from consciousness to define the body invariably fail, for the body cannot be defined either as a "field of forces" or a "nutrient medium fought over by a plurality of forces" (Deleuze, 1962/2006, p. 37). There is, properly speaking, no field of forces, nor is there a quantity of reality; instead, "reality is already a quantity of force" (ibid.). What constitutes a body – at a chemical, biological, social or political level – is the ongoing competitive relation between forces. In this sense, a body is the result of *chance*. Within it – within any organism as within 'nature' itself – we find active and reactive forces. It is crucial at this point that we take a closer look at them.

Active and reactive forces

> What is "passive"? – To be hindered from moving forward: thus an act of resistance and reaction. What is "active"? – reaching out for power.
> *(Nietzsche, 1968, pp. 346–347)*

An *active force* has three fundamental characteristics: it is (a) "plastic, dominant ... subjugating" (Deleuze, 1962/2006, p. 57); (b) it "goes to the limit of what it can do" (ibid.); (c) it *affirms* and *enjoys* its difference.

A *reactive force* has also three characteristics: (a) it is a "utilitarian force of adaptation" (Deleuze, 1962/2006, p. 57); (b) it also "separates", as well as denies the active force "from what it can do" (ibid.); (c) it turns the active force *against itself.*

The way reactive forces implement their quantity of force is by acquiring mechanical resources and final aims. They accomplish life's conditions by producing the functional undertakings of utility and adaptation. This is in itself valuable, but consciousness has difficulty in characterizing active forces. Historically, modern thought has more readily registered reactive forces; it has been excessively fixated with their mechanics and intricacies and has neglected active forces altogether. We have been strangely contented to think that it is enough to understand the life of an organism in terms of reactive forces; we are fascinated by their trembling and shuddering, and have gone on to erect theories of life entirely on their account, while neglecting to study and understand more closely the nature of active forces. The premises for such study are outlined by Nietzsche in that *tour de force* that is section 12 in the second essay of his *Genealogy of Morals*. His initial argument here concerns the origin and so-called 'lawful aim' of punishment which he refutes by asserting that there is "a world of difference between the reason for something coming into existence" and "the ultimate use to which it is put, its actual application and integration into a system of goals" (Nietzsche, 1887/1996, p. 57). He writes:

> [A]nything which exists, once it has somehow come into being, can be reinterpreted in the service of new intentions, repossessed, repeatedly modified to a new use by a power superior to it ...; everything which happens in the organic world is part of a process of overpowering, mastering, and ..., in turn, all overpowering and mastering is a reinterpretation, a manipulation, in the course of which the previous "meaning" and "aim" must necessarily be obscured or completely effaced.
>
> *(ibid., pp. 57–58)*

This passage already outlines the attributes of active forces, whose modus operandi (as he goes on to say) goes *beyond utility* – whether in a human body, an organ or a social and political body:

> No matter how well one has understood the usefulness of any physiological organ (or for that matter, legal institution, social custom, political practice, artistic or religious form), one has learnt nothing about its origin in the process ... All aims, all uses are merely signs indicating that a will to power has mastered something less powerful than itself and impressed the meaning of a function upon it in accordance with its own interests.
>
> *(Nietzsche, 1887/1996, p. 58)*

The above passage is one of the clearest definitions of the will to power found in Nietzsche's writings. It also culminates in a concise description of his central idea of genealogy, opposed to the notion of evolution, which is for him the quintessence of our fascination with reactive forces:

> So the entire history of a thing, an organ, a custom may take the form of an extended chain of signs, of ever-new interpretations and manipulations, whose causes do not themselves necessarily stand in relation to one another, but merely follow and replace one another arbitrarily and according to circumstances.
>
> *(ibid.)*

Crucially, and unlike the prevalent teleological accounts of evolution and history found in Darwin and Hegel, there is *no developmental progress* found in Nietzsche's genealogical model. Applied, for instance, to current humanistic psychotherapy theory, one could say that the 'tendency' at work is not 'formative' (purposely moving towards greater actualization and 'growth'), but *transformative*.

> The "development" of a thing, a custom, an organ does not in the least resemble a *progressus* towards a goal ... Rather, this development assumes the form of the succession of the more or less far-reaching, more or less independent processes of overpowering which affect it – including also ... the resistance marshalled against these processes, the changes of form ... and the results of these successful coun-teractions. The form is fluid, but the "meaning" even more so.
>
> *(ibid.)*

The above applies to individual organisms too, for at every stage "the 'meaning' of the individual organs also changes" (Nietzsche, 1887/1996, p. 58). This last point emphasizes the potential for reorganization in the body; it anticipates an implicit critique of the view that sees the body (and 'embodiment') as the final ground of philosophical/psychotherapeutic enquiry. We have seen that there is no final ground in Nietzsche's view, but an ongoing process of interpretation and eva-luation whose name is will to power. Affirming the latter is, however, an uphill struggle. This is because the "study of life as a whole" (Nietzsche, 1887/1996, p. 59) has neglected the fundamental feature of *activity* in favour of "a second-order activity, a mere reactivity". As a result,

> life itself has been has been defined as an ever-more expedient inner adapta-tion to external circumstances ... But this represents a failure to recognize the essence of life, its *will to power*; this overlooks the priority of the spontaneous, attacking, overcoming, reinterpreting, restructuring and shaping forces, whose action precedes "adaptation"; this denies even the dominating role of the organism's highest functionaries, in which the vital will manifests itself actively and in its form-giving capacity.
>
> *(ibid.)*

The philosophical tradition always held consciousness in high regard, its eulogies coated in both religious and secular/rationalist terms, and perhaps no epoch rated it as highly as the current one. Even psychoanalysis, whose premises once relied on the hypothesis of an unconscious, is weighed down by the peculiar malaise of our neopositivist times, namely "hypertrophied consciousness" (Bollas, 2007, p. 81). This could be characterized as the Promethean delusion to grab hold of organismic experiencing by planting on its luxuriant soil a handful of colourful little signposts. For Otto Rank,

> the error lies in the scientific glorification of consciousness, of intellectual knowledge, which even psychoanalysis worships as its highest god – although it calls itself a psychology of the *unconscious*. But this means only an attempt to rationalize the unconscious and to intellectualize it scientifically.
>
> *(Rank, 1932, p. 222)*

Consciousness only conveys the effect that active forces exert on reactive forces. Consciousness is itself reactive. As such, it does not really "know what a body can do or what activity it is capable of" (Deleuze, 1962/2006, p. 38). Consciousness merely sees the organism from its own perspective and apprehends it in its own terms, i.e., reactively. The origins of consciousness are, for Nietzsche (1882/1974), steeped in adaptation and survival:

> That our actions, thoughts, feelings and movements enter our own consciousness – at least a part of them – that is the result of a "must" that for a terribly long time lorded it over humans. As the most endangered animals, they *needed* help and protection, they needed their peers, they had to learn to express their distress and make themselves understood; and for all of this they needed "consciousness" first of all, they needed to "know" for themselves what distressed them, they needed to "know" how they felt, they needed to know what they thought ... Humans, like every living being, think continually without knowing it; the thinking that raises to consciousness is only the smallest part of all this – the most superficial and worst part – for only this conscious thinking takes the form of words, which is to say signs of communication, and this fact uncovers the origin of consciousness.
>
> *(pp. 298–299)*

The body always occupies a higher place because, unlike consciousness, it is active, permeated by the activity of essentially unconscious forces. A truer science would be involved in tracing this unconscious activity. However, science as we know it moved in the opposite direction:

> The idea that science must follow in the footsteps of consciousness ... is absurd. We can see the morality of this idea. In fact there can only be science where there is no consciousness, where there can be no consciousness.
>
> *(Deleuze, 1962/2006, p. 39)*

Naturalism and perspectivism

Two important conclusions can be drawn from the above investigation:

a   Nietzsche's philosophical position is thoroughly *naturalistic*. A psychotherapeutic theory and practice that were to draw from it would likewise give primacy to the body and the body's affects. Nietzsche embraces the scientific naturalistic critique of theology and metaphysics, with a warning, exemplified by his perspectivism.
b   Nietzsche's *perspectivism*, i.e., his taking into account the myriad perspectives that arise once we experientially investigate the life of the organism starting from our own experiencing, reins in the dogmatic reductivism inherent in scientific and materialistic doctrines (Cox, 1999).

The co-presence of naturalism and perspectivism in Nietzsche's discourse makes his investigation subtle and exhilarating. Naturalism and perspectivism mitigate each other, and their combined application help us avoid the pitfalls of, respectively, theoretical inflexibility and relativism. His naturalism, often overlooked by early commentators, is wholly consistent with the notion of the death of God and the pervasive presence of his shadows, which is both a straightforward observation as well as a challenge to accomplish a twofold task: (a) the *naturalization of the human*, and (b) the *de-deification of nature*. This is where our discussion takes us next.

Homo natura

The first task, the naturalization of the human, is achieved by "a thoroughgoing naturalism in epistemology and ontology"; the second, the de-deification of nature, via "foreground[ing] its commitment to the view that there is no 'pre-given world', but only perspectives (or interpretations)" (Cox, 1999, p. 71).

What would it mean to introduce a thoroughgoing naturalism in psychotherapeutic practice and philosophical inquiry? We may need to reconsider those qualities of natural and sensuous life that have been slandered by metaphysics and theology such as, for instance: instinct, sensation, and affect; growth, decay, and death; procreation and nutrition; impermanence, becoming, and contingency. We would need to free a practice such as body psychotherapy of the dogmatism inherent in accounts that see the body as a quantifiable entity and body affects as 'objectively' computable and at a remove from organismic processes. We would need to free a body-oriented psychotherapy (even when it calls itself 'emotion focused') from metaphysical and transcendental dregs. For Nietzsche, a perspective is metaphysical if it makes a clear-cut demarcation between the natural and the extra-natural world, i.e. between "the empirical, affective, physical, apparent, contingent" and "the rational, moral, mental, essential, necessary, eternal" (Cox, 1999, p. 71), with primacy granted to the extra-natural. He sees this move as motivated by a fear of *contamination*, and is developed further into the fundamental error that these supposedly separate domains have wholly separate origins. This *"metaphysical faith"* (Nietzsche, 1882/1974, p. 283) is the very same "upon which our faith in science rests" (ibid.). Science, then, is *not naturalistic enough*, for even we godless anti-metaphysicians still take our fire, too, from the flame lit by a faith that is thousands of years old, that Christian faith which was also the faith of Plato, that God is the truth, that truth is divine. But what if this should become more and more incredible, if nothing should prove to be divine any more unless it were error, blindness, the lie – if God himself should prove to be our most enduring lie?

(ibid.)

The naturalization of the human – our first task – begins with a suspension (*epoché*) of all metaphysical assumptions, be they scientific or religious. This clears the path for a series of thought experiments supported by a constant focus on the qualities and gradation of the natural forces at work. The results of some of these thought experiments can be startling. For instance, by observing the various levels of intensity of the life force, we might conclude with Nietzsche (1886/1978) that there is no moral difference between good and evil deeds but "at most, a difference in degree" (p. 75). We might also begin to challenge the assumption that there is a clear demarcation between life and death, when, at close observation, "the living is merely a type of what is dead, and a very rare type" (Nietzsche, 1882/1974, p. 168), given that, more generally, the organic is a "derivative, late rare accidental" (ibid.) extension of the inorganic. We might also question whether the revered duality of cause and effect ever exists or is "confronted with a continuum out of which we isolate a couple of pieces, just as we perceive motion only as isolated points" (ibid., p. 173). We may come to realize that "being conscious is not in any decisive sense the opposite of what is instinctive" (Nietzsche, 1886/1978, p. 17). We may begin to question the old philosophical opposition between true and false and look instead for degrees of semblance. These seemingly disparate examples share the same landscape: the world after the demise of God. They confirm an immanent view of reality that values becoming and multiplicity. This view allows us to see the bewildering and self-generating chaos of life-and-death on the horizontal, rhizomatic level of *infinity* instead of the conventional, arboreal view of vertical *totality*.

One immediate implication of this immanent view introduced by the death of God is that humans are equally embedded in the tangled web of nature with no special ontological status. A human being thus conceived is what Nietzsche calls *homo natura* (1886/1978, p. 143). Thanks to Darwin, the notion that humans are on a continuum with animals is not that controversial, despite the evangelical and creationist backlash of recent years. But Nietzsche pushes the argument further. Normally it is assumed that, unlike animals, humans are regaled with the extra-natural attributes of spirit, mind, or consciousness, as well as moral judgement, reason and language. But in an unpublished essay, written in his late twenties, *Truth and Lies in the Non-moral Sense*, Nietzsche (1979) contends that all of those extra-natural traits, normally seen as marks of sophistication in relation to brutes, are "the means by which weak, less robust individuals preserve themselves – since they have been denied the chance to wage the struggle for existence with horns or the sharp teeth of beasts of prey" (p. 80).

Already at this early stage of his philosophical development, Nietzsche is not shackled by either the Aristotelian or the Christian perspective. The former, found in the *Nicomachean Ethics* (Aristotle, 2004), is the basis for the predominant view within the philosophical tradition which sees humans as rational beings capable of disentangling themselves from the vicissitudes of life and the vagaries of fate and being elevated into a rational sphere of freedom. The answer to Aristotle's championing of reason is inscribed in a posthumous fragment via a revisioning of the relation between passion and reason:

> The misunderstanding of passion and reason, as if the latter were an independent entity and not rather a system of relations between various passions and desires; and as if every passion did not possess its quantum of reason.
>
> *(Nietzsche, 1968, p. 208)*

The Christian view sees the human being as the peak of creation. Nietzsche sees humans on the very same level as all other beings. This view is consistent throughout his oeuvre, from *The Gay Science*, where the separation between human and the rest of sentient beings is seen as one of four fundamental errors, to his late work *Anti-Christ* (Nietzsche, 1895/2007a) – where the notion of pure spirit is lampooned as pure stupidity – as well as in his posthumous writings. In a posthumous fragment he writes:

> *Second proposition:* man as a species does not represent any progress compared with any other animal. The whole animal and vegetable kingdom does not evolve from the lower to the higher – but all at the same time, in utter disorder, over and against each other.
>
> *(Nietzsche, 1968, p. 363)*

Organic/inorganic

Another implication of the horizontal, immanent view presented here concerns the relation between the organic and the inorganic. A brief discussion of this topic is important for two reasons. It opens up a new area of inquiry for psychotherapeutic orientations that value organismic experiencing and understand their work as fostering a process of greater alignment of the self-concept (or self-construct) to the wider life of the organism. It also foreshadows Nietzsche's idea of *will to power*, carving it not as a sweeping metaphysical proposition (as it is commonly read), but as an attempt at describing the working of natural forces and natural tendencies *from within*.

This is how the notion of will to power comes to life: as empirical hypothesis, via the naturalistic observation of the body as a composite of instincts, drives and affects, each of them trying to rule and absorb the others. Will to power becomes less esoteric a doctrine once we align it with some basic scientific observations:

> Chemistry, for example, shows us that every known entity is simply a certain combination and arrangement of a limited number of materials and forces.

Organic chemistry teaches us that the organic differs from the inorganic only by the structural incorporation of carbon compounds. Chemical analysis of both inorganic and organic matter also reveals that some compounds are more stable than others, that certain forces or the presence of particular materials can cause these compounds to break down and form new compounds and that, in the course of these reactions, these elements and compounds are attracted to some elements or compounds and repelled by others. Nietzsche suggests that *there is no fundamental difference between these sorts of chemical reactions and the bio-logical phenomena of procreation, growth, and extension of influence that we witness from the level of protoplasm to that of the human being.*

(Cox, 1999, pp. 78–79, emphasis added)

The activity of *interpretation* (requiring assimilation, taking over, adapting, restrain-ing, altering, shortening, excluding, concocting, fabricating) is in evidence all the way through nature from the erudition of humans to the reproduction of goings-on of the amoeba and "the actions and reactions of inorganic chemical com-pounds" (Cox, 1999, p. 79). In the light of this inquiry, what becomes increasingly questionable is the notion of *spirit* or *atman* bringing vibrancy into 'inert' matter and then 'leaving the body', as old friends from my spiritual days were fond of saying when speaking of death. What arises in its guise is a notion of *materiality* as "vibrant matter" (Bennett, 2010) that questions the view of the world as made up of 'things' to be conquered and subjugated. According to Jane Bennett, the task, wholly congruent with the perspective presented here, is threefold:

(1) To paint a positive ontology of vibrant matter, which stretches received concepts of agency, action, and freedom sometimes to the breaking point; (2) to dissipate the onto-theological binaries of life/matter, human/animal, will/determination, and organic/inorganic using arguments and other rhetorical means to induce in human bodies an aesthetic-affective openness to material vitality; and (3) to sketch a style of political analysis that can better account for the contributions of nonhuman actants.

(Bennett, 2010, p. x)

No ecology worth its name is possible without what this *naturalized epistemology* – initiated by Nietzsche and developed further by a host of counter-traditional philosophical, cultural assemblages, including post-structuralism and *new materialisms* (Coole & Frost, 2010). This implies the careful suspension of both Aristotelian and Christian perspectives that elevate humans above other beings in the tangled web of life.

Tendencies and emergent phenomena

Describing life *from within* is a task fit for psychotherapy, if the latter becomes more finely attuned to dynamic *tendencies* rather than being ensnared by accounts of reality organized around static essences and foundational substances. Some of us speak of an actualizing *tendency*. But what is a 'tendency'? The term, from the Medieval Latin *tendentia*, means *inclination, leaning*, draws from *tendens*: stretching, as well as aiming. It describes movement, a directional process that gestures towards a potential goal in space and time. The direction of movement of a tendency – including the actualizing tendency – is unknown. Actualization takes place in the (ever-present) future and without the need for a self. The latter is delayed, suspended or at best morphs into *distributed personhood* (Gell, 1998).

A tendency points indirectly towards a future and perhaps another state of being. It is *dynamic*, hence it cannot be reduced to a 'thing'. Evidently "the future … is something for the present" as Alfred North Whitehead wrote, adding:

> Cut away the future, and the present collapses, emptied of its proper content. Immediate existence requires the insertion of the future in the crannies of the present.
>
> *(Whitehead, 1933, p. 191)*

The last sentence is particularly striking. The *insertion* of a future – even though unknown and unknowable – is essential to our life in the present and confirms the notion of life as process and of the human organism as a continual work in progress rather than a static 'self'. In contemporary thought, "tendencies are neither *substantive* nor *quantifiable*" (Massumi, 2014, p. 32): they do not express a *static* being underneath (*sub-stans*), nor are they reducible to measurable quantities. They are "subjectivities-without-a-subject: sheer doings, with no doer behind them"; there is nothing behind them except "their own forward momentum" (ibid., p. 46). Thus a tendency emerges, is registered and described in the therapy room, but it does not directly belong to the self of the client or the self of the therapist.

Genealogy and evolution

Evolution is normally understood *teleologically*, as a steady movement towards a final goal and chiefly motivated by self-preservation. It is also understood in a *progressivist* sense, implying advance towards greater actualization and freedom. Nietzsche's view is radically different from these habitual accounts:

> A living thing desires above all to *vent* its strength – life as such is will to power. Self- preservation is only one of the indirect and most frequent consequences of it. In short: here as everywhere, beware of superfluous teleological principles such as is the drive to self-preservation (we owe it to Spinoza's inconsistency).
>
> *(Nietzsche, 1886/1978, p. 26)*

In relation to the progressivist view of history, Nietzsche writes in a late fragment:

Progress – Let us not be deceived! Time marches forward; we'd like to believe that everything that is in it also marches forward – that the development is one that moves forward. The most level-headed are led astray by this illusion. But the nineteenth century does not represent progress over the sixteenth; and the German spirit of 1888 represents a regress from the German spirit of 1788. "Mankind" does not advance, it does not even exist. The overall aspect is that of a tremendous experimental laboratory in which a few successes are scored, scattered throughout all ages, while there are untold failures, and all order, logic, union, and obligingness are lacking.

(Nietzsche, 1968, p. 55)

Instead of stable ascent, what we find in his writings is the naturalistic description of a series of uneven disarticulations within a wide and complex field of forces. The very same principle applies to knowledge and other supposedly noble human activities by which we attempt to draw a lofty distance from other species. The very origin of metaphysics is steeped in our cunning as feeble creatures that create herds and construct a language in order to banish danger and dread from our world. As we have seen above with the architectural metaphors from the beehive to the spider's web, our conceptual framework simplifies and codifies the multiple and complex array of sensuous experience. It makes it predictable and manageable.

Similarly, our fear of multiplicity and contingency allowed for the emergence of the Platonist Idea – an arché from whose lofty heights we look with scorn at phenomenal contingent manifestation as a set of poor copies. That same fear later engendered the Kantian notion of our linguistic and conceptual equipment as *a priori* within the structure of the mind, rather than a resourceful and contingent device. It was on these Platonic and later Kantian foundations that modern psychology was born: both a blessing and a curse.

While opening up a new exciting field, it also confined it from the start to disembodied archetypes and mental categories that privileged mental constructions over embodied experiencing. The cognitive faculties developed by human beings and celebrated in psychology are only tools for human survival; the intellect is an expedient way for protecting and perpetuating a specific kind of human life.

The intuitive human

Where you can guess, there you hate to deduce.

(Nietzsche, 1883/2006a, p. 123)

Many of the above insights have yet to reach psychotherapy. Despite the apparent diversity between approaches, psychotherapy is still implicitly ruled by Aristotelian, Kantian and Platonic, Christian-derived views of the human being. Despite the belittling of explicitly behavioural/cognitive orientations from approaches that see themselves as deeper and more philosophically astute, the human being within most psychotherapeutic discourses is rarely identified outside the confines of the faculty of cognition. Attempts to widen the exploration outside these strictures often result in comical anthropomorphic views according to which not only human existence, but the whole cosmos is seemingly spun out of human cognition. Not only you and I and he and she are benevolently actualizing, but the whole universe is growing towards greater actualization. Carl Rogers (1980) provided perhaps the most coherent account of this in that anthropomorphic reverie that is the *formative tendency*:

> I hypothesize that there is a formative directional tendency in the universe, which can be traced and observed in stellar space, in crystals, in micro-organisms, in more complex organic life, and in human beings. This is an evolutionary tendency toward greater order, greater complexity, greater interrelatedness. In humankind, this tendency exhibits itself as the individual moves from a single-cell origin to complex organic functioning, to knowing and sensing below the level of consciousness, to a conscious awareness of the organism and the external world, to a transcendent awareness of the harmony and unity of the cosmic system, including humankind.
>
> *(p. 133)*

Like other humanistic practitioners, Rogers arrived at this formulation by extending his observation and ethical involvement with transformative processes that were often guided by gradual alignment (or *congruence*) of the human self-construct with the more expansive and complex life of the organism. He then proceeded in later years to move from individual to cosmic congruence – a typical anthropocentric and anthropomorphic move.

To be clear: *all* psychotherapeutic approaches share the double error of anthropocentrism and anthropomorphism. This is a case of professional bias as much as professional hazard. In Nietzsche's terms, psychology as a whole is animated by the spirit of revenge that dominates the sciences, religion and morality. But within the wide field of psychology there are points of reversal from which the endeavour can be made to serve active rather than reactive forces. One could say that formulating notions such as the formative tendency (another case in point is 'universal relatedness') represents a laudable effort to widen the inherent self-boundedness of conventional psychotherapeutic discourse. With Nietzsche's help, we can also begin to recognize that this move is part and parcel of the same self-bound anthropocentrism whose basic aim is *preservation of the species*. Laudable as it might be, we must also recognize that this endeavour is deeply *conservative*. For Nietzsche, this inclination to self-preservation is "the symptom of a condition of distress", of our wish to curb "the really fundamental instinct of life" whose aim is *"the expansion of power"* (Nietzsche, 1882/1974, p. 291). Some of us will be encouraged to go in the opposite direction, to find novel ways to formulate a psychology (and a psychotherapy) not merely intent at self-preservation but stirred to explore and experiment more expansive possibilities. In order to do this, however, we need to go beyond 'useful':

"Useful" in the sense of Darwinist biology means: proved advantageous in the struggle with others. But it seems to me that the feeling of increase, the feeling of becoming stronger, is itself, quite apart from any usefulness in the struggle, the real *progress:* only from this feeling does there arise the will to struggle.

(Nietzsche, 1968, p. 344)

Will to struggle, despite its forbidding tone, is here linked to making "room for the expression of an intellectual play impulse" (Nietzsche, 1882/1974, p. 170). This constitutes the basis for the first tentative steps that affirm a view of the human as a being who accepts uncertainty, an *intuitive human* – more fully living than fully functioning. Since the driving force is no longer self-preservation, this type of human lives and breathes a more uncertain existence. Yet she sees the world as eternally new, and reveals "the contingent, conditional pragmatic and sensuous origins of the conceptual edifice" that was "reified and elevated by his more conservative and secure opponent" (Cox, 1999, p. 81). This *naturalized* version of the human already heralds that threshold of human experience that Nietzsche refers to as the *overhuman*, a domain that begins as play and unfolds as art, bringing to full flower the cognitive and functional edifice built until now. It is the emergence of this intuitive human dimension that truly harnesses those active, life-affirming forces that have been until now subdued. In *Truth and Lies in a non-Moral Sense*, Nietzsche writes:

[The] immense framework of planking of concepts to which needy humans cling their whole life in order to preserve themselves is nothing but a scaffolding and toy for the audacious feats of the most liberated intellect. And when it smashes this framework to pieces, throws it into confusion, and puts it back together in an ironic fashion … it is demonstrating that it has no need of these makeshifts of indigence and it will now be guided by intuitions rather than concepts.

(1979, p. 90, translation modified)

Nietzsche's naturalism is only superficially reminiscent of Darwinism. Darwin's version of evolution, championed in different ways by practitioners belonging to different therapeutic orientations (e.g. Phillips, 2001; Frankel et al., 2010) is a remarkable expression, in Nietzschean terms, of *reactive* forces. Nietzsche admired the eighteenth-century French naturalist Jean Baptiste Lamarck, whose *Zoological Philosophy* (1809/2012) prefigured the presence of the active forces of metamorphosis and transformation in place of reactive forces of adaptation depicted by Darwin. Echoes of this are found in contemporary thought (Coole & Frost, 2010), where 'dead' matter is reconceived as *materiality*, as something "active, dynamic, self-creative, productive and unpredictable" (Ansell Pearson, 2011, p. 47), and in psychotherapy, particularly with Claudio Rud's notion of the *transformative tendency* (Rud, 2016), a shrewd philosophical revision of the formative tendency that filters out the latter's reliance on teleology and clunky metaphysics. 'Transformative' here emphasizes becoming, an ongoing process with no aim or finality.

Nietzsche focuses on transformative rather than adaptive forces; he emphasizes what is noble (or active) over what is merely reactive. It also emphasizes *qualities over quantities*, a case in point when we consider the politics of qualitative and quantitative research methods and the increasing prominent role of the latter in our current neopositivist cultural landscape.

> Might all quantities not be signs of qualities? A greater power implies a different consciousness, feeling, desiring, a different perspective; growth itself is a desire to be more; the desire for an increase in quantum grows from a *quale;* in a purely quantitative world everything would be dead, stiff, motionless. *The reduction of all qualities to quantities is nonsense*: what appears is that the one accompanies the other, an analogy.
>
> (*Nietzsche, 1968, p. 304, emphasis added*)

Leaving God out of nature

Nietzsche's avowed de-deification of nature – the second of the two tasks mentioned earlier in this chapter – leaves God outside a naturalistic investigation of nature. At first, this appears to be aligned to the project of the empirical sciences. But Nietzsche is sceptical of empiricism; he sees physics itself as "only an interpretation and an arrangement of the world ... and *not* an explanation of the world" (1886/1978, p. 26). He attacks the empiricists' belief in immediate realities and certainties. A similarly strong critique of empiricism will emerge in Merleau-Ponty (1942/1983, 1945/1989), for whom empiricism fails to honour the perceiving subject, viewing it as an object triggered and impacted by other objects in ways that are 'explained away' by natural science. He also critiques empiricism for failing to answer the puzzling connectedness of experience. Here we need to remember that the 'empiricism' Nietzsche and Merleau-Ponty confront is not a quaint philosophical position of days gone by. Empiricism is alive and well today: cognitive behavioural therapy (CBT), the bio-medical model and the great majority of neuroscience are the most evident examples. What Nietzsche critiques in empiricism is the assurance that there is some "foundational, simple, present item", whether the 'I', direct sensory data, or the atom as "indivisible unit of matter", that offers the root of "all knowing and being" and constitutes "the goal of all inquiry" (Cox, 1999, p. 94). In this, empiricism is very much like Christianity and metaphysics in general, for in both we find an "impetuous *demand for certainty*" (Nietzsche, 1882/1974, p. 288).

The metaphysical idea of a pre-given, sub-stantial subject is common to science, religion, and psychology as we know it. Nietzsche's critique is particularly unrelenting on this topic, and one of his favourite targets is the notion of free will, that darling of religion and psychology alike. Assuming the existence of a free will behind our actions means denying the innocence of becoming and asserting instead the existence of an unconditioned doer behind the deed. What comes first – the doer or the deed? Nietzsche's answer is: the deed. Action, event, accident are *primary*. The self/doer/subject is, like consciousness, an *afterthought*, an arrogant seal of ownership. A thing is but "a sum of its effects". Equally, the self is the "sum of its actions and passions" (Cox, 1999, p. 126). The self or subject is an *assemblage*, an individuated set within myriad events, actions, and affects, what the Buddha called "heaps" or aggregates (Bazzano, 2017b, p. 123).

The inspiration throughout Nietzsche's inquiry into physics is Boscovich (1763/2015) – discussed in Chapter 3 – who disparaged both Newton's and Leibniz's notion of the atom as the definitive unit of matter, choosing instead a relational description of the atom as a "quasi-material nodal point within a network of force" (Cox, 1999, p. 93).

The project of de-deification of nature must also take on board all the various shadows of God loitering within seemingly atheistic, secular and scientific accounts. The result is *ontological relativity*; this undermines our customary notion of what constitutes empirical knowledge. There is no such thing as a direct content delivered to us by sensations. At the same time Nietzsche's position should not be confused with the Kantian transcendentalism that speaks of *a priori* categories in the mind that shape sensuous intuition. For Nietzsche (as for Merleau-Ponty), "sensation and interpretation … are inseparable activities" (Cox, 1999, p. 98). Both reductive empiricism (present in CBT and the bio-medical model), and Kantian transcendentalism (present in Husserlian phenomenological therapy) are discarded in favour of an active, naturalistic psychotherapy that values the creative process of infinite interpretation and evaluation. Nietzsche lays out and critiques both positions in a late passage:

> Against positivism, which halts at phenomena – "There are only *facts*" – I would say: No, facts is precisely what there is not, only interpretations. We cannot establish any fact "in itself": perhaps it is folly to want to do such a thing.
>
> "Everything is subjective", you say; but even this is interpretation.
>
> The "subject" is not something given; it is something added and invented and projected behind what there is. Finally, is it necessary to posit an interpreter behind the interpretation? Even this is invention, hypothesis.
>
> In so far as the word "knowledge" has any meaning, the world is knowable; but it is *interpretable* otherwise, it has no meaning behind it, but countless meanings: – "Perspectivism".
>
> It is our needs that interpret the world; our drives and their "for and against". Every drive is a kind of lust to rule; each one has its perspective that it would like to compel all the other drives to accept as a norm.
>
> *(1968, p. 267)*

Does Nietzsche's perspectivism imply that 'anything goes'? Is it the equivalent of moral relativism, the bête noire of all those God-fearing people out there? Does his opening onto countless meanings imply that there is no qualitative difference between one affect or instinct and the next? The answer is no. And what is the criterion for choosing, discerning and selecting the difference? The answer is *naturalism* – a naturalism freed of absolutes and unshackled by teleological notions and interpretation of the workings of nature. The choice in this process of transvaluation is, as always with

Nietzsche, in favour of active, life-affirming forces whose sole purpose is the increase of power. His invitation is to *feel* a particular force from the inside, from within the innocence of its innermost wave-like activity *before* moral, religious, scientific evaluations begin to interfere with it and classify it from the outside.

In terms of human experience, interference comes, for example, from notions of our alleged divine nature as humans or of our 'inner life' as one object of empirical observation like any other. Needless to say, the axiological and naturalistic view proposed by Nietzsche and heralded by the death of God is a hypothesis among others. But it is one that keenly invites us to re-open the investigation (in psychotherapy as in philosophy) and liberate it from the strictures of metaphysics and positivism.

A joyful science

Nietzsche's turn, in his middle works, from art to psychology, the "queen of the sciences" (1886/1978, p. 36), was a change of heart motivated by loss and disappointment. He abandoned his elective mentors, Wagner and Schopenhauer, and the late-Romantic leanings that permeated his youthful writings. He also harboured a genuine desire to embrace naturalism and draw on the best contemporary science. I disagree with those (e.g. Abbey, 2000; Safranski, 2003; Ure, 2008) who broadly suggest that Nietzsche's middle works (*Human, all too Human, Daybreak* and *The Gay Science*) would be animated by a sort of self-therapy based on Epicurean and Stoic *askesis* or care of self, as well as by an overall endorsement of Greek serenity. It is equally inaccurate to see Nietzsche as a visionary poet (e.g., Bachelard, 1988) and prophet of fervent vulnerability and bluster who cannot be let in within the aloof realm of science.

What cannot be denied is the *untimeliness* of Nietzsche's thought. He wrote at a time, the second half of the nineteenth century, when the "scientific ethos" that is dominant today, loosely understood as "self-possession, healthy scepticism and sobriety" (Moore, 2004, p. 1), was first established. Even the term *scientist* was invented at that time. After trying out different translations from the German word *Naturforscher* ('nature-researcher' and even 'nature-explorer' were suggested among others), in the early 1830s members of the British Association for the Advancement of Science finally opted for 'scientist'. The main characteristic of these early neophytes of modern naturalistic science was a pugnacious dismissal of all other disciplines: they professed "absolute, unconditional reverence for facts" (ibid., p. 4). This stance was liberally applied to psychology, which they saw as an unreliably intuitive, archaically subjective endeavour that had to be put right by the introduction of the scientific quantitative and measurable experiments of people like Alexander Bain, E.H. Weber and Wilhelm Wundt, or by "Qutelet's use of statistics to study human behaviour" (ibid., p. 4). The above may sound eerily familiar to some of us. At the time, Darwin's growing influence encouraged the thought that psychology too could and should be aligned to the methods of natural science. This eminently sensible stance overlooks one essential element that Nietzsche (1878/1984, 1881/1997, 1882/1974) will help us unravel: at the very heart of science are found, from its inception, the unchecked beliefs and assumptions of the Judaeo-Christian religion and morality. For while scientific *methodology* may be applied and tested, science itself cannot be fully trusted, Nietzsche surmises, but has to be subjected to closer scrutiny and ultimately to the intervention of art.

Only art applied to science can offset the falsehood of objectivity claimed by science, which is in turn based on what Nietzsche often refers to as the "ascetic ideal" (e.g., 1887/1996, p. 94). The scientific method is eminently useful: it can reveal to us that what we now call the world is the effect of a number of mistakes and fancies handed down to us, dutifully deemed a treasure trove, and on the foundations of which we have elevated our species and its set of values. Although his appreciation of science is, to say the least, nuanced, Nietzsche's genuine interest in naturalism is undeniable. Rather than forfeiting his original predilection for art, this gives rise to what Cristina Acampora (2006) aptly calls his "artful naturalism" (p. 315), an effortless development in Nietzsche's trajectory from the declaration of the death of God to the "de-deification of nature" (Nietzsche, 1882/1974, p. 168), a painstaking process of freeing concepts from supernatural dregs, especially the ones related to matters of "truth, knowledge and goodness" (Acampora, 2006, p. 315).

There is a great deal that psychotherapy can learn from this process. Nietzsche helps us deconstruct in this instance the shadows of God hiding within our ideas of nature, all those "teleological models of organic development and evolutionary theories" according to which there is some sort of essential order that directs development towards "an ultimately good end towards which all things progressively strive" (Acampora, 2006, p. 315). Nietzsche invites us to make the best use of philosophy in freeing ourselves from the shackles of transcendental thinking, and in particular from: (a) *teleological* concepts of nature; (b) the idea of *causation*. To that purpose, philosophy too (and psychology) must adopt the methods and modus operandi of the *gaia scienza* of the troubadours, i.e. of an approach to science that is not gravely subjected to the dictates of theology and morality but is inspired by a radical empiricism in the spirit of life-affirming gaiety: a meeting of art and science, a place where one can "naturalize cheerfully" (Schacht, 1988, p. 68). We should be wary, Nietzsche warns us, of the notion that "the world eternally creates new things" (1882/1974, p. 168). Nothing lasts forever, be it God or *matter*. 'Matter' too is but a shadow of God.

> When will all these shadows of God cease to darken our minds? When will we complete our de-deification of nature? When may we begin to naturalize humanity in terms of a pure, newly discovered, newly redeemed nature?
>
> *(Nietzsche, 1882/1974, pp. 168–169)*

An alternative model emerges for psychotherapy: instead of transcendental theology, the empirical sciences. When Nietzsche says that he wants to purge the natural sciences of metaphysics, he is not doing so in order to leave us with allegedly 'pure', unmediated facts. He is critical of the residues of transcendental ideas present within science *and* of the latter's alleged purity and neutrality. Both assume a God's-eye view; both fall into the metaphysical trap. Science too, though in many ways preferable to religion, needs to be strengthened by a more rigorous science, "a higher organic system in relation to which scholars, physicians, artists, and legislators – as we know them at present – would have to look like paltry relics of ancient times" (Nietzsche, 1882/1974, p. 173).

What makes Nietzsche's appreciation of science stand out is that he does not promote the subjugation of nature but advocates instead *loyalty to the earth*, a stance of "reverence for the ultimately enigmatic nature of things" (Parkes, 1999, p. 168) and of profound respect for transient natural phenomena. He is not alone in this stance that has been advanced within a counter-traditional current of thought that begins with Heraclitus and other pre-Socratic thinkers and reappears "in the Stoics and Epicureans ... with certain figures in the Christian mystical tradition and the Italian Renaissance" (ibid., p. 167), reaching its zenith with Goethe and the *Naturphilosophen* in Germany, and later in North America among thinkers like Emerson.

As Nietzsche's thought develops, it weaves an elaborate dance between art and science: art does not outdo science; science does not lead art. Together they make a hybrid, with art "involved in the process of interpretation that gives scientific research their organization and direction" (Acampora, 2006, p. 318). Nietzsche reminds us that a scientific view is an act of *exegesis* or artistic interpretation, a way of establishing our human relation to things. His work is a dangerous tightrope walk that refuses the straight highway paved by the seemingly solid postulates of religion and science and even the bucolic and enticing vagaries of art. He opts for naturalism, which "prevents him from casting the moral subject in terms of a soul" (Acampora, 2006, p. 318) and does not give in to the notion of an autonomous rational being.

The felt text

Throughout his writings Nietzsche affirms the primacy of the body, something that remains indisputable despite the influential misreadings of Heidegger (1961), who tried to dismiss this clear emphasis as a remnant of biologism. But the body is central in Nietzsche's project of translating the human back into nature.

Nietzsche began an important process within philosophy and psychology that will find even fuller expression in Bergson (Jay, 1993), and will later give rise to the development and mixed fortunes of bioenergetics, body psychotherapy, organismic psychology and ecopsychology.

The centrality of the body in Nietzsche's thought is merely the antechamber to his *anti-epistemological* stance. The body – and *physis* in general – remains crucial to his argumentation, but constitutes a stepping stone within the arc of his philosophy, one that allows him to mount a cogent critique of Cartesian dualism. However, even despite the fact that the body is embedded in the world, it would be wishful thinking to believe that through the body one can have knowledge of the world. The very notion of knowledge is anthropomorphic through and through (Brown, 2004), limitedly subjective, and forever trembling at the potential disruption posed by the presence of an (immanent) outside. It is not possible for a human subject to know what it is like to be a bat (Nagel, 1981), nor is it possible to "reduce sub-jective qualia to objective quanta" (Brown, 2004, p. 56).

In a similar vein, Nietzsche's *anti-epistemology* does not allow us any illusion about our possibility of knowing either nature or the things themselves. His anti-epistemology is both eco-physiology as well as physio-ecology (Babich, 1994), with ecology and physiology mutually affecting and moulding one another. *Ecology* is the ceaselessly *relative circumstance* of a becoming world. *Physis* – both as world and body-subject – is for Nietzsche "self-generating, self-manifesting" (ibid., p. 84). This particular human body that we are, he understands as "the expenditure of organic force expressing a particular perspective" (ibid.).

The body is in the world as the heart is in the organism, Merleau-Ponty will later say: not so much at the centre but as a living fragment of the world that, akin to other splinters, is keenly felt yet remains fundamentally unknown.

Primacy of the body (and bodily affects or *Triebe*, drives) is a prelude to what in section 119 of *Daybreak*, in a passage titled "Experience and invention", Nietzsche calls "felt text" (Nietzsche, 1881/1997, p. 120). He begins by cautioning the reader against the exaggerated claims of knowledge. "However far" our understanding may go, "nothing can be more incomplete that [our] image of the totality of *drives* which constitute [our] being" (ibid., p. 118). We can barely *name* the more obvious or basic affects, let alone have a clear idea of what feeds them. Because of our ignorance, their sustenance has to be left to chance:

> [O]ur daily experiences throw some prey in the way of now this, now that drive, and the drive seizes it eagerly; but the coming and going of these events as a whole stands in no rational relationship to the nutritional requirements of the totality of the drives: so that the outcome will always be twofold – the starvation and stunting of some and the overfeeding of others. Every moment of our lives sees some of the polyp-arms of our being grow and others of them wither, all according to the nutriment which the moment does or does not bear with it. Our experiences are ... means of nourishment, but the nourishment is scattered indiscriminately without distinguishing between the hungry and those already possessing a superfluity.
>
> *(ibid., p. 118)*

Imagine, he says, that a particular affect reaches the point where it needs satisfac-tion – "or [to] exercise its strength, or discharge of its strength, or the saturation of an emptiness" (ibid.). It will look at the events of that day to see whether they can be utilized in order to serve its plan. Whether a person is walking, relaxing, speaking, being angry, sad or joyful, the affect or drive will "taste every condition". As often as not, "it will discover nothing for itself there and will have to wait and go on thirsting". After a while, "it will grow faint", and after a few days or months of "non-gratification", it will simply dry up "like a plant without rain" (ibid., p. 119). This situation would be unbearable – Nietzsche goes on saying in a striking passage that anticipates Freud – if it wasn't for the fact that most of the affects can get their nourishment from "*dream food*" (ibid.). Dreams are *inventions*: they "give scope and discharge to our drives to tenderness or humorousness or adventurousness" (ibid.). They are also *interpretations*: they give a commentary on a (living, pulsating, felt) text. They do this more freely and with greater ingenuity than our waking consciousness, Nietzsche warns.

> Do I have to add that when we are awake our drives likewise do nothing but interpret nervous stimuli and, according to their requirements, posit their "causes"? That there is no essential difference between waking and dreaming? That when we compare different stages of culture we even find that freedom of waking interpretation in the one is in no way inferior to the freedom exercised in the other while dreaming? That our moral judgements and evaluations too are only images and fantasies based on a physiological process unknown to us, a kind of acquired language for designating certain nervous stimuli? *That our so-called consciousness is a more or less fantastic commentary on an unknown, perhaps unknowable, but felt text?*
>
> (Nietzsche, 1881/1997, pp. 119–120, emphasis added)

Bodily affects are *prelude* to the felt text, I wrote earlier, which is to say: they are not the felt text itself. This is not because there is another, transcendent reality beyond the body and its drives, but because the latter are interpretations, the result of former evaluations. Nietzsche uses the body as a *guide* in his philosophical project; however, the body does not constitute the *ground*. If it were, his philosophy would be a rather simplistic rather than problematic (and, properly speaking 'semiotic') naturalism. Duncan Large (2001) explains:

> *All* "phenomena" (i.e. evaluations), Nietzsche suggests, need to be interpreted ("read") as a physician interprets a body: they should not be taken "literally" but at "face value" – their value is as symptoms which the philosophical physiognomist reads like the experiences etched on a face.
>
> (p. 178)

Establishing the primacy of the body certainly represents a way forward, and a *way out* of the Cartesian impasse within which the majority of psychotherapeutic orientations are stuck. But the body is not (and cannot be) the final ground of our investigation; not because (as spiritually minded psychologists are fond of telling us) it is perishable and ephemeral, but because the body is not a *unit* but instead an intricate combination of competing forces.

No true self

> Behind your thoughts and feelings ... there stands a mighty ruler, an unknown sage – whose name is self. In your body he dwells; he is your body.
>
> (Nietzsche, 1883/2006a, p. 34)

Words are the means of social interaction. As a talking cure, currently influenced by positivism and focused almost exclusively on consciousness, psychotherapy relies on the inevitable lies and inaccuracies conveyed by words. It is becoming increasingly rare, in my experience, to find any emphasis in current therapy training on the unintentional language of gesture and expression, let alone on the intricate play of the unconscious. This 'subliminal' content, awareness of which is essential in therapy, is relegated at most to the stale category of 'body-language' and to a handful of techniques for reading the latter. Or, the body is consigned wholesale to the increasingly specialized field of 'body psychotherapy'. In this state of affairs, therapy ends up reinforcing the pervasiveness of the lie in social interaction. Nietzsche gave primacy to the organism and the bodily affects and relative value to words and consciousness. The latter is for him a *reactive* force that answers, retorts and blabbers in response to vital, instinctual, 'unconscious' forces. A similar emphasis is found in Proust, for whom "a glance may … yield the greatest truth quotient" and who valued "the involuntary, bodily, chance nature of truth" (Large, 2001, p. 182). Ultimately, the time regained by Proust's narrator is entirely etched in the body through the senses and involuntary memory. These are *sensations* rather than *impressions*: "provoked by senses other than vision" (ibid., p. 186). Like Nietzsche before him, Proust subverts the hierarchical order that privileges vision over the other senses. The vast expanse of time opened up by involuntary memory brings about a *déjà senti* more than a déjà vu (Doubrovsky, 1986).

Crucially for our investigation, Nietzsche stresses a lot more than an emphasis on different 'points of *view*'. It does not add one more optical metaphor to a Western cultural tradition that favours sight over the other senses (think of the pervasiveness of terms such as *vision, insight*, and *seeing-through*, all transmitting the primacy of sight). This hinting at a fully sensory experience of time and reality may resemble mysticism. But Nietzsche dismisses mystics as people who have "faith in intoxication" (1881/1997, p. 32), and his indictment still rings true today, especially in relation to the transpersonal and spiritualist disdain of the everyday in the name of an allegedly 'truer' reality and a 'truer' self.

6

POISON AND REMEDY

Active and passive nihilism

Last week a friend asked me how the writing of this book was going. I didn't know what to say at first: during that week, I had reached, if not an impasse, certainly a moment of vacillation. 'It seems to have a life of its own', I replied, 'it sets off where I hadn't suspected or even wanted it to go'. 'Like where?' she asked. 'Well, against everything we seem to hold dear in therapy at present: integration, intersubjectivity, growth, self-actualization, making the unconscious conscious, relationality, mindfulness … you name it.' With a big smile on her face, my friend said: 'But that's brilliant, no? It will be truly *nihilistic*.'

She had a point. I confess to a feeling of glee when passages in Nietzsche appear to corroborate my armchair anarchism. Psychology itself is debunked in his writings as a moral prejudice based on the misguided notion of causality, on the existence of a doer behind the deed. At the same time, psychology is for him, at least potentially, one of those rare domains where moral and religious prejudices can be demystified. This process of demystification is far from nihilistic for it is in the service of life.

In *The Anti-Christ*, one of his last works, Nietzsche (1895/2007a) succinctly illustrates two main characteristics of what he calls *nihilism*:

> When the centre of life is placed not in life itself but in "the beyond" – in nothingness – then one has taken its centre of gravity altogether. The vast lie of personal immortality destroys all reason, all natural instinct – henceforth, everything in the instincts that is beneficial, that fosters life and that safeguards the future is a cause for suspicion.
>
> (Nietzsche, p. 44)

For Nietzsche, nihilism manifests as denigration of life, as something that gives more importance to accounts of life rather than life itself. It does so in three ways: via religion, morality and traditional philosophy.

Religion supplies consoling explanations of our bewildering human situation through notions of sin and punishment, redemption, creation and salvation. *Morality* is a poor substitute for our potential ability as humans of being artists in the broad sense, of *creating* values in the crucible of our experience. It opts for tables of commandments and prescribed behaviours, providing a structure that is seemingly more reassuring than the scarier option of ethical freedom and responsibility. Morality is essentially a legacy of religion, with the will of God and then the creation of law and moral codes displacing our difficult and painful freedom. The will of God, alongside "biblical dogma ... the moral law delivered once and for all" (Vattimo, 2005, p. 18), creates for us an insufferable yoke; it even creates the fatalism of 'it was' – our inescapable past reflected in notions of history as in the myths and psychologies of childhood.

Traditional philosophy substitutes a difficult and daring will to create with a will to truth based on fear. *Truth* (and in particular that 'will to truth' which for two millennia has been almost exclusively the province of traditional philosophy) is a fundamental prejudice; it must be replaced by the *will to create*. Why do we hanker for truth? Because we are afraid of becoming. Because, troubled by the unpredictability of life, we fathom a *static*, pre-existing, metaphysical truth whose 'unveiling' will provide a buffer against *dynamic*, vertiginous existence. Nietzsche invites us to cast aside the will to truth and to find the strength to be motivated instead by the will to create.

'Will to truth' rests on the notion that truth is already there somewhere from eternity, prior to our human experience; all we have to do is to find it. The nihilism of religion, morality and philosophy betrays for Nietzsche an elemental fear of becoming, i.e., fear of the unpredictable and dynamic dimension into which we are thrown. The nihilist considers becoming what phenomenologists will later call *Lebenswelt* or the life-world – to be nothing (*nihil*). Why? Because life is imperfect, impermanent, and perishable, especially when compared to the imaginary perfection, permanence and eternity of an abstract notion of being. The nihilism inherent in religion, morality and conventional thought gives frightened people the illusory fortitude of a providential order and a totality which may or may not be called 'God'.

Nihilism is appealing. It exempts us from the troubles of having to experience our life first-hand and then having to describe it in our own terms. It exempts us from the perceived burden of acting freely and responsibly, and – the Nietzschean task par excellence – from having to create new values. We are let off the hook, as it were, and can placidly walk through life half-asleep, applying existing explanations of the world in the same way as we pick recipes from a book.

The originality of Nietzsche's position on this matter is twofold. He *redefines* nihilism: it no longer means lack of values and principles but excessive dependence on them at the expense of lived life. He also states that, given that nihilism is the backbone of the culture we have created, there is *no turning back* from it. Nihilism must be wholeheartedly, actively embraced. This is a task that neither religion, nor philosophy, and least of all morality can perform. It is a task for psychologists, or physicians of culture. He draws the line sharply between passive and active nihilism. Passive nihilism is what we normally do, i.e., accept a logocentric, metaphysical explanation of the world. Active nihilism implies seeing through the inherent emptiness of all our notions of truth, recognizing them as expressions of our creaturely survival and self-preservation. As Vattimo (2005) succinctly puts it: "We have projected the conditions of our preservation as predicates of being in general" (p. 136).

On a micro-level (as a psychological state), there are usually four ways by which we arrive at nihilism. The first three belong to passive nihilism, while the fourth pertains to active nihilism.

The *first* occurs through our positing a *purpose*. "When we have sought a 'meaning' in all events that is not there", Nietzsche writes and later, discouraged, come to recognize "the long *waste* of strength" and with it, "the agony of the 'in vain', insecurity, the lack of any opportunity to recover and to regain composure", we feel ashamed of ourselves, as if we have *"deceived* [ourselves] all too long" (1968, p. 12). We had some goal in mind, whether the realization of some "highest ethical canon", the "growth of love and harmony" (ibid.), the dream of universal happiness, or even the negative goal of universal obliteration. We then realize that all our efforts have been in vain, that the long pursuit and hard work and aspiration have all come to *nothing*, that our aim has not been achieved. This kind of pessimism is perhaps the most common kind of nihilism, born out of our frustration and disillusionment.

The *second* meaning of nihilism as a psychological state relates to our notion of *unity* or "a totality, a systematization, indeed any organization in all events, and underneath all events" (Nietzsche, 1968, p. 12). Conjuring up the existence of an intrinsic unity gives us a reassuring sense of inter-relatedness, of "being dependent on some whole that is infinitely superior" to us. We tell ourselves that "the well-being of the universal demands the devotion of the individual". We find this notion reassuring, Nietzsche tells us, because we have, deep down, "lost the faith in [our own] value" (ibid.); we conceive the existence of a whole simply because this is the only way left for us to believe in our own value. Some will recognize how this second meaning of nihilism, namely the 'holistic' belief in universal relatedness, permeates many a psychotherapeutic perspective.

The *third* way we arrive at nihilism as a psychological state is through our clever fabrication of the notion of *Being*. This is the last resort we arrive at, once we have vainly gone through the above two attempts. Having learned in the first instance that "becoming has no goal" (Nietzsche, 1968, p. 13), and in the second instance that there is no grand unity "in which [we] could immerse [ourselves] completely as in an element of supreme value" (ibid.), we now attempt a way out of this gridlock. "We pass sentence on this whole world of becoming as a deception and to invent a world beyond it, a *true* world" (ibid.). This kind of nihilism is typical of existential/phenomenological therapists influenced by Heidegger. If only the notion of 'Being' could save us! Soon, when some of us eventually find out "how that world is fabricated solely from psychological needs", and how we have "absolutely no right to it", the *fourth* form of nihilism emerges. This type of nihilism, he writes, "includes disbelief in any metaphysical world and forbids itself any belief in a *true* world". He continues:

> Having reached this standpoint, one grants the reality of becoming as the *only* reality, forbids oneself every kind of clandestine access to afterworlds and false divinities – but *cannot endure this world though one does not want to deny it.*
>
> *(1968, p. 13)*

The last passage portrays a difficult existential stance: it is a moment of intense crisis, yet also loaded with the potential to turn from passive to *active* nihilism. Normally, the person who has experienced the three aspects of nihilism described above comes to devalue the world itself because it failed to display convincing proofs of the validity of the human-made notions of aim, unity and being. Now, disappointed and frustrated, this person turns her back to the world. The world, she concludes, has no value. Ontological insecurity turns into metaphysical depression and ontological despondency. But the above is only one of two possible responses. The other response – what Nietzsche calls active nihilism and corresponds to the fourth and last meaning of nihilism – does not devalue the world simply because aim, unity, or being were not found within it. Instead, *it devalues aim, unity and being while upholding and celebrating the world.* One might say that both responses are 'negative' but the second does a lot more than negating. It turns poison into remedy.

In Derrida's account, part of his civil yet thoroughgoing critique of Heidegger's interpretation of Nietzsche, nihilism is both benevolent *and* malevolent; both poison *and* remedy (Derrida, 1981). In his malevolent form, nihilism is the poison (*pharmakon*) of *onto-theology*, whose most coherent manifestations are Platonism and Christianity. What is poisonous in these philosophical and religious stances is that they can only bring themselves to appreciate life and the world *on condition* that the latter are shored up by notions of unity, being and telos. Yet nihilism becomes *remedy*, provided we can bring it to its far reaches by turning it into *active* nihilism.

For Nietzsche, a nihilist is one who cannot value life intrinsically, on its own terms, but needs to add to it a thick veneer of moral and religious 'meaning'. The first true nihilist is for Nietzsche *the priest*, whose mellifluous condemnation of life extends by contagion to the scientist, the artist, the thinker and – you guessed it – the psychologist and the therapist.

Platonic for the people

Far from being a freak phenomenon on the fringes, nihilism entirely *coincides* with our religious and our moral and philosophical tradition; nihilism is but another name for the tradition. Influential manifestations of it are the Platonic and Judaeo-Christian ideologies that for Nietzsche engulf the totality of Western culture, *including* secularism. With 'our way of life' now exported wholesale on a global scale, this is arguably a universal condition.

The meaning Nietzsche gives to nihilism is nevertheless ambivalent. He seems to regard as inevitable the depreciation of life and the placing of 'true' life in a transcendental domain. Could nihilism have taken a slightly different shape if Platonism (and its simplified, popularized version, Christianity) had not been so successful? Nietzsche's meaning is ambivalent for another reason. It does not allow us to reduce it to the moral and religious value-system of bourgeois society (or its modern equivalent: secularist, consumerist, middle-class value-system), against which we could then launch a critique in the name of sexual, emotional and socio-political liberation for the sake of humankind. Nietzsche's thought is too mercurial to be employed in this way. Equally, to think of psychotherapy in these terms in our ironic age would mean regressing to outmoded Marcusian syntheses of Freud and Marx, or to cathartic 'techniques of liberation'. Worse still, it would mean giving in to simplistic notions of love – and love in therapy – now in vogue within humanistic psychotherapy, which provides a vehicle for a return to religious belief and a renewed endorsement of nihilism.

If we want to get a little closer to Nietzsche's meaning of nihilism, we would have to bring in instead an altogether different – and differential – element: a play of forces that is able to deconstruct as well as present *new values* in a way that, unlike the simplistic solutions presented above, does not resort to accepting and using the structures of *Logos*. We need to exit the citadel of Logos and enter that most Nietzschean site – the *labyrinth*.

Thousand-fold

> I descended into the depths, I tunnelled into the foundations, I commenced an investigation and digging out of an ancient faith, one upon which we philosophers have for a couple of millennia been accustomed to build as if upon the firmest of all foundations – and have continued to do so even though every building hitherto erected on them has fallen down.
>
> *(Nietzsche, 1881/1997, pp. 1–2)*

In spiritualist readings, the labyrinth is seen as sacred geometry – at once reproduction of spiritual cosmology and ancient symbol of the mystery of life. The Gothic cathedrals of Europe, Tibetan sand mandalas, the elongated figure of the Kabala, Islamic patterns, the Chartres labyrinth of the Knights Templar, Pythagorean mysteric practices and the Hopi medicine wheel – are all evoked as eclectic manifestations of a single, trans-cultural spirituality instilling harmony and stability in a vast and bewildering universe. As a result, it would appear that our all-too-human wish for order and regulation is appeased.

If we feel dismayed while roaming the tangled maze of experience or are seized by anguish at the terrifying prospect of coming face to face with the half-bull, half-man monster forever hungry for our flesh, we may similarly take comfort by holding on to Ariadne's thread. We may feel safer in the knowledge that we *will* find our way out and exit the maze as the very same self that entered it.

When the image of psyche as a labyrinth came up during a session with my client Karen, her immediate response was of strong revulsion – a mixture of distress and claustrophobia. Her assumption, it turned out, was that the labyrinth is at all times a confined space, rather than a locus of infinite possibilities. It turned out that also this latter option proved distressing for her, for it implied unwelcome surprise, whether 'good' or 'bad', a stumbling upon a new situation that demanded of her a fresh response, unmediated by previous information and experience. As is often the case, she had good reasons for feeling this way. A traumatic childhood, punctuated by shocks and permanent instability had awoken in her an overriding desire for constancy and predictability in her life, to the point where she needed to exercise control at all costs. Unsurprisingly, this had very mixed results, confirming the psychological truism that the attempted remedy can become a new and even more virulent poison than the problem it is supposed to eradicate.

Even before being a symbol of the psyche, the labyrinth emerges in Nietzsche as a more immediate representation of the darkness of the body, understood not as a hidden foundation that can one day be illuminated through painstaking investigation, but as the "philological enigma of plurality" (Blondel, 1991, p. 210). Typified by Nietzsche with the digestive tract, he sees the non-conscious body as a thousand-fold process (*tausendfältiger Prozess*), indiscernible to a conscious mind that is wholly incapable, even in our age of efficient managerialism, to supervise its unbroken plurality. His investigation does not result in the disclosure of anything resembling either Schopenhauer's unitary will, or the equally unitary unconscious portrayed by Freud. Instead of the invisible/indivisible core of body and psyche, he finds plurality – the labyrinth, i.e., a *pluralization of foundations*. Nietzsche, the self-appointed "subterranean man" (1881/1997, p. 1) who tunnels the foundations of psyche and the non-conscious body, does find depth, but it is a *bottomless* depth that does not regale us with the solidity of a foundation – even less with a geometrical order linking psyche to the cosmos. Instead of a path, we find many paths. The reason for this, Alan White (1991) writes, is that

> Nietzsche's labyrinth is our labyrinth, the labyrinth of the human condition; to affirm human life is to value living within this labyrinth, rather than to attempt to escape from it.
>
> *(p. 14)*

When not trying to escape from it, which may well be our default position, the religious person seeks to embellish the labyrinth by projecting on it the human dreams of order, aim, and unity – the hallmarks of nihilistic denigration of life – which is another, more sophisticated way to escape a difficult and tragic affirmation of life.

Against 'wellness'

> I love him whose soul squanders itself, who wants no thanks and returns none: for he always gives away and does not want to preserve himself.

I love him who is abashed when the dice fall to make his fortune and asks: "Am I then a crooked gambler?" For he wants to perish.

(Nietzsche, 1883/2006a, p. 15)

Alongside the denigration of life commonly found in religion and morality, on a psychological level nihilism is that stealthy, widespread feeling Nietzsche charts at the dawn of modernity, characterized by a near-comatose and pervasive absence of values – a kind of universal mourning for something we can no longer either remember or name. It is under the spell of this particular affect that, despite their lush resonances, metaphysical texts begin, all of a sudden, to sound hollow. Through Hegel we had assigned deep meaning to metaphysics by means of logical reason. Now reason began to question the validity of these very same metaphysical values. Nietzsche's method for seeing through the hollowness of metaphysical claims is *philology*, a discipline that in his hands sheds its conventional stuffiness and becomes a weapon of demystification. Rather than mere destruction, demystification is at the service of the wider project of *homo natura*, a thoroughgoing affirmation of the natural living body and of a *physiological* sense of identity – a powerful rebuttal of Descartes' *cogito* and of our entire philosophical tradition that has demurely obeyed the dictates of religion in leaving the body out of the picture.

The Platonist-Christian tradition rejected the splendour and magnificence of bountiful life, creating instead a *disembodied* culture. What were the reasons for this? Was this an act of simple malevolence against life? Not quite. The tradition worked hard at creating a certain *type* of human being who is incapable of dancing to the rhythm of tumultuous, luminous, *ascending* life. This type of human (in the beginning the priest, later followed by the 'objective' scientist) cannot hear the music and sees those who are dancing as mad. Standing by the river shore and giving greater value to the static domain external to the flowing water, he exacts revenge against life, in the attempt to get compensation for the life he misses.

Life itself, the life of the breathing, perishable body and its affects, has no intrinsic worth for the nihilist, unless it can be either linked to a transcendental value, or is duly measured and 'evidenced'. The parallels with psychotherapy are striking. In a nihilist culture, psychotherapy *has* to be nihilistic: clinical practice must be validated and justified by an overarching metaphysical frame, be it a belief in a reified unconscious, a transpersonal dimension, or faith in the formative tendency and the power of love. Despite the fact that therapy is at heart a delicate experiment, it is currently being spied on and accounted for by a barrage of quantifiable data. It matters little in the end whether it is faith in God or faith in Data: both swerve therapy away from the living body and the life of body affects; both supersede the organism – the body, the world – with transcendental or scientistic detours that help us forget the dread and magnificence of the silver river of life.

What is the alternative? A Nietzsche-inspired psychology of the future cannot be what psychology and psychotherapy are at present – depositories for second-hand metaphysics, scientific certainties and moral prejudices. It would instead facilitate the coming into being of the *human as dissonance*, i.e., as a vibrant point of convergence where the uncertainties of life do not have to be resolved, but are allowed to be experienced. Is this even possible? It has been realized in other areas – mainly art – so why could not the same intelligence at work there also operate within psychology? There is one major obstacle. Psychology and psychotherapy are at heart nihilistic, i.e., they are crafts born out of *ressentiment*. Their originary stance does not celebrate life, but tries to amend it. Even art has only occasionally been the expression of active, life-affirming forces. From his middle works onward, Nietzsche harboured the hope that psychology could reach where art could not. He had witnessed, with Wagner's music, how thoroughly narcotic art can become, a form of superficial, sentimental entertainment that allows us to forget our joyous and thorny task of creating meaning. Psychology, he thought, could just be able to cut through the illusion of the human dimension and make space for the overhuman, that is, for the moment of opening and crisis that potentially ushers in a more abundant life.

Psychotherapy's rather suspect, 'Protestant' aspiration to be a corrective, a means for self-improvement, becomes much more acceptable when we substitute 'corrective' with 'healing'. *Therapeia* means, after all, healing, in this case soul (*psyche*) healing. The nihilistic, life-denying influence of our culture has made sure that psychotherapy replicates these principles, thus functioning as a mouthpiece for a pervasive ideology of *ressentiment*. Yet it is from 'sickness' that a doorway is found into that richer labyrinthine existence Nietzsche writes about. In order to feel more fully the plenitude of existence, in order to feel the first stirring of a desire to explore it, we need to be 'sick'. Our sickness, or suffering, is a sign of profound ambivalence: it is, first of all, the result of the contagion our nihilist culture exerts on us, as it turns us into the only consistently self-hating animals in existence. It also sharpens our understanding by eliciting experimentation and a broadening of experience.

Psychotherapy performs two equally important tasks: one *reparative*, the other *experimental*. The latter, however, has not been sufficiently explored in psychology and psychotherapy and for that reason we may benefit from examples in the world of art. In a letter to Paul Demeny, a 15-year-old Rimbaud (1871/1986) wrote of wanting to "arrive at the unknown" (p. 6) by the deliberate disorientation of all the senses. Could something similar be advocated for psychotherapeutic investigation? Could psychotherapy become a guide to getting lost, an experiment in the exploration of the human domain that although born in sickness can access the labyrinthine palace of experimentation? Like Rimbaud, the artistic avant-garde of the twentieth century knew this well. In some cases, it took Nietzsche's teachings to heart, constructing an enduring modern myth that through the twists and turns of 'sickness' expressed exuberant ways of being that belonged to "the outlaw, the deviant, the transgressor, the immoralist, the one who violates the command of health understood as self-preservation, as miserly self-satisfaction" (Masini, 1978, p. 299).

The question naturally arises as to whether this angle on therapeutic exploration may only appeal to a certain type of person. This became a very real question at some point in my clinical practice. I began to notice that, even with their wide differences, several clients shared a similar cluster of issues that could be said to belong to a particular realm of experience. At its core, there is an exhilarating but perilous dance between creative expression and intense distress. My current belief, after Otto Rank, is that the awakening of a certain level of creativity in the client – whether expressed through artistic or literary works, or directed towards self-creation – is the key factor in anything that could be called successful therapy, and that this can be applied to virtually anyone willing to engage with it.

For Nietzsche, 'health' – or that trendy word beloved of the corporate world, *wellness* – is a much poorer ally in the exploration of psyche than sickness (a.k.a. incongruence, suffering, crisis, existential dilemma and so forth). While the former entraps us within a stagnant, self-satisfied and precarious pretence of certainty in the midst of an uncertain world, the latter may spur us on towards further exploration.

By beginning to understand, with Nietzsche's help, the pervasiveness of nihilistic culture, we also begin to grasp more fully the significant hold *redemption* has on the collective psyche. Dominant narratives – whether religious or secular – placed great importance on redeeming life from its inherent flaws and fragility. They constructed an onto-theological frame that has now taken hold of psychology and psychotherapy. As a result, these disciplines no longer maintain their autonomous inquiry into the human condition, but are reframed within the parameters of the onto-theological narratives. There is a way out, however. Following Nietzsche's examples, this would imply a gradual movement of emancipation from three prejudices, from three powerful yokes (Vattimo, 2005), that keep us ensnared and limit our investigation. As we have seen for Nietzsche, the three prejudices are: religion, morality, and, via traditional philosophy, truth.

What do these three have in common? They are all facets of nihilism, in the *primary* sense Nietzsche attributes to the term, that is, as the imposition of values *above* life itself, an imposition that unfailingly results in the denigration of life.

The secondary meaning Nietzsche attributes to nihilism equally results in a devaluation of life, but this time in the name of a life "stripped of meaning and purpose, sliding even further towards its nothingness" (Deleuze, 2006, p. 140). The primary meaning is established by an astute construction of fictions that together weave an orderly cosmos, a totality that alone, it is assumed, can grant meaning to the mere 'furniture' of the world – to a fragmented, all-too-particular reality.

Active nihilism

In a notebook entry of autumn 1887, Nietzsche draws a clear distinction between *active nihilism*, which he sees as a "sign of increased power of the spirit", and *passive nihilism* which is characterized by the "decline and retreat of the spirit's power" (Vattimo, 2005, p. 134). At first glance, passive nihilism may sound and feel as an affirmative and bold proposition: faced with what it perceives as moral relativism and pervasive disintegration of values, it will inveigh against these in the names of religion, morality, and aesthetic principles. This is a version of passive nihilism we are all more or less familiar with: the prude who thinks of D.H. Lawrence's, James Joyce's or Eimear McBride's writings as obscene; the traditionalist who sees abstract expressionism as 'splodges on a canvas'; the myopic scholar or sanguine priest who objects to a couple of young lovers exchanging a French kiss in a public library or a church. Within the small world of psychotherapy, passive nihilism operates in the name of the sacred cows of a particular orientation, in the name of Spirituality or a reified Unconscious, in the name of Being or Felt Sense, of Growth or Presence, of Authenticity or Integration – preferably rendered in capitals, thus making sure that neophytes bear in mind that these are not mere signposts but true and proper Objects of Worship.

Active nihilism, as portrayed by Nietzsche, is a very different kettle of fish. It professes a doing away with all so-called 'eternal' values and truths. This is not done out of a fashionable 'appetite for destruction' that in good time turns into lucrative 'greatest hits' compilations, but out of a rigour and a fever of thought that blazes through the lie and sees that those eternal truths and noble values are merely conditions without which our species could not survive. They are not grounds of being but simply tools of self-preservation. An active nihilistic stance will see through the notion of truth as an elevation on a grand scale of our way of life as individuals and societies.

When applied to the world of psychotherapy, active nihilism would mean refusal of starry-eyed contemplation of the Unassailable Monuments of the past, be they Berggasse 19, Vienna, or Zollikon, or the Wisconsin Project or Kingsley Hall. It would also be different from mere resignation in the face of the encroaching regimentation of the profession. It would mean putting aside the old dreams and the old idioms, and working at creating new dreams, new idioms, this time knowing that these are temporary and expedient creations rather than foundational principles.

In order to live, we have to go on dreaming – even when we come to realize that all we do is dream. Active nihilism in this context is a little more than acceptance of life's vicissitudes, a little more than the detached, maudlin appreciation of life's magnitude and wonder expressed by the spiritual and the wise. It is dynamic identification; it is participation in life's own creative process. This is housed in *bios* and *physis*; it acknowledges and celebrates nature and the body, but goes one step further – not towards transcendence but in the direction of collusion with life's incessant self-creation. Nietzsche's exploration does more than recognize the body and nature; it celebrates it. Many passages in Nietzsche point towards what will be later called *vitalism*, a philosophy which is to my taste far more enriching and affirmative than any thought founded on the abstraction of 'Being'. When applied to therapy, Nietzsche's insights provide us with the rudiments of a *Lebensphilosophie* rather than any *Dasein-analysis*. This is because they emphasize *life*, not *being*.

What routes are then open to our exploration? Having bracketed for the time being the vitalist option, it is tempting at this point to settle on a hermeneutics of self-awareness. This is approximately the route taken by existential-phenomenological therapists of a Husserlian persuasion, for whom Nietzsche belongs snugly (with Kierkegaard) to the fabricated Olympus of existentialist forebears. The trouble with this stance is (I will put it crudely) that hermeneutic awareness is *self-centred*, i.e., it escorts us back to the centrality of self-awareness. Not a bad thing, some will say; part of the job of therapy is, after all, helping a person regain an internal locus of evaluation, foster autonomy and self-direction, becoming more sharply individuated, more discerning: all of these are centred on a greater and more solid sense of self.

What then? Shall we settle instead for some kind of militant pragmatism, focusing exclusively on behaviour, discarding self-consciousness in the name of 'what works' in the crucible of everyday existence, of what increases our sense of wellbeing and strength? But taking this route would lead us back to a more superficial form of vitalism. A possible way out of this seeming impasse is given by Nietzsche himself, who draws attention to what could be called nihilism's originary felt sense. This is an increasing feeling of the futility of existence, in the light of which one is tempted to find consolation in the ready-made answers promulgated by various institutionalized herds. This has the feel-good effect of corroborating one's own identity and bolstering one's presumed sense of substantiality. This stance may be momentarily satisfying but, crucially for Nietzsche, it fails in partaking more actively in life's creative and interpretative process. The real task, for Nietzsche, is finding a way to sustain and be complicit with the latter. This is not a task for the so-called 'strong person', least of all for the fascist mind, or for the person of great confidence and self-assurance, nor for the integrated, mindful, or fully functioning individual or for those who, thanks to therapy, have regained a fictitious state of normality. Who is the strongest? – Nietzsche asks. *The most moderate*, the one who can bear the unforeseen, the impermanent and the nonsensical; the one who can partake of life's creative impulse by moulding new masks for herself outside of the models and parameters of received wisdom. The active nihilist is at heart a *creative artist*: she embodies the tragic, Dionysian dimension and is able to embrace joy and sorrow, ecstasy and agony, beauty and horror. She is an artist in the specific (creating artefacts) and the general sense (creating herself, i.e. finding a way out of incongruence, neurosis, enmeshment in the malaise of an unlived and uncontested life).

Thus the client who undergoes therapy 'successfully' becomes, potentially, *creator of his life*. The crisis brought about by those 'presenting issues' that drive clients to therapy is the widening crack, a first taste of nihilism, a vague sense of the meaninglessness of existence. Equally nihilistic is the client's attempt at finding an answer and a solution outside the crucible of everyday existence: through a causal explanation, the dispensing of a formula, a diagnosis, a set of practices that will exorcise the problem and fill the yawn.

This is not 'finding wellness' or recovering a fabricated notion of mental health. For Nietzsche, health is a kind of prejudice that reinforces and is motivated by self-preservation. The task here is deeply counter-intuitive and not at all evidence-based: transcending our instinct for self-preservation, bringing our exploration close to the point of vanishing. The implications here are philosophical *and* political. It is our instinct for self-preservation, our overriding need to bolster identity and ipseity that drive metaphysics and, with it, all the repressive categories of conventional thought. Forfeiting the notion of being in favour of becoming, in favour of a constantly vanishing point, of a non-presence that aligns us with the process of life itself: this is a new task for a praxis-based therapeutic work unshackled from metaphysics and from the philistine pragmatism of evidence-based normative demands.

Homo neoliberalis

The 1980s witnessed the emergence of *self-help*. Beneath a wobbly, sub-pre-Raphaelite aesthetic and a penchant for spirit channelling and fluffy cherubs, its promoters supplied the reactionary ethos of that decade with a fittingly obscurantist ideology which culminated in the 'smile or die' scenario so brilliantly lampooned by Barbara Ehrenreich (2010). It was easy at the time to dismiss the self-help business and its new-agey, half-baked belief system as surrogate religion or meta-physics for the dim-witted. Few could have predicted it would gradually meta-morphose into the widespread phenomenon it is today, endorsed by governments, big business and academia alike (Davies, 2015), and slowly but surely encircle the world of psychology and psychotherapy. All that the self-help industry had to do was change its name, tweak a clause or two in its 'philosophy', add a scientific patina plus a handful of data: *voilà*, the *happiness industry* was born! This shift from crackpot religion to crackpot science may be mystifying to some, but it is pro-foundly interesting. It suggests two things:

a When it comes to manipulating and bamboozling the public, governments and big business are impressively supple; they can draw from *any* ideological source, provided it sends out the simple message that if we suffer, go through a crisis, or can't find meaning in our life, it is essentially our fault. Back in the day, this was described in terms of *karma* and chanted in Sanskrit over incense smoke; nowadays we're shown a PowerPoint presentation with plenty of multicoloured brain imagery, followed by a bullet-point guide to the princi-ples of Positive Psychology and Mindfulness.

b Although the version of spirituality and religion imparted by the self-help industry of the 1980s, and the version of science imparted by the happiness industry of today, are both third-rate, they are exploiting sources that even in their more original and sophisticated versions, and despite their widely diver-ging worldviews, have one fundamental thing in common: they are both metaphysical, i.e. they provide a system, a comforting and ultimately illusory explanation of what is a deeply ambivalent and unknowable world. For Nietzsche, they are at best stimulants, but it would be a mistake to attribute ultimate value to them.

Some positive psychologists have imaginatively assembled a *lineage* of positive psychology itself (Linley & Joseph, 2004). They have done so presumably in the attempt to show that the latter is rooted in deep thinking and wisdom and is far from being the simplistic and politically compromised practice that it appears to be, given its associations with highly controversial practices in the US military and the

CIA (Shaw, 2016). Interestingly, they go all the way back to Aristotle and his notion of *eudaimonia* or 'happiness'. Despite the wide gap between the depth of understanding in Aristotelian thought and Positive Psychology's creed, the association is apt. Aristotle has to bear some responsibility, it seems to me, for the vulgar eudaimonism and optimistic tranquillity that has slowly and inexorably become the dominant understanding of the human place in the world since the post-war years, all the way from the bourgeois ideal of normality to the happy-clappy human prototype of today, *homo neoliberalis*, a mollified version of the human that hides its hatreds and passions behind the pretence of the cool, scientific neutrality of the market.

A pact with the devil?

> One is an artist at the cost of regarding that which all non-artists call "form" as content, as "the matter itself." To be sure, then one belongs in a topsy-turvy world: for henceforth content becomes something merely formal – our life included.
>
> *(Nietzsche, 1968, p.433)*

Against the current corporate promotion of wellness, happiness, and mental health, Nietzsche's provocative invitation to a heuristic and experimental *application* of illness aimed at widening the frontiers of knowledge, experience, and wisdom begins to make a lot of sense. To some, this will inevitably look perverse and, depending on outlook and/or social conditioning, even evil, given that the latter is the name historically given to a heretical position that chooses a different route to individuation and meaning that the well-trodden paths of orthodoxy and tradition.

A multi-layered philosophical plan lies just beneath Nietzsche's challenging appreciation of illness and the further links he makes between illness and the creative and meaningful life. At its core, this has to do with transposing dialectics from the plane of logical reasoning to that of concrete bodily reality, and with conceiving knowledge as 'emotional', incarnate knowledge. The organism is already endowed with instinctual intelligence: *creativity and instinct are intertwined.* This goes against the common assumption that, after Freud, sees creativity as a *sublimation* of instinct or "diversion" of the latter into "symbolic realms" (Massumi, 2014, p. 91). More fundamentally, it goes against the logo-centrism of Western metaphysics that conventionally assigns either a 'primitive', near-unintelligible place to the life of the body, or sees it as the beast to be tamed. The direction Nietzsche invites us to take is to untie dialectics from its canonical association with logical reason and link it instead to nature and the body, going right down to the rich and contradictory life of instincts, emotions and 'passions'. In the process, the range of universally accepted values (moral and logical) is subverted in favour of contradiction, *agon*, and continuous interpretive shifts towards greater refinement.

Mothers of invention

There exists an altogether different account of chaos than the one we have inherited from the religious and philosophical tradition. Babich (2004) dates this notion of chaos back to the poet Hesiod (2012), thought to have lived in the late fifth and fourth centuries BC, and to his didactic narrative poem *Theogony* ('genealogy of the gods'). Chaos (sometimes referred to as 'the dark' as well as 'water' and – later echoed by Aristotle's *Metaphysics* – 'the night') is prominent in Hesiod's account and has no predecessors. After Chaos, other limitless gods emerge: Gaia (the Earth) and then, in the depths of Gaia, Tartarus and Eros. These four gods, including Chaos, are variously referred to as 'elements' or as 'mothers of being'; they are self-made and do not arise from each other. It is Chaos who gives birth to the deities of darkness, including Erebos, and Hesiod's account is similar to the one found in the Orphic tradition. Both narratives emphasize the *self-generative* element; both give primacy to "the pattern of spontaneous (and feminine) creativity" (Babich, 2004, p. 143). Already in these early accounts, however, the feminine, self-generative aspect is quashed, as shown in the story of Eros where it is the "insurgent male power" who, "ordered by desire," claims authorship of origins. This masculine version of "cosmological genesis" (ibid.) we inherited was further perfected and popularized by the Judaeo-Christian religious tradition. This detail unmasks another important layer of meaning in the time-honoured story of tidy, bright and virtuous genesis of history out of the dark night of frenzied misrule. It speaks of fear and hatred of chaos as fear and hatred of the feminine.

This does not mean that, as with our previous discussion on the labyrinth, we can conveniently turn Nietzsche into a devotee of the primeval goddess, despite the fact that his favourite god Dionysus presents distinctly androgynous traits. What matters to Nietzsche is that we turn our attention to, and partake of, the powers of untamed nature in "creative self-genesis, in becoming ourselves a work of art" (Babich, 2004, p. 144). In this sense both 'chaos' and 'the feminine' come to affirm nature as self-generative and 'self-actualizing', i.e. devoid of a creator, a self – a *cause*. Chaos is, in short, another name for primeval nature. This primeval nature does not belong solely to archaic stories and fables: it is present, if dormant, within all of us; it is our creative power. But we are likely to mislay it in our concerted attempts to stave off chaos, which we hurriedly and misguidedly apprehend as dis-order and the breakdown of order. It is very difficult not to do so, when we have inherited a bi-millennial religious and philosophical tradition that sees the primordial world as the "impotent, and featureless, waters of an unreal and feminine abyss" that preceded the "first divine moment of the creation of the world" (Babich, 2004, p. 144). This worldview, according to Nietzsche, has then in turn strongly influenced science. Rather than refuting our ancient mistrust of chaos, science reinforced it. Overall, it did not question the myths of genesis and paternity but strengthened the veneration of Gaia, the earth mother organism whose early atmosphere, shrouded in carbon dioxide (an effect of frequent and multiple volcanic eruptions), slowly makes way for 'life proper' through a series of masculine begetters. In science too, chaos carries on being a non-creative force and takes on a negative meaning.

One of the implications of Nietzsche's radical stance – namely, his linking of chaos with nature in the way it has been described above – is an effective repudiation of the conventional antagonism between art and nature. The two are intimately related; nature itself is art, once we manage to separate it from the influential misconception that attributes to it a rational (scientific) or divine (religious) foundation.

Against mechanicism, against teleology

From the above it may become clear that Nietzsche refuses both *mechanicism* and *teleology*. His reading of F.A. Lange, Helmholtz, Boscovich, Kopp, Roux, among others, helped him take this stance confidently. It is fairly common to find in the psychotherapy literature of the last few decades a critique of mechanicism (at least within humanistic and psychodynamic accounts). In the mechanistic view, nature is seen as made up of 'things', with the human subject one more thing among them. This view has never entirely faded from the world of counselling and psychotherapy. On the contrary: while it once remained confined to behaviourism, it is now enjoying widespread popularity, fuelled by the neopositivist ideology that is being aggressively promoted in the humanities. In some of its more reductive manifestations, this view separates the mind from the body; it identifies the former with the brain; it regards psychology as indistinguishable from the study of brain processes and the causal relations between them, and between what happens in the brain and in other areas of the body. The giddily uncritical reception of neuroscience among therapists must surely give pause for thought, especially given that many of neuroscience's over-optimistic claims still await verification.

I heard a conversation on the radio a while ago between a novelist and a neuroscientist. The novelist was saying that, when all is said and done, we don't really know much about human nature. The neuroscientist responded that, given time, neuroscience will unmask all there is to know about human nature; all mysteries, he assured listeners, can be revealed. In his reply, the novelist paraphrased Nietzsche: there is nothing behind the mask.

But if mechanicism is met with some resistance in psychotherapy circles, the same cannot be said about teleology. To posit an evolutionary goal, to think of a tendency in the universe, reflected in all living organisms, to actualize, grow, and develop is to replicate the error of mechanicism. Both views establish univocal explanations of life. While mechanicism maintains that existence is blindly "unfolding in the pursuit of nothing other than its mere perpetuation" (Acampora, 2004, p. 173), teleology declares that "all values derive from the end towards which everything is supposed to strive" (ibid). The latter relies on metaphysical explanations of the world, but the same is less obviously true of mechanistic explanations. The classical materialistic view is not free of the very same prejudices that are normally the province of moral philosophy and metaphysics. For Nietzsche, mechanistic physics and evolutionary biology are still not scientific or *naturalistic* enough.

The teleological view – manifestly present in orthodox accounts of person-centred, existential and humanistic psychotherapy – makes too much of humans: we are effectively depicted as "nearly divine" as well as "divorced from the rest of creation" (Acampora, 2004, p. 173). This is largely due to the overriding influence of the Judaeo-Christian perspective, both in its religious and less obvious secular manifestations. Conversely, the mechanistic view makes too little of us: the human is seen as "descendant of the grinning ape", who by sheer luck finds "the path of least resistance" (ibid.) in the struggle to achieve mere survival and self-preservation. The task is to find a way out of this double bind. For Acampora (2004), this may be done by

> developing a conception of human being that: (1) situates it within the world of becoming, but (2) puts it in dialogue with the empirical sciences, and (3) allows for the possibility that we might also be able to raise the bar and indicating the goals for which the human might strive, thereby making room for meaningful art.
>
> *(p. 174)*

Alongside Nietzsche, a great inspiration in reaching a way that does not stoop to either mechanicism or teleology is Heraclitus, one who was, in Nietzsche's view, unique among the ancient in actively resisting the siren call of metaphysical explanation of reality. We need this sort of inspiration to counteract the entire weight of the philosophical and religious tradition that conditioned us to see *becoming* as inconceivable outside a teleological or a mechanistic view. For Heraclitus, as for Nietzsche, the incessant becoming of the world is neither of the above. It is more akin to a playing child – a most fitting image that refuses the impositions of dogmatic religion and reductive science alike and remains innocently and unashamedly loyal to the unwarranted excess of the world.

7

AMBIGUOUS LEGACIES

Player and plaything

Of all misreadings of Nietzsche, the one that had the most enduring and deleterious influence, particularly in relation to psychotherapy, is Heidegger's. Nietzsche's anti-Semitic, pro-Nazi sister, Mme. Förster-Nietzsche – "one of those abusive relatives that figure in the procession of cursed thinkers" (Deleuze, 2004, p. 117) – had one overriding concern: "to make of Nietzsche a true philosopher, in the common sense of the word" (Blanchot, 1969/1993, p. 137). Heidegger shared her concern. He did all he could to systematize Nietzsche's thought (Heidegger, 1961/1991); in doing so, he overlooked its very heart and spirit.

Not only did he read Nietzsche as a metaphysician, constricting the latter's expansive insights on psychology, anthropology, science, religion and ethics within the narrow confines of metaphysical assertions. He also managed to misinterpret Nietzsche's notion of the will, and to ascribe Nietzsche's conception of Being within a metaphysical tradition to which Nietzsche not only does not belong, but against which he decidedly came to blows (Schrift, 1990).

Even more crucially, Heidegger tried very hard to anchor Nietzsche's mercurial output around the allegedly central idea of the eternal recurrence, while blatantly missing one of the key themes in the entire Nietzschean oeuvre: *play*. Not only is the notion of play central in Nietzsche; it is also multifaceted, and specifically, expressed in the following threefold manner, as:

a   *Schauspiel* or theatrical play, i.e., conveying a vision of life, the world, and our role in it as akin to a theatre performance.
b   *Weltspiel*, or understanding the world (and the human being) as a play of natural forces to be arranged and composed, as in the illustrious case of Goethe, who "disciplined himself to wholeness [and] created himself" (Nietzsche, 1888/2015,

p. 83). Here the psychological and existential choice is between being either a player or a plaything, i.e., between actively playing with natural forces and being passively played with by them.

c *Kinderspiel*, the vision of life and the universe as child-play. This is the most central among these three notions, the one that brings them to life (Schrift, 1990).

These three dimensions of play are closely linked to another key notion in Nietzsche's thinking: *dance*. In a letter to his friend Erwin Rhode on 22 February 1884, he wrote:

> My style is a dance; it plays with all sorts of symmetries, only to leap over and scoff at them.
>
> *(Schrift, 1990, p. 72)*

Metaphysical reductionism

All of the above is utterly lost to Heidegger, whose "*metaphysical reductionism* fits neither the spirit nor the letter of Nietzsche's philosophical project [and] fails to attend to the *genealogical* character of Nietzsche's remarks" (Schrift, 1990, p. 54, emphasis added). Heidegger was no psychologist, and his misreading reaches its nadir when he tries to respond to Nietzsche's reflections on psychology. Instead of taking them seriously, he curiously reads them as "disguised metaphysics" (ibid., p. 54). But for Nietzsche (1908/ 2007b), a "psychologist beyond compare" (p. 41) and "the foremost psychologist of the eternal feminine" (ibid., p. 42), the fundamental problems are *not* metaphysical. They do *not* concern 'Being', as Heidegger has it, but are problems of value, i.e., *axiological*. They are to be tackled not by metaphysics but *psychology*. As "the doctrine of the structure and development of will to power [Nietzsche's psychology] does not seek the Being of beings" (Schrift, 1990, p. 55), but is keen to discover whether current instances of will to power are ruled by active (life-affirming) or passive (life-denying) forces. A psychology thus understood is not after knowledge (a supposedly neutral knowledge that will shield us, we hope, from a sensuous experience of the world) but is committed to the genealogical task of recognition of the forces at play. Rather than being mixed up with investigations concerning ontological status, Nietzsche's psychology is axiological, i.e., it *assigns value* in the service of active, life-affirming forces.

By understanding Nietzsche's take on nihilism only as 'poison' – i.e. as *passive* nihilism – Heidegger (1961/1991) misses the psycho-genealogical nature of Nietzschean thought, whose implications are electrifying for psychotherapy. His reading of Nietzsche, a profoundly anti-metaphysical thinker, is fanatically metaphysical. Even will to power, that most supple of Nietzschean hypotheses, becomes, in Heidegger's hands, a rigid statement on the so-called Being of beings. But Nietzsche is royally uninterested in the 'Being' of will to power. He could not care less about metaphysical questions. What interests him is the 'Where from?' (*Woher?*), and the 'Where to?' (*Wohin?*) of will to power. Alan Schrift asks: "out of what do these impulses that we call 'will to power' arise and toward what ends are these impulses directed?" (1990, p. 60).

For Nietzsche, philosophy and psychology do not need metaphysics but *axiology* (from *axioein* = to hold worthy): a science of evaluation bold enough to disregard *Seinsfrage*, the idle and abstract question of 'Being' in favour of *Wertfrage*, a concrete and searching question of value, i.e., an incessant process of investigation and interpretation. The latter is crucial to the practice of psychotherapy, for in this case the attribution of value would centre on weighing up what is life-affirming from what is life-denying.

Heidegger (1961/1991, IV) dismisses the primacy of value in Nietzsche: "The question about value and its essence" – he writes – "is grounded in the question of Being" (p. 16). He is scolding Nietzsche for not having made explicit, or for having *forgotten* 'Being'. But Nietzsche did not forget Being. He clearly saw that there is no Being in the first place. What the philosophical tradition calls 'Being' is a mildly interesting, ultimately misleading notion aimed at appeasing our inveterate inability as a species to come to terms with the terrifying and wondrous reality of becoming. It is understandable that this notion should attract philosophers, in whose ranks both closet and candid transcendentalists have been known to mingle from time immemorial. But it is disappointing that it should attract psychotherapists too, i.e., practitioners of an art whose key tenet is, as I understand it, the bracketing of unverified and superstitious ideas. But then again, with both the closeted and unconstrained varieties of cut-price theology back in fashion as we speak (alongside its complementary opposite, i.e. the faux empiricism of 'evidence-based' therapy), there is no denying that psychotherapy too suffers from what Schrift calls "the 'beyond' corruption" (1990, p. 61).

Psychotherapy carries on its frail shoulders an unnecessary load of metaphysical ballast, and one of the reasons why Nietzsche's thought is invaluable to our practice is for how light-heartedly it does away with spiritual and pseudo-scientific encumbrances. In order to make good use of it, however, one ought to bypass Heidegger's influential misreadings and perceive the spirit of play at the heart of Nietzsche's style and content. This means learning more about the important shift in Nietzschean scholarship that took place in Europe (particularly in France, but also in Italy) in the 1960s and 1970s and, in later decades, in North America. The shift went unnoticed in the UK, where to this day one has to waste precious time arguing with otherwise well-informed people against the Nazification of Nietzsche, let alone trying to reframe his thought away from the philosophical tradition into which Heidegger arbitrarily placed it. The cultural shift, particularly in Europe, was momentous in turning the gaze away from the three *Hs* – Hegel, Husserl, and Heidegger – that dominated philosophical discourse until then, and towards the masters of suspicions: Marx, Nietzsche, and Freud (Ricoeur, 1970/2008). Foucault's 1964 paper, presented at the 7th International Colloquium at Royaumont (Foucault 1967/1990) caught the zeitgeist: he argued that *signs* are *no longer to be viewed as the repository of* some profound, concealed *meaning*. He also launched a distinctly Nietzschean spin on the notion of interpretation:

> Interpretation can never be brought to an end, simply because there is nothing to interpret. There is nothing absolutely primary to interpret, because at the bottom everything is already interpretation. Each sign is in itself not the thing that presents itself to interpretation, but the interpretation of other signs.
>
> *(ibid., p. 64)*

In later works, Foucault raised the stakes even higher, highlighting another fundamental shift that signalled the move away from old-style hermeneutics towards what he calls an "uprooting of Anthropology", a shift instigated by Nietzsche himself who had, in Foucault's view, "rediscovered the point at which the human being and God belong to one another", with the death of the latter becoming identical to the vanishing of the former, a point at which "the promise of the overman signifies first and foremost the imminence of the death of the human" (Foucault, 1966/1994, p. 106, translation modified). This stance, so rich of latent ramifications for psychotherapy, was further intensified by the link Deleuze and Guattari (1972/1982) made between the death of God and the demise of the Oedipal father, a link whose implications remain oddly unexplored to this day.

While it is true that the figure of the patriarchal father has been somewhat decentred by decades of feminism and the efforts of emancipatory politics, the creed of the family's "nuclear complex", the "daddy-mommy-me triangle" (Deleuze & Guattari, 1972/1982, p. 51), established long ago by psychiatry and classical psychoanalysis, hangs about unscathed at the core of all psychotherapeutic orientations, even within those approaches that congratulate themselves for their independence from conventional and conservative models of understanding the psyche.

While it is true that Heidegger moved away from the Freudian model and attempted to inscribe humans in history and the world, his fascination with the abstraction of 'Being' disinterred the deceased God. From then on, it is only a small step away from anthropological subjectivity, a move replicated in conventional existential psychotherapy's current insistence on subjectivity's addenda: intersubjectivity and universal relatedness. A 'return' to Nietzsche is then essential in any psychotherapeutic enterprise, for in debunking this strange "empirico-transcendental doublet" (Schrift, 1990, p. 79) – the myth of God (or the myth of Being, a shadow of God), alongside the myth of the human – his thought undermines anthropology, or at the very least, the way we have thus far understood anthropology, i.e., in Kantian terms.

In the first pages of his *Introduction to Logic*, Kant (1800/1963) wrote that "the field of philosophy ... may be reduced to the four following questions": 1 What can I know? 2 What must I do? 3 What may I hope? 4 What is a human being? He then gave the following answers:

> The first question is answered by *Metaphysics*, the second by *Morals*, the third by *Religion*, and the fourth by *Anthropology*. In reality, however, all these might be reckoned under anthropology, since the first three questions refer to the last.
>
> *(ibid., p. 15)*

Until Nietzsche came along to clarify that undoing any of the first three bastions entails undoing the fourth (given that they are all inextricably linked), it had been canonical (with the increased popularity of ideas from the Enlightenment) to think of anthropology in terms of the exaltation of the human and its separation from nature. Without implementing or, at least, giving some consideration to Nietzsche's insights in the matter, we are caught in the net of the epistemological slumber that permeates psychotherapeutic theories across most orientations.

But this would entail opening the exploration to the overhuman. It would mean planning for a clean break with the humanist tradition and the kind of metaphysical humanism that smugly believes itself to be 'secular' and free from any shadow of God.

Foucault, particularly in *The Order of Things* (1966/1994), articulated this Nietzschean position brilliantly. It is astonishing that Foucault's writings have justly become an inspiration on a wide array of topics – from the link between institutional power and knowledge, to burning issues of difference and equality on all fronts – while his shrewd critique of the dominant role ascribed to the human, which happens to be at the very centre of his brightly subversive oeuvre, is ignored. But it can no longer be ignored, for it is only when we begin to *decentre the human* that anything resembling a 'phenomenological' therapy can begin. It is only when we begin to decentre the 'person', that attention can be finally paid to experiencing and affect. It is only when we actively proclaim the demise of the human that hope arises for a true ecology. And it is only when we begin to decentre the human that we can make room for immanent spirituality, free of the virus of metaphysical humanism.

All-too-humanist

Heidegger is seen in some psychotherapeutic circles as having presented, through his notion of *Dasein* or being-in-the-world, a valid alternative to the Cartesian subject and to Freud's view of the psyche. But once he asks the question of the *meaning* of Being in all its implications, the repressed Cartesian subject returns. For Derrida, Heidegger "had to acknowledge the exemplary being which will constitute the privileged text for a reading of the meaning of Being" (Derrida, 1982, p. 125). The above being is none other than us – none other than the same old unreconstructed 'I' of the metaphysical tradition. Heidegger wants us to believe that this is not subjective consciousness but entails an incessant *bringing to light*. Hidden in plain view in Heidegger's pastoral, Black Forest imagery of "stand[ing] in the clearing, yet not standing like a pole but rather to sojourn in the clearing and be occupied with things" (Heidegger, 2001, p. 225), is a replica of the old trope of idealistic philosophy: *human essence*, in whose defence he launches his thoroughly humanist critique of technology (Heidegger, 1982).

In many ways, this amounts to a "fundamentalism centred on human reality" (Behler, 1991, p. 50). Despite the emotional allure of aspiring to disperse, after Heidegger, the human subject as "a sort of open, bright forest glade into which beings can shyly step forward like a deer from the trees" (Bakewell, 2016, p. 185), it is not all that easy to shake off anthropocentrism. Incantatory lingo alone won't do, though some psychotherapists, understandably bored by the amount of data and evidence-based barrage that has taken siege of our profession, are ensnared by it and willing to trade the neoliberal utopia for a promise of Arcadia.

We are irredeemably implicated in *telos*, particularly when speaking of the 'end of the human' and becoming preoccupied with the melodrama of the protagonist's sad demise. The human subject simply won't go away and, in Heidegger's case, we are entirely within the terrain of fundamentalist humanism. Here, metaphors of proximity, immediacy, presence abound; words like "neighbouring, shelter, house, service, guard, voice, and listening" (Derrida, 1982, p. 130) are frequent, as are notions of homeland and identity.

Nietzsche is, conversely, the thinker of difference and multiplicity. He *leaves* the house of Being altogether. Choosing to "dance outside the house" (ibid., p. 136), he calls for an *active forgetting* of Being. Heidegger mourns a passive forgetting of Being which merely results in the restoration of a new metaphysical structure that is entirely caught within *logocentrism* (Bazzano, 2017b, pp. 115–135). He reinstates the logos and the 'truth of Being' as *primum signatum* or 'first signified'. As Eric Blondel (1991) explains, Heidegger's reading of Nietzsche is also oblivious to the role that both the *body* and *genealogy* play in Nietzsche's work:

> Heidegger ... reduce(s) Nietzsche's philosophy to a moment in the history of Being. But the price paid is the effacement of the *Versuch*, the interpretative nature of the body and the genealogical question. Reduced in this way to a few key concepts, Nietzsche's work becomes valuable only as an example of metaphysics and as such has to be superseded ... by the thought of Heidegger.
>
> *(p. 5)*

Negative psychology

Among the many interesting readings of Nietzsche in the field of philosophy, those connected to critical theory (Adorno, 1970) and deconstruction (Derrida, 1981) stand out, each of them arguably underlining one aspect of Nietzschean thought (Vattimo, 2005) and for that reason useful perhaps (and without presumptions of synthesis), to be briefly considered together.

It has been said (Foucault, 1983; Dews, 1986; Bazzano, 2016b) that greater awareness of the writings of the Frankfurt School could have alerted existential and post-existential thinkers to the urgent need for the formulation of an *ontology of actuality*. The latter is a necessary antidote to the inevitable trappings of a philosophy of consciousness within which much of existentialist thought (and existential phenomenological therapy) remains entangled to this day.

But the opposite is also true, a point made by Vattimo (2005, pp. 122–125), for whom the eulogizing of *Schein* (semblance) in Adorno is not sufficiently linked to an equally urgent deconstruction of the subject. In Nietzsche we find both a coherent negation of the subject *and* an equally coherent negation of the 'real world'. Could this double negation, crudely sketched above, be the basis for the beginning of a *negative psychology*? It is widely accepted that almost everything in

Nietzsche points towards a dissolution of the Cartesian *cogito*, of its many shadows and doubles. He also provides us with potent means that allow us to unmask as *cogito*'s dead ringers even those later, avowedly anti-Cartesian formulations. Among these I unapologetically include: *Dasein*; the organismic self; the authentic and/or integrated/individuated self, plus various other shibboleths of contemporary psychotherapy. Nietzsche's exploration does not salvage the 'real' world either, which he sees as no longer useful as an idea, one that has to be abolished alongside its counterpart, the 'apparent' world.

The path of a negative psychology inspired by Nietzschean thought is at variance with most of the assumptions held by contemporary psychotherapy, including those I have long been sympathetic to. It negates at every step of the way, for instance, the grounding of subjectivity and intersubjectivity in universal relatedness. One authoritative account of this stance critiques the influence that our unwarranted belief in "individual subjectivities" (Spinelli, 2016, p. 305), as well as "intersubjectivity" (p. 306), holds on therapy, and finds that these arise as "outcome expression or manifestation" of an "*a priori* ground of relatedness" (p. 308) – which is another word for holism. But common to all three (self-identity, inter-subjectivity and universal relatedness) is the belief in the existence of a ground of being which is precisely what Nietzsche convincingly refutes: *there is no ground to begin with*. Echoes of this very same confusion are found in Buddhist thought in relation to the notion of interdependence, in itself a mistranslation of the Buddha's notion of *paticca samuppada* or 'dependent arising'.

My emphasis here is on relativization rather than oneness, on 'no ground', rather 'we are all one'. As a result, rather than a conflation of 'self' into 'Self', the stress is on 'no-self', *anatman*, the negation of theological and metaphysical sub-stance. This is not 'nihilism' as it is commonly believed; it does not *denigrate* the living; it simply refrains from substantiating it. To see this impermanent life and its individual expressions as nothing (*nihil*) unless we *add* substance to it (soul, self, an origin, a cause, a doer behind the deed, a puppeteer behind the curtain) – *that* is nihilism. To think that *becoming* is not good enough, that this incessant arising-and-vanishing needs *being* in order to collate the myriad manifestations and give them meaning – *that* is nihilism.

We forget that meaning is not something we add as an afterthought or place in the backdrop as source, origin, or beginning. The world is intelligible if we can sing it and sing with it – as we do when we carry the pre-linguistic into speech, *logos endiathetos* into *logos prophorikos*. This is certainly a 'bonding' with the world, but one that requires, for Nietzsche, a forgetting of being, and greater appreciation and enjoyment of incarnate existence:

> Hear my brothers; hear the voice of the healthy body: a more honest and purer voice is this.
> More honestly and more purely speaks the healthy body, the perfect and perpendicular body, and it speaks of the meaning of the earth.

> *(Nietzsche, 1883/2006a, p. 22)*

The path of double negation Nietzsche invites us to follow (negation of the self *and* negation of the real/apparent world) leads to deeper affirmation. The strangeness of the situation we find ourselves in as humans would then appear to require of us something akin to that equally negative gift of negative capability, the quality "which Shakespeare possessed enormously … of being in uncertainties, Mysteries, doubts, without any irritable reach after fact & reason" (Keats, 2009, p. 41). Clearly, this is not a path for everyone; we can't all be Shakespeare. But if we are able to simply wait and resist the 'irritable reach', the nervous tickle and itch for evidence and solid proof, or the knee-jerk hunt for conclusive interpretation, diagnosis and certainty, we may be able to go back to what is central to our work as therapists: active listening and the ability of "being *with* uncertainty, and being *in* uncertainty" (Voller, 2016, p. 35). This is a positively counter-cultural stance, for it means to actively resist the demands thrust upon practitioners by the neopositivist zeitgeist and the institutional bodies that supinely accept its creed.

Therapy as entertainment

One of the outcomes of maintaining this stance is that we become positively open to myriad interpretations. Another way of saying this is that any interpretation, whether implicit or explicit, is simply another association, an additional useful creation to be employed within the frame of therapy. The latter can be seen in this context as a skilled form of *entertainment*, a term whose original meaning is 'holding together', from the Latin *inter* = 'among', and *tenere* = to hold). Nietzsche's contribution in this regard is profoundly counter-traditional; he refuses to provide a new cultural model that will supplant the old one. What he offers instead is the precious germ of all future negations, alongside the means to detect and banish all remnants of metaphysics that lie concealed within the structures of self-consciousness and history.

The above is another way of portraying Nietzsche's radical perspectivism and honest atheism (Masini, 1978). In psychotherapy, this may find a correlation in the practitioner's refusal to attribute lasting importance to interpretation and become implicated instead in the game of infinite entertainment within the finite frame of therapy. This stance goes against our profession's customary reliance on those theoretical opinions and pointers that quickly morph into dogma within a network of tribal fantasies of belonging. For Nietzsche, theory itself is fiction – both in the sense of being fakery *and* creation – unreal, as well as artefact.

Natural archetypes

The seeming transcendent experience of the Dionysian celebrant and/or the strange rapture felt by a spectator attending a Sophoclean drama is *immanent*, that is to say, *within* nature and the world. Both Dionysus and Apollo are immanent; they are gods, i.e., natural forces whose breadth and depth we may at times glimpse but never fully capture. The act of capturing belongs to the altogether different, and perhaps more limited faculties of apprehension and knowledge that originate in our understandable fear of subjugating experience within our control.

In chapter two of *The Birth of Tragedy*, Nietzsche refers to the Dionysian and the Apollonian as "*artistic drives of nature*" (1872/2000, p. 24). Understanding the "degree and extent" to which they have developed among Ancient Greek artists, he writes, will enable us to "appreciate more deeply the relation of the Greek artist to his archetypes, or to use the Aristotelian terms, 'the imitation of nature'" (ibid.). Nietzsche here informally equates what he calls *Urbilder* (archetypes) with Aristotle's notion of *mimesis* or imitation of *nature*. Had psychotherapy paid more attention to this description of archetypes as thoroughly immanent to nature, it may have avoided the confusion engendered by the Platonic detours that it suffered with the introduction of a similar term (*Archetypen*) in Jung's analytical psychology.

The key Jungian notion of archetypes (a term Jung began to use regularly from 1919) is indebted to Plato, Augustine, and Kant. Plato's eternal *Forms* and *Ideas* are prior to the phenomenal world and determine its order, value and structure. Similarly, archetypes, as innate, *a priori* constructs, are thought to mould and direct psychic activity. In relation to Plato's 'Ideas', the world, with its comings and goings, is mere representation. Equally, deeds and events in human life acquire full meaning solely in relation to these transcendent, eternal entities of which they are tributaries.

Jung may have not fully endorsed the "eternal, unmoving grounds of Plato's vision of true being" (Huskinson, 2004, p. 74), but the centrality of this notion in his system does speak eloquently in favour of the "human dream of eternal life" (Nagy, 1991, p. 161). It is not *wrong* to dream of eternal life. This dream has often been expressed with poetic beauty and a surge of spiritual longing. The only problem, in Nietzsche's terms, is that from Plato onwards this dream is often accompanied by a profound, nihilistic *denigration* of the transient existence that we are and that we inhabit.

Hooked on 'Being', eternalists of all persuasions avert their gaze from becoming. Smitten by the chance of deciphering unreachable *noumena*, they overlook the bountiful and mysterious life of phenomena themselves. They are like the proverbial old cleric who has lost sight of the path in a pitch-black forest on a moonless night. When lightning strikes, he looks up at the heavens and praises almighty God instead of making use of the sudden light to find the path.

Archetypes burst forth, according to Nietzsche, as "direct artistic states of nature" (1872/2000, p. 23), in relation to which "every artist is an 'imitator', that is to say, either Apollonian dream-artist or Dionysian artist of intoxication, or finally – as for example in Greek tragedy – simultaneously artist of dream and intoxication" (pp. 23–24). The artist is nature itself, assembling and dissolving individuals. Art imitates nature, not in the sense of representing it in realistic fashion, but because it replicates nature's creative, actualizing leanings. The Apollonian principle of *individuation* is all-pervasive: it is found in nature as in human experience. The same applies to the Dionysian principle of elemental *unity*. Apollo celebrates the individual in her existential struggle towards actualization, creativity, and meaning; Dionysus honours the individual's disappearance into nature. One values autonomy, solitude, and difference; the other marks the communal, orgiastic moment when individual boundaries are dissolved.

As with marked differentiations of day and night, light and darkness in different parts of the globe, these two forces have clustered and assembled in different ways across the world. I have often wondered, after James Hillman (1997), whether Southern cultures have, for instance, developed forms of spirituality and sensibility that can be loosely described as Dionysian. And whether Northern cultures have given rise to more distinctly Apollonian sensibilities. Does each mode yearn for idealized versions of its opposite? Like other Northern European writers and artists before and after him, Nietzsche worshipped the sunny dispositions and hot passions of the South: rightly or wrongly, he considered French culture to be the best, closely followed by the Italian.

When entertaining this train of thought, I find myself musing whether psychotherapy itself, as a cultural product of Northern Europe (and Northern America) is rooted in Apollonian principles. After all, the *principium individuationis*, the heart of the Apollonian experience – in Nietzsche's language, "respect for the limits of the individual, moderation in the Hellenic sense" (1872/2000, p. 31) – is a common factor in all psychotherapeutic orientations, however differently expressed. These rather wide generalizations notwithstanding, it may also be worth considering whether, as a product of an essentially Northern sensibility, there is at the heart of psychotherapy culture a 'dream of the south', a dream of Dionysian depth in relating, intersubjectivity and love. Interestingly, this longing is finding ever greater expression at a time when the profession as a whole is being crushed into regulative submission, as well as diluted and debased by encroaching market-driven demands. In any case, what is lost in this dream of love and intersubjectivity is the *symbolic* nature of the psychotherapeutic domain, a factor that alone can guarantee greater space for the unfolding of a person's creativity and autonomy. What is also lost is the difficult practice of psychotherapeutic *neutrality*, something which needs to be retrieved from the blank screen, depersonalized model – *not* towards humanist intersubjectivity but towards a *quality of empathy* that, inspired by Nietzsche, would maintain a dignified distance from the other and appreciate more fully our intrinsic existential aloneness and autonomy (Russell, 2017).

This point is crucial, and can in my view be extended to most therapeutic orientations – provided these are not landlocked into parochial defensiveness. It is not alien, for instance, to the debate within the person-centred therapy community in relation to principled non-directivity, understood as respect for the client's autonomy and maintenance of a boundaried, and paradoxically freer, symbolic domain. Inspired by Nietzsche, I am proposing a privileging of *individuation* over the more fashionable notion of *integration* as one of the guiding principles of a psychotherapy practice that takes on board Nietzsche's thought. This may well mean "more difference, more solitude, and more suffering" (Russell, 2017, p. 69), in a cultural landscape that has arguably ceased to value difference over integration, elevating the latter to the highest value through a coercive demand for assimilation of difference, migrancy and otherness within the parameters set by institutional power.

It is surprising that psychotherapy and the bodies that represent it have readily joined the integration bandwagon. In the name of happiness and wellbeing, they have bypassed the vital step of individuation while paying lip service to diversity, internal loci of evaluation, and imbalance of power in therapy.

Individuation

The current one-sided emphasis on the relationship in therapy alongside the championing of universal relatedness as the underpinning rationale for practice has meant that *individuation* has now virtually vanished from the vocabulary of contemporary psychotherapy, slowly but inexorably superseded by *integration*. This has powerful political reverberations on a global scale. Migrants and refugees are routinely asked to integrate into a culture that (grudgingly) hosts them. They are asked to shed their originary identity in exchange for adopting another. In the personal sphere within which psychotherapy normally operates, the implicit and explicit message, as I read it, seems to be promoting social conformity and obeisance to the psychic norm dictated by the herd. This shift in psychotherapeutic discourse from individuation to integration is a setback, a catastrophic loss of those narratives of *agency, autonomy* and *emancipation* that it took us so long to establish, in favour of an abdication to an overall political project – namely, neoliberalism – that under its veneer of dialogue and relatedness betrays an attitude of compliance to institutional power, for it is always the latter that decides the terms of the dialogue in question.

The notion of individuation itself, particularly in the way it has been appropriated and monopolized by Jung, is itself in dire need of revision and reframing. The problem, however, is that contemporary psychotherapy's culture is now so far removed from individuation that a critique would be nearly incomprehensible without first a positive appraisal that in retracing the path of psychotherapy, makes use of individuation as a necessary stepping stone en route to greater freedom.

Individuation – this fundamental process of transformation through which one becomes an individual, a person with an internal rather than external locus of evaluation, someone who has gained independence from the group mind of her originary 'tribe' – has seemingly become a taboo. In a sense, this has always been the case. The history of science, philosophy and religion is full of examples of heretics, or *hairetikos*, those who are chastised because they are *able to choose* and refuse to buy wholesale into the latest creed available in the marketplace.

What has dramatically changed in the last few decades is that narratives of belonging, once the chosen domain of reactionary and/or totalitarian thinking, are now actively endorsed by forces whose modes of expression are cloaked in progressive language.

Jung understands individuation in terms of (intrapsychic) integration:

> Individuation means becoming a single, homogenous being, and, in so far as "individuality" embraces our innermost, last, and incomparable uniqueness, it

also implies becoming one's own self. We could therefore translate individuation as "coming to selfhood" or "self-realization".

(Jung, 1928b, par. 266)

Individuation is, according to Jung, the process through which unconscious material is assimilated into consciousness. This process implies that the dynamic play of multiple, often opposing forces, is reduced into a new unity. As we have seen in the previous chapter, for Nietzsche the idea of *unity* is in itself, alongside notions of *purpose* and *being*, a shadow of the dead God, a nihilistic denigration of life and becoming. It is an attempt to project onto the incommensurable movement of living-and-dying an anthropocentric dream of harmony.

For Jung, "a healthy psyche is acquired only when the 'fact' of God is accepted" (Huskinson, 2004, p. 114), something that needs to come about "both externally and internally" (Frey-Rohn, 1988, p. 85). In other words, it is only through accepting the nihilistic abstraction of unity, via the God archetype, that something resembling mental health or psychic integration can be reached. Jung (1963/1995) believed that by daring to choose a different trajectory, Nietzsche laid himself open to 'pathological' ego-inflation that resulted in a psychic split and, allegedly, in his collapse.

Nietzsche did choose a different path: not towards 'God' but in the direction of 'nature'; not towards unity, but in the direction of multiplicity; his was not an arboreal, vertical move towards 'spirit' but a rhizomatic, horizontal trajectory in the direction of all living things. Practitioners sympathetic to (or at least aware of) Spinoza would see no contradiction here, for 'God is Nature, and Nature is God'; a healthy, robust dialogue would develop as a consequence of seeing through this apparent dichotomy. Sadly, this is not what happened. Scores of Jungians, with little knowledge of Nietzsche's work (e.g. Jacobi, 1968; Jaffé, 1970; Moreno, 1974; Von Frantz, 1975) mechanically followed Jung's hasty and intemperate assessment of Nietzsche, thus precluding a rich dialogue that could have potentially problematized the superficial and schematic divisions that today divide transpersonal from body psychotherapy and, more generally, spiritualism from materialism. Most Jungians uncritically assumed, after Jung, that Nietzsche substituted God for the overhuman, without bothering to investigate further the meaning of the overhuman. They read the latter as an inflation of the human ego rather than the threshold experience where the limitations of the human dimension and the human self open up to the plurality of the body, the world and nature.

Like Heidegger, Jung too dedicated time and energy to lengthy discussions of Nietzsche's work – particularly *Zarathustra*. Many of his remarks are, however, so intemperate and unwarranted that they have seriously puzzled commentators (e.g., Parkes, 1999; Huskinson, 2004). It is legitimate to ask whether Jung's judgemental tone was unconsciously motivated by his need, as a respectable bourgeois Swiss doctor, to "distance himself from an outcast" such as Nietzsche, and from "the fear of being considered one himself" (Bazzano, 2006, p. 31).

Despite the wide, nearly unbridgeable gap between Nietzsche and Jung, there is one element in Jungian 'individuation' that remains valid to a Nietzsche-inspired psychotherapy, one that constitutes a stepping stone on the path of exploration and experimentation, one that is arguably being neglected in contemporary psychotherapy discourse: the importance "for individuals to assert their individuality against the collective, to differentiate themselves from it" (Huskinson, 2004, p. 43).

We don't need another hero

It would not be at all strange to find that, for all its alleged scientific objectivity and aspiration to explore the depth and breadth of being human, psychotherapy ends up operating under the influence of the dominant Western narratives inherited from Platonism and Christianity. One of these, elevated by Jungian analytic psychology to the unassailable sphere of archetype, is that of the (usually male) hero's quest. Even though this is still a matter of contention among scholars, parallels have often been drawn between the Greek myth of Dionysus and the tale of Jesus. Hölderlin linked Dionysus, the "thundering god" from whom "the pleasure of wine comes", to Jesus, the "quiet genius … comforting in a god-like way" (Hölderlin, 2010, n.p.). It is not perverse, I think, to suggest that Christianity may have *subverted* the myth of Dionysus Zagreus, the child-god dismembered by Titans and then, his heart intact, re-created by Zeus.

The important element in the hero's quest, replicated in countless tales, is *redemption*, a hybrid term steeped in the dual world of trade and religious morality, revealing how closely entwined the two are, a term whose literal meaning is *compensation*, which includes financial reimbursement and moral and/or professional atonement related to a poor or dubious past performance. In redemptive tales, the ordeal suffered by the protagonist, we are often told, turns out to have been worthwhile; as it is worked through, valuable knowledge or insight is invariably gained in the process.

Even more crucially, the alleged unity of the self, momentarily threatened when glancing over the abyss, is now regained. The emphasis is on happy endings. Levinas (1998/1963) chastises Kierkegaard for being too fixated on the first half of Abraham's story, i.e. on God's command to kill his son Isaac, thus, in his view, misunderstanding ethics in a fundamental way. Similarly, Spinelli (2017) sees Kierkegaard's alleged disrespect of ethics as a form of folly. What matters, Levinas effectively says, is that at the last moment God intervenes and prevents the killing. In this way, however, the instant of decision – the moment of madness – is forgotten. In the example of Jesus, the crucial moment of existential pain and abandonment is often forgotten in canonical readings in favour of yet another instance of redemption. *Lamma Sabachtani* is cast aside, in favour of *Thy Will Be Done*. 'Why have you forsaken me?' is read as the necessary moment of human weakness that makes the final act of surrender all the more significant.

Predictable feelings of edification and moral satisfaction, produced by the dominant interpretations of these tales, are then replicated everywhere, from Hollywood to Mills & Boon. Yet life persists in playing a dissonant note. Reality, it seems, is naturally deconstructive – it doggedly refuses to play the redemptive rules of facile dialectical reasoning. There is no concrete synthesis in sight to make up for the distress of the antithesis. The tales inherited from the tradition may be dialectical, but only on a superficial level, for there is greater meaning in Hegel than the *telos* of happy endings. True, the structure of his *Phenomenology of Spirit* (1807/ 1977) can be plausibly compared to that of a *Bildungsroman*, with an abstractly imagined protagonist ('Spirit') evolving through the vicissitudes of history and various shapes of consciousness and phenomenal worlds. This formative tale goes through social formations which constitute the history of European civilization, concluding happily with an 'Absolute Knowing', where Christianity and the State join hands in a marriage that is arguably a triumph of totalitarian values. But there is more to Hegel than happy-clappy dialectical endings in a totalitarian key. Absolute Knowing may be also read as a form of radical relativization, as the utter demise of the subject (Žižek, 2013), and conspicuously devoid of the compensatory happy endings typical of evolutionary fantasies. An alternative example to Spirit finding its apotheosis in the State is the desolate end of Jesus on the cross: utter loss and abjection – the unveiling of another, more literal meaning of absolute, from *absolvere* = to free from, setting free, *relinquishing*. Georges Bataille (1943/2014) may be right after all: a *lamma sabachtani* always lies in store at the end of the story – and at the end of history. Our final exit leaves us naked and hopeless – absolved, absolute, unchained from everything, sand slipping through our fists. *Free for death.*

There is then a different route to the *Bildungsroman* or 'formative story' and, when dreamt up by an artist, a little more than an edifying little fable of loss and redemption. My difficult contention, following Nietzsche in my own unorthodox ways, is that an art worth its name will give us another version of the so-called 'hero's quest'. The latter may be steeped in the reductively masculine, masturbatory fantasy of an erotic catharsis that neglects the greater riches of a wayward path. Left well alone to walk a labyrinthine walk, we may come across unexpected and undeclared treasures.

A name for this different route is *Dionysian art* – an art fiercely opposed to the narcotic craft that shields our collective vision from the horror, beauty and tenderness of the world. Or one could call it *art of awakening*: taste, sight, touch, smell, and hearing open to the impact of precarious, magnificent reality.

Necessarily insufficient

The mystifying interpretations of Nietzsche found in Heidegger and Jung influenced how the world of therapy has subsequently responded to Nietzsche. Heidegger tried to turn him into a metaphysical thinker, hemming him in within a Dasein-analysis tradition that to this day doggedly persists, in current incarnations as Heideggerian phenomenological therapy, in seeing Nietzsche as a thinker of so-called authenticity, and even free will – nothing more than a John the Baptist figure to the coming of that good shepherd of being, Heidegger. For his part, Jung oversimplified Nietzsche's psychic perspectivism through his own version of personification, i.e. the propensity of psychic stances to take on distinctive and autonomous personalities, separate from the ego-self, while at the same time never daring to stray too far from the double-headed archetype of the tradition – Self/God.

A third, more genuine influence must be mentioned here, one that is refreshingly devoid of the ambiguities and misinterpretations that characterized the previous two. Otto Rank (1884–1939) parted company with Freud in the 1920s because, despite "call[ing] itself a psychology of the unconscious", classical psychoanalysis promoted in his view "the scientific glorification of consciousness" (Rank, 1932, p. 222). Not only did he exert a pivotal influence on Carl Rogers (Kramer, 1995), creating a link between post-Freudian and humanistic therapy; he was also the most coherent Nietzschean psychologist of the twentieth century. His emphasis on the *creative will* of the individual; his understanding of incongruence and mental distress as a *failure in creativity*; his focusing on the client and on the client's ability to *self-direct* her creativity towards a more meaningful, individuated existence – all of these are unambiguous expressions of Nietzsche's influence. Rank's work provides an immediate and coherent link between aspects of Nietzsche's psychology and psychotherapy; they also anticipate some of the struggles that psychotherapists face today.

Firstly, Rank highlighted what he called the *burden of difference*. Alongside Ferenczi, Rank understood experience (*Erlebnis*) as the "strange consciousness of living" (Kramer, 1995, p. 224n), as something one can live and breathe but not understand, let alone compute (Ferenczi & Rank, 1924). The living moment, the 'present' of our incarnate existence, is fundamentally *unknowable* and strange. For many of us, being with this strangeness is intolerable and therefore the possibility of responding creatively to the challenge posed by our existence feels remote. We may react in ways that could be construed as *neurosis* (in Rank's language) or *incongruence* (in Rogers'): terms indicating an indirect, ineffectual response to the burden we feel. This burden is for Rank *the burden of difference*, the sheer fact of being an 'I'. Rank understood some of his clients' obsession with the past as equivalent to yelling a loud 'No' to the living moment:

> It becomes clear that [the client's] so called fixation on the past, the living-in-reminiscence, is only a protection from experiencing, from surrender to the present … There are individuals who know how to overcome the hardest, most traumatic experiences with a new experience. Such a new experiencing, and not merely a repetition of the infantile, represents the therapeutic process and its value in my conception.
>
> *(Rank, 1978, p. 39)*

Needless to say, this burden cannot be easily laid off without also evading our own sense of dignity and freedom and the possibility of that first crucial step – individuation. Actively accepting our burden of difference is, in Nietzsche's terms, embracing not a preordained fate but the creative path of our *destiny* – of becoming who we are without a preconceived notion of who we may be.

Secondly, *incongruence* is understood, in Rankian terms, as a *failure in creativity*. Rank's "extensive experience and study" led him to state that "the scientific side to human behavior and personality problems is not only insufficient but leaves out the most essential part: namely, *the human side* – the characteristic of which is just that it can't be measured and checked and controlled" (Rank, 1996, p. 221).

Creativity is central, and echoes of Nietzsche are heard every step of the way in Rank's writing here. At times, this is the literal creativity of artists and writers who actively transmute, transfigure and transubstantiate living matter, and in so doing partake of the work of nature-as-artist. More often, this is a process of self-creation. As with Greek tragedy, where the protagonist does not *find* but *attain* herself, Rankian and Nietzsche-inspired psychotherapies are a continuous process of creating oneself. In this respect, the therapist for Rank cannot be an instrument of love, for this would create dependence, nor can she be an instrument of education, which would mean "directing and trying to alter the individual, and in so doing hinder the positive, active will" (Raskin, 1948, n.p.). I find the above stance very instructive and significantly at odds with two positions found in contemporary therapy. The vision of the therapist as an instrument of love is all the rage in sections of humanistic psychology, including aspects of person-centred therapy, that unreservedly champion a romanticized version of the I-Thou and of inter-subjectivity in general. The therapist as educator is an equally pervasive stance found across the theoretical spectrum – especially in psychoanalytic psychotherapy, cognitive behavioural therapy, and mindfulness-inspired approaches. Both stances focus on the therapist rather than the client and implicitly rob the latter of her inherent ability to self-direct and actualize.

A third aspect worth mentioning relates to Rank's anti-neopositivist stance: his verdict of 'scientific' psychology is that it is *necessarily insufficient* (Rank, 1932) in explaining and dealing with human experience. For him, the really essential battle to be fought in the field of psychotherapy is not between theoretical orientations but between different worldviews. One assumes that psychology can measure, check and control human experience; the other recognizes that psychology and psychotherapy are *necessarily insufficient* in comprehending it. Rather than an impasse, this recognition is a fertile ground for creativity in therapy. For Rank (1932), "the error lies in the scientific glorification of consciousness … which even psychoanalysis worships as its highest god – although it calls itself a psychology of the *unconscious*" (p. 222). This point, I believe, remains as valid and urgent today as when was first formulated by Rank nearly 100 years ago.

8

TEARS OF JOY

Wormwood

Inscribed in the entrance hall of the CIA headquarters in Virginia is the oft-repeated passage from John's Gospel: *And ye shall know the truth, and the truth shall make you free.* Given the long history of lies and cover-ups that has been one of the hallmarks of this particular organization, the CIA's appropriation of the passage is "beyond irony" (Ignatieff, 2018, p. 43). While it is not a given that knowing the truth about something will make one free, it is often the case that it can be devastating. Echoing the tragic destiny that had befallen Orestes centuries before, Hamlet whispers "wormwood, wormwood", the name of a bitter plant, emblem of a harsh and bitter truth, the moment he realizes that his mother is responsible for his father's death.

Nietzsche is justly credited for having invented what came to be known as *perspectivism*, as well as for relativizing truth, particularly when the latter is adorned with a capital 'T'. There is also a spurious charge attributed to his thought. According to this view, his writings heralded the beginning of an irrational cultural movement which, corroborated by Derrida's deconstruction, by post-structuralism and even post-modernism, eventually prepared the ground for the shameless political relativism of dubious political figures like Berlusconi, Trump, Farage et al., who thrived on fake news and on making truth relative in the political and social dimensions. 'Nietzsche and Derrida made me do it' is how one could describe the recent litany of protest from hyper-conventional academia, neo-traditionalists and spiritualists alike for whom the universities are now the stronghold of subversive post-modernists and barely reconstructed Marxists whose mission is to assail the remains of culture as we know it. Perspectivism is their bête noire. But what *is* perspectivism? And why is it allegedly so dangerous?

Perspectivism

> I am ... necessarily the man of impending disaster. For when the truth squares up to
> the lie of millennia, we will have upheavals, a spasm of earthquakes, a removal of
> mountain and valley, such as have never been dreamed of.
>
> *(Nietzsche, 1908/2007b, p. 88)*

The term 'perspectivism' was popularized by Ortega y Gasset (1961) who, drawing from Nietzsche, among others, gave it two distinct but related meanings: (a) a *historical* meaning, which emphasized that all periods in history contribute a particular element of truth; (b) an *individual* meaning, in the sense that every individual construes the same 'horizon' in his/her own different way.

The above reading already implies a little more than it is normally understood by perspective and perspectivism. When we speak of 'gaining a sense of perspective' on something, we commonly mean understanding its relative importance by seeing it in context. In art, perspective is the ability to represent "three-dimensional objects on a two-dimensional surface so as to convey the impression of height, width, depth and relative distance" (*Oxford English Dictionary*, 2011, p. 1071). For the *OED*, perspectivism is "the theory that knowledge of a subject is inevitably partial and limited by the individual perspective from which it is viewed" (ibid.).

To be alive in the world is to be thrown into a perspectival situation, Ortega reminds us: it is not unlike being shipwrecked in the midst of fortuitous things we vainly take hold of in the hope of gaining some degree of certainty and stability. With Nietzsche, only a few decades earlier (the term begins to appear in his writings in the mid 1880s), perspectivism had taken on an even more drastic meaning, one that acknowledges the plurality of perspectives within a *dividual* self that is not one, but *many*. It is not only that, as an individual, I see things differently from you. I see things differently from myself too. My individuality is *divided* and plural. A plural self and a plural world go hand in hand, and what is affirmed in both cases is the inherent insubstantiality of both in a continuous process of evaluation of the forces at play. This is less arcane that it may sound at first.

We all go through profound changes in life, each time experiencing the death and rebirth of various fragmentary selves. Aspects of the past are also re-interpreted in the light of new experiences. In its existential immediacy, this is already a first glimpse of Nietzsche's mature perspectivism of his posthumously published writings: not a mere caveat about the inevitable partiality of our knowledge, but the sketching of an *alternative theory of knowledge* altogether, one that appreciates the profound inadequacy of the artefact we call our knowledge.

Far from being the wicked moral relativism that metaphysicians old and new consider it to be, perspectivism starts with the frank recognition that our stance on life, ourselves and the world will change periodically, and that each time the particular vantage point we inhabit will inevitably colour our perception. Nietzsche adds a radical twist to this seemingly common-sense view. He says: there is no point in seeking an essential self because there is no such thing. What this means of course is that there is no such thing as a 'true' self, or an 'organismic', 'fully functioning' or 'authentic' self either. The fluidity and uncertainty of existence does not allow us to design a credible utopian model of shinier and happier 'persons of tomorrow' either.

On chapter 3 we have seen that if one imagines a person of "eighty thousand years", Nietzsche argues, the character of that person would be "totally alterable" in such a way that "an abundance of different individuals would evolve ... one after the other". The brevity of human existence "misleads us", he concludes into making "many ... erroneous assertions" (Nietzsche, 1878/1984, p. 45) about our qualities. Not only can Nietzsche's perspectivism shed light on the psychotherapeutic endeavour. It also constitutes the most accessible route to one of his far-reaching and rarely understood hypotheses: the *will to power*.

Before moving our enquiry further, I think it useful to stay for a moment longer with the topic of plurality and fragmentation of the self and, guided by Duncan Large's remarkable study on the subject (Large, 2001) – already referred to in other sections of the book – draw a comparison between Nietzsche's views and that of another influential writer who, in his uncommon ways, held a stance to which the majority of us tend to subscribe: Marcel Proust. *In Search of Lost Time* (Proust, 1927/2003) is an undisputed masterpiece and a magnificent, multi-layered and complex work of world literature. It is also the most seductive refusal of perspectivism I have ever come across and, as such, it makes one want to yield to his beautifully nuanced arguments.

The various forms of rejection of perspectivism made by a host of writers, from analytic philosophers to neo-Hegelians, from neo-mystics to out-and-out reactionaries, all stridently or melodiously cheering for 'Truth', do not so much pale as liquefy by comparison. Proust's painstaking quest is a search for the essence of the self, a quest pursued "in elegiac mode" (Large, 2001, p. 161), suspended between anticipation of the inevitable mourning for an essence that eludes us and a yearning to establish an idealistic, comforting perspective, which can be summed up by "the self as everything" (Large, 2001, p. 161). It may well be that the artistic achievement of this momentous novel lies in the *unresolved* struggle between these two modes of mourning and yearning. What Proust has nevertheless in common with Nietzsche is an emphasis on the primacy of the body, and while in Nietzsche's case this is expressed in his project of naturalization of the human, in Proust it is examined via the phenomenon of *involuntary memory*. Yet despite Proust's efforts at reading the latter as a confirmation of an *eternalist* view, involuntary memory is "not a transcendent abstraction, but a *bodily effect*" (Large, 2001, p. 161, emphasis added). Although ephemeral and one with sensory perception, this phenomenon is linked to an *experience of eternity* – not in the essentialist, conventional meaning normally attributed to the term, but in the more expansive, open-ended meaning that does not turn eternity into a *thing*, least of all an object of worship, but allows for the incidence of infinity within immanence.

By positing a pre-existing 'Truth' based upon a particular reading of the human condition, much contemporary psychotherapy perpetuates the fundamental error and prejudice of dogmatism. The difference with a Nietzsche-inspired methodology is that the latter has potentially inbuilt the dispositive for its own undoing. This is not carried out in the name of misguided cynicism and/or relativism but out of profound respect for genuine difference and out of an understanding of the fluid nature of reality.

One of the ways in which this kind of perspectivism becomes manifest is through *irony*, which is eminently lacking in all truth-based psychological systems. For Nietzsche (1895/2007a), the main inadequacy in the entire New Testament is the absence of a single joke. The sole exception, also remarked upon by Bacon (Vickers, 1996), is Pilate who, in response to Jesus' rather solemn declaration 'I am the Truth', shrugs and replies, ironically: 'But what is truth?' Bacon too, like Nietzsche, had precious little time for those humourless souls who gravely intone that question and invariably find portentous metaphysical formulas to which others must give in. It is catastrophic that psychotherapists too have historically followed that path, shipwrecking the hope of an art, a science and a craft potentially devoid of prejudices in the murky sea of third-rate metaphysics.

In Nietzsche's thought, perspectivism represents the peak of an existential stance that had gradually matured from his early writings of the 1870s. In the later writings, his mistrust of the 'will to truth' becomes more pointed and, to this reader, wholly justified as the latter is unveiled in essence as *will to power*. The implication is that we need to unmask the grand metaphysical claims of religion and philosophy, but also, perhaps, our everyday claim to being capable of grasping what some psychotherapists call "a provisional truth" (Orbach, 2017, p. 278).

> The will to truth is a making firm, a making true and durable, an abolition of the false character of things, a reinterpretation of it into beings. "Truth" is therefore not something there, that might be found or discovered – but something that must be created and that gives a name to a process or rather to a will to overcome that has itself no end.
>
> *(Nietzsche, 1968, p. 298)*

Nietzsche's remarkable trajectory can help the therapeutic endeavour clear some of the clutter accumulated over more than a century. The notion of the 'thing in itself' (the supposedly raw, un-interpreted experience examined in therapy) is at first conceived almost in Kantian terms: as inaccessible, even indefinable. Later this is abandoned, and what is also abandoned is "recourse to a historical fixed point or origin prior to 'falsification'" (Large, 2001, p. 126). No Husserlian 'noematic' search into the alleged veracity of experience before or alongside 'noetic' investigation; no archaeological excavations into the coded lingo of remote childhoods; no anthropological venturing into the wild and virgin exoticism of the psyche. What emerges instead is the beginning of a *genealogical* reading of experience that reveals the interpretative quality of everything that happens.

What we call 'event' is then *seen through* as a group of appearances interpreted and gathered by an interpretative faculty. The latter is not a *person* – the one whom we imagine existing *behind* the deed. The question 'Who interprets?' is irrelevant, because "the interpretation itself is a form of the will to power, exist[ing] (… not as 'being' but as a *process*, a *becoming*) as an affect" (Nietzsche, 1968, p. 302).

Some of Nietzsche's posthumous fragments elaborate further on the topic of the will to power – a good exposition of which was already present in his *Genealogy* – a slow build-up on the basis of perspectivism that reaches a crucial point in a brilliant passage that is an indictment of both *positivism* (still the dominant narrative of our times permeating evidence-based therapy) as well as *subjective idealism* (its flipside, evident in the rather futile but 'noble' resistance to the above found among many humanistic 'beautiful souls').

Large (2001, pp. 123–124) sees two levels in Nietzsche's induction to an alternative theory of knowledge: ontological and epistemological. At the ontological level, Nietzsche, inspired by Boscovich, critiques the attempt made by contemporary natural scientists to fasten, through 'atomistic' notions, the fluctuation of becoming into the seemingly solid designs of being. At the epistemological level, "'truth' is still a certain species of error … a trick of language" (ibid., p. 124).

> We set up a word at the point at which our ignorance begins, at which we can see no further, e.g. the word "I", the word "do", the word "suffer": – these are perhaps the horizon of our knowledge, but not "truths".
>
> *(Nietzsche, 1968, p. 267)*

It is at this point that we begin to fathom that what was meant by 'perspectivism' is effectively the ambitious project of unmasking *will to truth as*, at heart, *will to power*.

> [T]his, my Dionysian world of the eternally self-creating, the eternally self-destroying, this mystery world of the twofold voluptuous delight, my "beyond good and evil", without a goal, unless the joy of the circle is itself a goal; without will, unless a ring feels good will towards itself – do you want a name for this world? A solution for its riddles? … This world is the will to power – and nothing besides! And you yourselves are also this will to power – and nothing besides!
>
> *(Nietzsche, 1968, p. 1067)*

We have seen in other sections of the book how the 'I' is for Nietzsche a conceptual synthesis, a plurality of forceful drives, understood not in terms of soul atomism but *soul multiplicity*. For him, it is the drives or *affects* that *interpret*, not consciousness which is but a surface. In dismantling the subject, Nietzsche (1968) discards the very notion of epistemology in favour of a *"perspective theory of affects"* (p. 255). This does not mean, however, that the affects are not given to error. At this point in Nietzsche's trajectory the original, common-sense meaning of perspectivism is reinstated, but having gone through a process of significant intensification: incidental limitation has become certainty of error. In other words, what was a warning of possible human limitation and ignorance becomes certainty of error. Plurality of perspectives implies that *every truth is a type of lie.*

The idea that affects and other expressions of incarnate experience are somewhat deeper than the historically privileged locus of self-identity (i.e. mental cogitation) may be appealing, but drives are themselves only the result of evaluation. They are the *aftermath*, in Nietzsche's view, of evaluations long cultivated and cherished, an organization of pleasure-and-pain assessments that we end up performing automatically. Beginning as compulsions, gradually becoming needs, they eventually turn into 'natural' tendencies. For those of us hoping to find in Nietzsche the high priest of embodied experience and of the free, natural life of the instincts, this realization may come as a disappointment.

Nietzsche's deconstructive process is painstaking; it resists all final accounts of 'human nature' and of any ground that may help bolster it – be it God, the *cogito*, bodily intuition or even felt sense. All of these are but manifestations of the ongoing, unrelenting process of neutral evaluation that he calls 'will to power'. A posthumous fragment reads:

> That the *value of the world* lies in our interpretation (that other interpretations than merely human are perhaps somewhere possible); that previous interpretations have been perspective valuations by virtue of which we can survive in life, i.e., in the will to power, for the growth of power; that every *elevation of man* brings with it the overcoming of narrower interpretations; that every strengthening an increase of power opens up new perspectives and means believing in new horizons – this idea permeates my writings. The world *with which we are concerned* is false, i.e. is not a fact but a fable and approximation on the basis of a meagre sum of observations; it is "in flux", as something in a state of becoming, as a falsehood always changing but never getting near the truth: for – there is no truth.
>
> *(Nietzsche, 1968, p. 330)*

Post-truth

The 'post-truth' world we supposedly inhabit at the time of writing (a time that has seen the rearing of nationalism's ugly head with Brexit, Trump and the pervasive rise of xenophobia and of 'fake news') does not originate, as some fear, in that 'post-modern' and deconstructivist repudiation of pre-existing and solid truths whose alleged chief instigator was Nietzsche. Its genesis must be sought within that seemingly uncomplicated world that casually adheres to an ossified notion of truth that is thought to be the sole domain of a particular discourse, in this case a populist truth, a 'raw' notion of what reality 'really' is – posed against the excessive sophistication and perceived sophism of the cosmopolitan 'elites'. A parallel in philosophy is found in the inability of a brilliant but provincial mind (Heidegger's) to grapple with the wider intellectual horizons and sophistication of writers like Nietzsche and Schopenhauer (Magee, 1983). A parallel is found in Jung's dedicated but deeply flawed reading of Nietzsche, a reading, as we have seen in Chapter 7, partly based on the petit bourgeois terror of falling prey to the same perceived existential and academic uprootedness of the latter.

There is a direct link between the fabricated lies of 'fake news' proliferating today and the Love of Truth professed by new tyrants and profiteers. They both inhabit the common ground of dogmatism. The direct 'enemy' of Nietzsche's perspectivism bears the same name: dogmatism. The populist 'post-truth' world has nothing to do with the perspectivism professed by Nietzsche or the post-structuralists after him. On the contrary, it is the post-truth of the fundamental lie. There is a difference between a post-truth world of lies and a perspectivism that is in the service of experience and whose thoroughgoingness does not stop at experience but aspires to create a new horizon of knowledge. To ascribe the same ethos to the post-truth world and Nietzsche-inspired perspectivism is not only a grave ontological and epistemological error; it is an act of bad faith. By fabricating lies in the service of the dogmas of parochial identity, cultural homogeneity and above all profit, the former is wholly in the service of the self-serving Truth inherited by the religious and philosophical tradition and by the middle-of-the-road psychology and psychotherapy businesses that perpetuate them. Conversely, by illuminating the nature of 'truths' as *mere evaluations* that have come into view as "provisionally dominant in the hierarchy of the interpreting drives" (Large, 2001, p. 131), the latter reaches outside the narrow diagrams of received knowledge; it broadens the horizon, it liberates, it allows an exhilarating process of infinite evaluation and interpretation.

A 'thing' never has only one meaning, but several. More precisely, "there is no 'thing' but only interpretations, hidden in one another, like masks layered one on the other" (Deleuze, 2004, p. 118). This does not mean that 'anything goes', that all interpretations have the same value and that one can no longer discern what is true from what is false. It means that the criteria of true and false no longer have primacy and are superseded by new criteria of high and low, noble and mean. What begins to matter more is the sense and value of what one thinks, feels and says.

All the old mirages

We invariably get the truth we deserve, and in relation to the values we express. Value too must be revaluated; it must be freed from the burden of conformity and tradition, from the pious whiff of righteous moralism. The idea of value expounded by Nietzsche has nothing to do with the bourgeois notion of value that has been sadly embraced by contemporary psychotherapy. In this, as Deleuze (2004, p. 136) reminds us, Nietzsche is in oblique agreement with Marx, as both conceive *value* in terms of a radical critique of society – of its *fetishes* (in Marx's language) and *idols* (in Nietzsche's). Both call for an equally radical transformation: *revolutionary action* in Marx; *trans-valuation* in Nietzsche, i.e. the creation of new powerful and life-affirming myths that help redescribe the world and the human within it.

The primacy of truth is turned on its head: what kind of person turns truth into an absolute priority? Nietzsche's answer is: a *resentful* person, one animated by the spirit of revenge. The old logic, inherited from the religious, philosophical and psychological tradition, is then replaced by a "topology" as well as "typology" (Deleuze, 2004). We will then find that some interpretations and evaluations may, at close scrutiny, reveal a *base* way of thinking, being and feeling, while others will show big-heartedness and liberality.

Everything is revealed as a mask for various forces at play – some vile, some noble; but there is no final judgement, only the infinite interpretative play of will to power and the option of aligning oneself with more munificent forces. To be able in some way to align oneself or even identify with this impersonal continuous process of evaluation and interpretation that is will to power requires a generous leap, for at heart will to power, as manifested in the human domain, is essentially generosity, an act of giving, the giving away of oneself, what the Buddha calls *dana* (Bazzano, 2006). For Nietzsche's fictional character, Zarathustra, the highest virtue is the *virtue that gives*. Gold assumed the highest value, he tells his disciples, because "it is uncommon and of no use and luminous and mild in its lustre; it always bestows itself" (Nietzsche, 1883/2006a, p. 65). Similarly, the highest virtue is uncommon, of no use and mild in its lustre. We are striving, Zarathustra says, for this highest virtue of giving or 'bestowing':

> Insatiably your soul strives for treasures and jewels, because your virtue is insatiable in wanting to bestow.
>
> You compel all things towards you and into you, that they may flow back out of your wells as gifts of your love.
>
> Verily, a predator of all values must such a bestowing love become; but whole and holy do I call such selfishness.
>
> *(ibid.)*

This thirst may be seen by some as the selfishness of someone who strives for "treasures and jewels" but he or she does so out of the yearning to acquire the gold-like glance of someone who is able to give. This type of selfishness is still preferable to a selfishness that is mean and miserly. This other selfishness, Zarathustra says,

> always wants to steal; [it is] a selfishness of the sick, a sick selfishness.
>
> With the eye of the thief it looks at everything that shines; with the greed of hunger it measures him who has plenty to eat; and it is always skulking around the table of those who bestow.
>
> *(ibid.)*

The primacy we ascribe to the twin notions of *sense* and *meaning* must also be radically re-interpreted. This is because sense (including 'felt sense'?) has become, alongside meaning, the place of rest for a new type of metaphysics "sometimes called 'hermeneutics'" (Deleuze, 2004, p. 137). Drawing here an interesting parallel between Nietzsche and Freud, Deleuze explains:

The Nietzschean or ... Freudian notion of sense is just as much in danger of being misappropriated. You hear everyone talking about "sense": original sense, forgotten sense, evaded sense, veiled sense ... All the old mirages are just rebaptized under the category of sense; essence is being revived, with all its sacred and religious values. In Nietzsche and Freud, it's the exact opposite; the notion of sense is an instrument of absolute contestation, absolute critique, and also specific creation: sense is not a reservoir, *not a principle or an origin*, not even an end, it's an "effect", an *effect produced*, whose laws of production must be uncovered.

(Deleuze, 2004, p. 137, emphasis added)

Lawless and free

Will to power is at heart *affirmation* – affirmation of *difference*, as well as affirmation of those noble virtues that have been marginalized by the tradition: play, pleasure, generosity of spirit and, above all, an invitation to train in developing the courage and ability to express nobility by *expending oneself*, without expectation of reciprocity. There is little room here for the utilitarian, survivalist, merely transactional values of a class – the bourgeoisie – that in the twentieth century triumphed in getting its petty beliefs hallowed and raised to the heights of 'universal' values.

I believe it also goes counter to (or at the very least it problematizes) a 'philosophy of the meeting' (e.g., Buber, 1961, 2004) and the all-pervasive dialogical, 'intersubjective' psychotherapy currently in vogue that draws from it. Nietzsche's noble or perhaps more severe ethical stance is more akin to a Levinasian and Derridean understanding of ethics and encounter (Derrida, 1978; Levinas, 1961, 1999) which, similarly based on generosity, are thoroughly non-reciprocal and non-transactional. What this may foster in therapy is a difficult discipline of *interruption* of the (therapist/host's) self through *hospitality*, in the service of the client/guest, rather than an emphasis on mutuality. These new values positively subvert the existing order of what is considered right and proper in our societies; the latter deserve to be called philistine even when they are made up of *cultured* rather than coarse philistines.

I have often written of Hegel's *Anerkennung* (recognition/acknowledgement) as a crucial tenet of dialogical approaches to therapy as well as of encounter-based understandings of self-consciousness (e.g. Bazzano, 2013c, 2015). But Hegel's *recognition* is unrecognized in therapy, in favour of sentimental versions of the Philosophy of the Meeting that rhapsodizes on love and ignores conflict. Nietzsche goes one step further, and effectively questions as to whether the notion of recognition is in fact alien to will to power and belonging instead to 'slave morality'.

There are essentially three aspects to Nietzsche's notion of the will to power. The first attempts to outdo prevalent theories of life that emphasize evolution and/ or self-preservation. It is worth rereading this passage:

> Physiologists should think before postulating the drive of self-preservation as the cardinal drive in an organic being. A living thing seeks above all to *vent* its strength – life as such is will to power; self preservation is only one of the indirect and most frequent *consequences* of it.
>
> (Nietzsche, 1886/1978, p. 26)

Secondly, Nietzsche also sees life as a "shifting nexus" (Conway, 2006, p. 532) of forces engaged in creative antagonism with one another, continually assembling and disbanding, and in the process giving rise to animate and inanimate beings. Despite its emphasis on *agon*, his view is fairly close to the Buddha's teaching of *paticca samuppada* or 'dependent co-arising'. The one difference with Buddhist orthodoxy here may consist in rejecting the distinction between animate and inanimate beings and in refusing to ascribe primacy to humans and the notion, in some Buddhist schools, of our 'precious human birth'.

There certainly are differences, in Nietzsche's view, between organic and inorganic manifestation of the will to power. However, while with inorganic beings "every power draws its ultimate consequences every moment" (Nietzsche, 1886/1978, p. 34), a living being is *subject to laws* that guide it to "its final incarnation [via a series of] developments" (Conway, 2006, p. 533).

Thirdly, the discharge of strength (*Kraft*) – more fundamental for Nietzsche than the need for self-preservation – is experienced by an organism "*as if it were*" an inorganic outflow of power (*Macht*). Intriguingly, Conway sees this as an example of "inanimate nature [serving] as an orienting model for the vital activity of organic beings" (Conway, 2006, p. 533). Given that in inorganic beings "power draws its consequences at every moment" (Nietzsche, 1886/1978, p. 34), and that they are not subject to the laws we are subject to as living beings, then it could be concluded that "the 'favourable conditions' of discharge sought by an organism" are the ones that are "most conducive to an experience of itself as lawless and free" (Conway, 2006, p. 534).

The central point in Nietzsche's notion of the will to power, which remains controversial to this day, is seeing the fundamental instinct of life not in self-preservation but self-expenditure.

Consider the butterfly

It is tempting to translate the overflowing of the organic into the inorganic (or rather, the use of an inorganic model for an organic being's experience of strength and power) into Nietzsche's description of 'great' humans, whose strength, power and creativity are often expressed in the language of inorganic nature: gathering storm, bolt of lightning and so forth. This reading, however, is a little too prone to the humanistic fallacy of personalizing the will to power, thus repeating the error of humanistic psychotherapy when, particularly with Maslow (1962, 1997), it tends to confuse self-actualization (i.e. the organism's capacity for autonomous organization) with actualization of a particular and atomistic 'self'. Personally, I am inclined towards a reading that emphasizes will to power as refusal of both evolutionism *and* self-preservation – but without allowing these to crystallize within a self whose 'strong characteristics' would *personify* will to power.

Nietzsche points towards a threshold and a *limit* where human experience loses its imaginary boundaries and steps over into the greater life of the world. This is a point of crisis and vulnerability, a point of radical receptivity rather than the conventional strength of a superhuman individual. This point is made clear by Nietzsche's interest for species and organisms whose natural cycles of growth ultimately place them at mortal risk, e.g., the butterfly. Humanity is for Nietzsche "the experimental material, the tremendous surplus of failures: a field of ruins" (1968, p. 380).

A vulnerable piece of vanity

A common criticism in relation to the notion of will to power (for instance, Rorty, 1989) sees it as a slide into metaphysics – inevitable, so it is alleged, for those engaged in philosophy, hence in the business of truth and truth-claiming. Having successfully deconstructed everything under the sun, Nietzsche could not avoid, so the story goes, coming up with a construct that symbolizes the 'essence' of the world. But essence too is *relativized* in Nietzsche:

> A "thing-in-itself" [is] just as perverse as a "sense-in-itself", a "meaning-in-itself". There are no "facts-in-themselves", for a sense must always be projected into them before there can be "facts".
>
> The question "what is that?" is an imposition of meaning from some other viewpoint. "Essence", the "essential nature", is something perspective and already presupposes a multiplicity. At the bottom of it there always lies "what is that for *me*?" (for us, for all that lives, etc).
>
> *(Nietzsche, 1968 p. 301)*

All the same, the above criticism carries some weight, for in the next instance Rorty (1989) interestingly points out that only artists, poets and novelists – for example Proust – can successfully avoid the trap of metaphysics because, unlike philosophers, they are not expected to provide an investigation into the nature of reality or a logically coherent system. This is true only in part, for it relegates philosophy to the narrow realm of the Tradition, which to this day disdains writers who don't belong to the club. It took several decades and some decisive action (from Kristeva and others) before Simone de Beauvoir could be accepted as a philosopher as well as a 'mere' novelist/ essayist. This is because according to the Tradition, philosophers are not supposed to write, as she did, about sex, politics and gender (among other things). Even Nietzsche's writings are, for some, not worthy of the admission to the Philosophy Club.

If it is true that will to power could be read as a metaphysical, non-transcendental claim, what I find deplorable is the view, still widely held and especially within the world of psychotherapy, that it can be read as individualism, as the will of an *individual* to have power *over* others. But individualism, Nietzsche writes, "is a *modest* and still *unconscious* form of the 'will to power'" (1968, p. 411, emphasis added). This is partly because the individual itself "is an extremely vulnerable piece of vanity" (ibid., p. 410).

A joy forever

I did not recognize it at first; we had come across it by chance that morning, walking along Lake Silvaplana, marvelling at the eerie sensation of ambling along at the same level as a trail of clouds. We knew by now that clouds and mist could move down at any moment, seemingly out of nowhere; but not on this bright October day. Then we noticed this block of stone, a rock like any other, triangular, and almost shaped like a pyramid. As soon as the word 'pyramid' popped into my mind, it dawned on me. The spot where we had paused awhile to have hot tea with honey, where Sarita did her sketches and I my scribbling, was *the* rock. It was here, in August 1881, 6,000 feet above sea level and human concerns (as Nietzsche was to write in a letter to his friend Peter Gast), that the thought of the eternal recurrence first occurred to him. He laughed and trembled. Throughout that time, Nietzsche's eyes were often enflamed because he cried too much. His tears were tears of joy. Despite the fact that he was suspicious of the ecstasies of the mystics, some of his most powerful experiences did resemble ecstasies.

It is hard to describe that particular instant of recognition by the pyramid rock at Lake Silvaplana without sounding melodramatic. But that rock is for me the Western equivalent to *Bodhgaya*, the site of Buddhist pilgrimage in the Indian state of Bihar where the Buddha is said to have experienced awakening. Suitably devoid of wreaths and crowds of devotees, I found the inconspicuousness of the rock touching. Coming close to it for the first time, I was thrilled and strangely disappointed – an ambivalence that reminded me of when I had for the first time come up close to Van Gogh's painting of the wooden chair at the National Gallery. I had been struck by its skewed perspective, perplexed by its ordinariness – the pipe, the pouch of tobacco. The same ambivalence felt next to the pyramid rock felt pertinent.

Within the history of philosophy, the thought of the eternal recurrence is outlandish, metaphysical-sounding and, at a first glance, even archaic; yet it also points towards everyday experience. This uncanny notion – strange, entirely new and subversive, though swathed in the weathered pelt of ancient myth – *occurred* to Nietzsche. It was an instance of what was once called inspiration before this term became obsolete, deemed to signify mere passivity, and then superseded by perspiration and the cult of work. That the eternal recurrence is usually read as a replica or, at best, as mytho-poetic riff on the transmigration of souls, on ancient visions of cyclic repetition, testifies to the efficacy of one among Nietzsche's crafts: masking new ideas within old semblances.

I remember fondly our week in Sils Maria, a village in the Upper Engadin, in the Swiss Alps. It was October 2002. Sarita and I stayed at what is known as 'Nietzsche's house', the place where he lodged during the summer months between 1881 and 1883, and that is now self-catering guesthouse, study centre and library all in one. This fond memory is tinged with ambiguity. She was recovering from a serious illness that had thrown our lives into disarray. We had glimpsed death's silhouette at our front door – its step so ordinary, it looked harmless. What I was going through at the time was also a death of sorts – trivial by comparison – the end of what I had been until then, the giving up of old ropes and tropes and the start of an urgent need to write and chronicle, to leave marks in the sand before the tide comes in. Only a few years before, my father's brain stroke had left him unable to read and speak – unbearable for one who like him loved language. He was to die in Turin, the town where he spent his final days, the same town of Nietzsche's collapse, two years after our stay at 'Nietzsche's house'.

Given the stark circumstances, it was strange to stumble upon the eternal. This was no consolatory ruse on my part. On balance, the notion of the eternal we contend with here turns out to be even more unsettling than the thought of finitude. When it presents itself to me, the word 'eternity' does so unannounced; its arrival feels inopportune. After love, one autumn morning, gazing idly at the ceiling, a daydream of sun-kissed treetops in a dense European forest, untouched by the stream of time. Or during a silent meditation retreat, a new and strange feeling, minutes of my allotted time outstretched and dissolved in the valley below drifting to insignificance in the summer air. I have no word for it at first. Until the word 'eternity' finds me. 'For lack of a better word', I tell myself later. Bizarrely, of all the words that can come to mind, the one that knocks at the door is the very same I have built a lifetime to crush; the most Platonic, Christian, metaphysical of all: eternity! And with the reality of unappeasable, implacable death all around me; with the actuality of perishable imperfection doing its song and dance 24/7: eternity! I remember objecting once with some petulance to John Berger's recurring use of the word during a talk he gave at London's South Bank. With hindsight, I realize he had meant it in close connection to ephemeral beauty, to John Keats' 'joy forever'. Allergy to the eternal is almost equal to my aversion to nostalgia, but I found with time that this second antipathy too is in need of reassessment.

A world without being

The notion of the eternal recurrence does not imply, as it is sometimes believed, negation of time, nor is it really linked to the ancient notion of timeless eternity. It can be read as a powerful new myth of affirmation. Nietzsche certainly thought of it as the highest form of affirmation that is ever possible. First mention of the idea surfaced in a notebook entry of the beginning of August 1881, where he refers to it as "the new gravity" (cited in Parkes, 2005, p. xxii). Thinking and feeling were experienced by Nietzsche as one and the same; two weeks later, in a letter to his friend Heinrich Köselitz from his room in Sils Maria, he hinted at a thought process that had touched him to the core:

> Now then, my dear, good friend! The August sun is above us, the year moves along; it becomes more still and peaceful on the mountains and in the forests. On my horizon thoughts have arisen the like of which I have never seen before – but I will let nothing be known of them and shall maintain myself in an unshakeable silence. Now I shall have to live for at least a *few* years longer!
>
> (ibid., p. xxiii)

A year later, in 1882, in section 341 of *The Gay Science*, titled "The Greatest Burden", and poised between bliss and dismay, he announces the thought of the eternal recurrence.

At its most straightforward and pragmatic, the eternal recurrence can be read as a way to help clarify the degree of active appreciation of our life at this moment in time. How much do you value your life right now? Would you be prepared to repeat it eternally? What things, if any, are you *not* prepared to repeat? This sort of questioning can initiate a process of selection that gives priority to what one values most.

At a deeper level, and given Nietzsche's keen interest in physics as a "science of intensive quantities" (Deleuze, 2004, p. 122), the notion of the eternal recurrence presents us with a principle of *pure intensity* and *pure difference*. This process of selection is intimately connected with the high degree of intensity implied in the notion of the eternal recurrence. Do I desire what I desire to its utmost level, to its ultimate power? If so, the desire itself will change, it will initiate a process of extraction of "the superior form of everything that is" (Deleuze, 2004, p. 122). Both notions of the One and the Same melt in this intensity, alongside correlative notions of 'God' and 'Self':

> In short, the world of the eternal [recurrence] is a world of *differences*, an intensive world, which presupposes neither the One nor the Same, but whose edifice is built both on the tomb of God and on the ruins of the identical self.
> *(Deleuze, 2004, p. 123, emphasis added)*

It is natural to want to translate this genuinely unsettling notion within familiar frames: the eternal cycle or wheel of life, the return of the same, the vision of eternity itself. But in Nietzsche's conception, not everything comes back: the eternal recurrence is selective. The law that reigns in this depiction is that of a world *without unity, without identity* – a world *without being*. This world activates every desire to its upmost and removes half-desires. Here is how Gilles Deleuze (2004) describes it:

> Imagine laziness that willed its eternal [recurrence] and stopped saying "tomorrow I will get to work" – or cowardice, or abjection that wills its eternal [recurrence]: clearly, we would find ourselves faced with forms as yet unknown and unexplored. These would no longer be … laziness or cowardice. And the fact that we have no idea of what they would be means only that extreme forms do not pre-exist the ordeal of the eternal [recurrence].
> *(p. 125)*

The world thus envisioned is a world of *tendencies* and *intensities* rather than a world of things. It is a world that naturally exorcises all that is feeble, calculative, all that is too reasonable and moderate: none of these would endure the test. It is a world that values the sanctity of affect as well as the sanctity of being affected by the unbearable beauty and suffering and sadness of the world, as well as by the intensity of the 'magnificent monsters', those passions and emotions that religion, philosophy, and now psychotherapy are keen to control, regulate and place under the domain of reason.

From its very inception, the eternal recurrence is presented to us as a *thought experiment* – 'What if …?' It concerns this life. What if *this* life, as you have lived it until now, were to return eternally? We are faced with a choice. Many of us, confronted with the demon's question, would choose not to choose. What is the alternative? What would it mean to take on the demon's challenge? A tentative, poignant answer is found in *Zarathustra*:

> Have you ever said Yes to one joy? Oh my friends, then you also said Yes to *all* pain. All things are enchained, entwined, enamoured – if you ever wanted one time two times, if you ever said "I like you, happiness! Whoosh! Moment!" then you wanted *everything* back! – Everything anew, everything eternal, everything enchained, entwined, enamoured, oh thus you *loved* the world – you eternal ones, love it eternally and for all time; and say to pain also: refrain, but come back! *For all joy wants – eternity!*
>
> (Nietzsche, 1883/2006a, p. 263)

What is it that returns? It would be a mistake to frame the notion of the eternal recurrence in terms of the canonical categories of *identity* and the *same*. This vision does not present us with "the permanence of the same, the equilibrium state … or the resting place of the same" (Deleuze, 1962/2006, p. 43).

Noontide

In the section of *Thus Spoke Zarathustra* titled "Of the Vision and the Riddle" (Nietzsche, 1883/2006a, pp. 123–127), the protagonist invites the dwarf to look at a large gate on top of a mountain from which two roads spring. No one until now has followed them to their end, he says. They both stretch to infinity: one forward, towards the future; the other backward, towards the past. In actual fact they are one, not two; it is one road that encircles the gate, and the name of the gate on the mountain top is *Augenblick*, the moment, a moment of vision. With this quasi-mythical image, Nietzsche presents a view of time that is profoundly antithetical to our ordinary perception. Our infinite wandering and meandering can stop here, this very moment. The recognition opens us to new possibilities beyond linear time: for instance, to the very real possibility that the future may influence the past. In this picture, the moment is not the mystical or 'mindful' here and now: it is not what we ordinarily call 'the present'. This is because, in fact, *there is no such thing as the present*. The moment is not a dot in the linear progress of time but is represented by the gate on the mountain top through which the eternity or totality of time can be accessed. The world, one might say, did not begin with Genesis. History is not preceded by pre-history. More to the point: existence, *our* existence, did not begin at birth; instead, it "begins in every instant" (Vattimo, 2005, p. 22). Every moment is 'the middle'; "the middle is everywhere" (ibid.). The moment is the moment of noon, with the sun at its zenith. This is the moment of insight when we can see through the relative truth of linear time and, free from the clutches of *fate*, reshape a *destiny*.

The task of psychotherapy can then be reframed: to prepare the individual for what Nietzsche calls *noon* or noontide (Nietzsche, 1883/2006a, pp. 223–225). This term has been misread, with some of the most ridiculous misreadings coming from pop psychologists who went as far as to see it as 'midlife crisis' (Goldhill, 2015).

Strangely enough, noontide is a necessary crisis of sort, individual as well as societal and cultural. To prepare individuals and groups for the noontide – the task of psychotherapy – means to arrange a crisis, to quicken dissolution rather than band-aid the wound and cork the flow of life's energies. A psychologist in Nietzsche's sense is a critic and physician of culture. A good historical example of how this side of his thought has been suitably assimilated comes from the literary, artistic and philosophical avant-garde of the first decades of the twentieth century, that very same cultural milieu from which psychoanalysis sprang. These cultural expressions, Freudianism included, knowingly or unknowingly signal the dissolution of the human. They point in various ways towards the overhuman or ultrahuman. Vattimo (2005) sees most of the above as the result of "negative thought", a thought that is focused on what he calls "bourgeois disintegration" (p. 229).

Our dominant culture is too easily repelled by notions of dissolution and disintegration. True, they do not offer consolation, nor do they readily chart heroes' journeys through thinly disguised Stations of the Cross to final happy destinations of redemption and integration. Nor do they affirm the myth of the fully functioning, authentic or integrated individual that grows and develops to her full potential, to a shinier, grander version of the very same self.

For those of us predisposed to this other jingle whose first notes drift in the early spring air, another archetype or prototype makes itself known to us, dancing a jig in the melting snow – a *jester*, whose domain is not the exhausted arena of pathology versus normality, but a *playground*.

Nietzsche's emphasis on play does not justify the accusation of irrationalism levelled at him from many quarters. 'Disintegration', in this context, signals dissolution of the old frames of culture and of the human self in favour of wider organismic experiencing. But even this formulation falls short of Nietzsche's range and scope, for even 'wider organismic experiencing' is still confined to a human organism, hence to humanism – in itself a product, in Marx's critique of Feuerbach (Marx & Engels, 1845/1998), of alienated thought.

On recursion

It may happen at times that a client recognizes the similarity between this moment of opening, this possibility of the new disclosed by therapy and another significant moment of transformation that took place in the past. The two moments may be different, but both present the person with the glimpse of a more expansive life – in Nietzschean terms, with the possibility of a realignment in favour of active forces. This is no straightforward recognition: 'active' does not necessarily coincide with 'positive', least of all with the version of positivity promoted by popular psychology brands such as positive psychology. This is because a glimpse into a more expansive life, where active forces gain the upper hand, may appear as a crisis, for there may be after all a grain of truth in the cliché according to which the two characters for *crisis* in Chinese are made up of 'danger' and 'opportunity'.

What matters to our present investigation is that a past event is vividly echoed by a current experience and that the greater intensity of affect present in both instances (translated by the individual consciousness in either 'positive' or 'negative' terms) – alerts the person to the momentarily tangible presence of an immanent *outside* – powerful, dynamic and potentially overwhelming – that cannot be understood or assimilated within the habitual diagram (self-construct or self-concept) without undergoing a fundamental and potentially disruptive transformation.

The other person (a significant other in the past; the therapist now) certainly plays a role in this scenario – as a catalyst. But what matters even more is the *entirety* of the 'transferential' landscape, something characterized by (autonomous, neutral, immanent yet ungraspable) affect. What matters is not so much the relationship, classically understood within a familial matrix of attachment and cathexis, and obediently replicated by most therapeutic approaches, including those that profess independence from psychiatry and psychoanalysis. What matters is the very real and rare possibility of *transformation*.

An *active psychotherapy* is a therapeutic stance that values the emergence of life-affirming forces within a person, and is interested in recognizing the latter and bringing them again into focus. The re-enactment and resolution of static mummy-daddy scenarios is not sufficient to this purpose, and the same is true for those relational rhapsodies produced by an all-empathic, self-congratulating counsellor who believes he can see into the soul of his unsuspecting client. What matters is that transformation, glimpsed sometimes in the past and then forgotten, becomes again possible. In this context, transferential phenomena are subordinate to the main task of identifying and bringing to the fore those active forces whose presence and power has been denied and ostracized. 'Transformation' – the allure of a new door opening – is not resolution, completion, 'closure' or even 'developmental growth'. It is not *formative*: it does not head towards a final destination that actualizes an allegedly inbuilt potential within an orderly, holistic and benevolent universe. It is *transformative*, engaged in a process of metamorphosis, interpretation – of greater power and affirmation.

This can be linked to Nietzsche's notion of the eternal recurrence: what *returns* is the possibility of transformation, the call of the outside, life's incitement to expanding and modifying a self-concept that has been hijacked by reactive forces and whose functionality expires with every breath. The name I have adopted for this potentially liberating moment of opening across time is *recursion*, a term that in computer science (Andrew Seed, personal communication, 2018) refers to a method where the solution to a problem depends on solutions to smaller instances of the same problem. In computer science, the appeal of recursion consists in the possibility of "defining an infinite set of objects by a finite statement" (Wirth, 1976, p. 126). In the same way, "an infinite number of computations can be described by a finite recursive program, even if this program contains no explicit repetitions" (ibid.).

The passing moment

> To impose upon becoming the character of being – that is the supreme will to power.
> *(Nietzsche, 1968, p. 330)*

A brief detour will be necessary here before we examine another important aspect of the eternal recurrence. At the heart of the popular notion of the 'present moment', notably championed in contemporary psychotherapy by Daniel Stern (2004), is the "moment of meeting" (ibid., p. xvi), which underscores the "nature of co-creativity" … and acknowledges "the pervasive importance of inter-subjectivity in therapy". This notion has been favourably commented upon by several practitioners, including Spinelli (2007), who reads the moment of meeting taking place between therapist and client as confirmation of a "foundational spe-cies-based system for inter-subjective … knowing whose aim is achieved in those instances of 'present moments'" (p. 164). Spinelli expands on Stern's idea (albeit briefly), grounding it within the phenomenological tradition, and with a little help from the unspoken tutelary presence of Husserl, perhaps the first to emphasize the pivotal role of intersubjectivity in constituting objectivity itself.

Husserl's phenomenological structure of time-consciousness (Husserl, 1928/1990) seems to provide the inspiration for Spinelli's explanation of the 'present' as made of both "retentive … and … protentive horizons" (ibid., p. 165). Grounding the objectivity of the spatio-temporal framework itself almost entirely within an inter-subjective *Lebenswelt*, as Spinelli appears to be doing in the manner of Husserl, is mercifully a long way from the intrepid sentimentality of notions such as "relational depth" (Mearns & Cooper, 2005) to which Spinelli unpersuasively attempts to marry both Stern's 'present moment' and his own Husserlesque version of intersubjectivity. In Stern's case, and despite his avowed appreciation of phenomenology, we are firmly within the terrain of psychoanalytic intersubjectivity. With Spinelli we are as firmly ensconced within a Husserlian frame. As for Mearns and Cooper and other therapists who, like them, wax literal on the complex dynamics of the therapeutic encounter, I believe theirs is both over-simplification and a misreading of Buber's *I-Thou*. I have addressed this topic elsewhere at greater length (Bazzano, 2013c). Here I will only say that while borrowing copiously from Buber, this particular version of relational therapy blatantly ignores both the *religious* element as well as the *accidental* nature of the I-Thou encounter.

From a Nietzsche-inspired psychotherapeutic practice, all three stances sketched above are found wanting. This is because all three are haunted by the caricature of the depersonalizing, blank-screen analyst and marred by their own disproportionate reaction to it. True, the Husserlian intersubjective grounding of objectivity that inspires Spinelli and other phenomenological therapists can be seen, with good reason, as a step forward compared with the solipsistic abstraction of space-and-time. Something similar could be said in relation to Stern's intersubjective stance. Moreover, considering how stuffy, doctrinaire and archaic psychoanalysis proved to be in some of its historical manifestations, the caricature of the cold blank-screen analyst could be seen as not too far off the mark. But to throw out analytic *neutrality* with the proverbial bathwater is, in my view, a serious mistake. Much can be gained from reclaiming analytic neutrality in the name of true empathic attunement and in ways that are more attuned to Nietzsche's original insights, as Russell (2017) explains:

> From a perspective informed by Nietzsche's thinking, psychoanalytic neutrality appears "more empathic" than empathy conceived as humanist, intersubjective relation, because it maintains a differentiating, "noble" distance from the other by insistently deferring equality and agreement, opening up the potential for symbolization by means of interpretation and perspective.
>
> *(p. 68)*

At the heart of the intersubjective experience there appears to be a common emphasis on the vividness of the present moment. This notion has now gained greater import and is found within a wide range of settings, practices, and with varying degrees of ethical or not-so-ethical principles, from mindfulness to business management, from the experimental to the corporate. In the light of Nietzsche's notion of the eternal recurrence, however, an awkward question emerges – a devilish question, a philosopher's question: Is there really such a thing as 'the present moment'?

Above all, the notion of the eternal recurrence is a powerful affirmation of becoming. If the universe had a final aim, a state of equilibrium to be reached at some point, it would have attained it by now. In a posthumous fragment titled "The new world conception", Nietzsche writes:

> The world exists; it is not something that becomes, not something that passes away. Or rather: it becomes, it passes away, but it has never begun to become and never ceased from passing away – it maintains itself in both. It lives on itself.
>
> *(1968, p. 548)*

It is difficult to think of our experience in the world in terms of *becoming* rather than being. This is because from its early days philosophy, with the one remarkable exception of Heraclitus, never confronted squarely the thought of becoming. Our current notion of the present moment as a moment of being is a direct consequence of this millennial bias that from the Eleatics onwards has characterized mainstream thought and education. We need – in psychotherapy as in everyday life – a more precise description of the *moment* as a result of our bracketing of the habitual notion of being, a description that implements more fully the reality of becoming. What would that description be? Nietzsche's passage above already gives us a hint: the *passing* moment. Not the present moment, but the passing moment. The notion of the present moment is an abstraction entirely dependent on an idea of being understood conventionally, i.e., as distinct from becoming. There is being *within* becoming; its name is *returning*.

"Do not make it too easy on yourself! [...] See this moment!" ... "From this gateway Moment a long eternal lane stretches *backward*: behind us lies an eternity. Must not whatever *can* pass already have passed this way before? Must not whatever *can* happen, already have happened, been done, passed by before? ... And are not all things firmly knotted together in such a way that this moment draws after it *all* things to come?

(*Nietzsche, 1883/2006a, p. 126*)

Commenting on the above passage, Deleuze (1962/2006) writes:

How can the past be constituted in time? How can the present pass? The passing moment could never pass if it were not already past and yet to come – at the same time as being present. If the present did not pass of its own accord, if it had to wait for a new present in order to become past, the past in general would never be constituted in time and this particular present would not pass. We cannot wait, the moment must be simultaneously present and past, present and yet to come, in order for it to pass.

(*pp. 44–45*)

The eternal recurrence is, in this sense, a response to the quandary of passing. What is it that returns? Is it *being*? Is it the *same*? If we are inclined to think in this way, we repeat the mistake of understanding this notion as the eternal wheel of cyclical time, as a rehashed notion borrowed from antiquity. What returns is not this or that thing, this or that being; what returns is not *identity*.

Identity in the eternal return does not describe the nature of that which returns but ... the fact of returning for that which differs. This is why the eternal return must be thought of as a synthesis; a synthesis of time and its dimensions, a synthesis of diversity and its reproduction, a synthesis of becoming and the being which is affirmed.

(*Deleuze, 1962/2006, p. 45*)

Walter Benjamin wrote:

Memory is not an instrument for surveying the past but its theatre. It is the medium of past experience, just as the earth is the medium in which dead cities lie buried. He who seeks to approach his own buried past must conduct himself like a man digging. Above all, he must not be afraid to return again and again to the same matter; to scatter it as one scatters earth, to turn it over as one turns over soil.

(*Benjamin, 2006, p. 85*)

We are back to archaeology – a more fitting inspiration for therapy than anthropology (with its inherent human-centredness) will ever be. In this case, there is no promise or guarantee that digging will result in finding a final 'ground of being', of encountering an origin or a primary cause. We go on digging. The conversation is infinite.

REFERENCES

Abbey, R. (2000). *Nietzsche's Middle Period*. Oxford and New York: Oxford University Press.

Acampora, C.D. (2004). Between Mechanism and Teleology: Will to Power and Nietzsche's Gay Science, in Moore, G. and Brobjer, T.H. (eds.) *Nietzsche and Science*. Aldershot, Hampshire: Ashgate, pp. 171–188.

Acampora, C.D. (2006). Naturalism and Nietzsche's Moral Psychology, in Ansell Pearson, K. (ed.) *A Companion to Nietzsche*. Malden, MA: Blackwell, pp. 314–333.

Adler, A. (1964). *Superiority and Social Interest*, edited by H.L. Ansbacher and R.R. Ansbacher. New York: W.W. Norton & Co.

Adorno, T.W. (1970). *Aesthetic Theory*, trans. A. Mitchell and W. Bloomster. London: Athlone.

Adorno, T.W. and Popper, K. et al. (1976). *The Positivist Dispute in German Sociology*. New York: Harper & Row.

Aeschylus (1977). *The Oresteian Trilogy*, trans. P. Vellacott. London: Penguin.

Aeschylus (1978). *Prometheus Bound, The Suppliant, Seven against Thebes, The Persians*, trans. P. Vellacott. London: Penguin.

Ansbacher, H.L. and Ansbacher, R.R. (1964). *The Individual Psychology of Alfred Adler: A Systematic Presentation in Selection from his Writings*. New York: Harper & Row, Publishers.

Ansell Pearson, K. (ed.) (1991). *Nietzsche and Modern German Thought*. London and New York: Routledge.

Ansell Pearson, K. (1997). *Viroid Life: Perspectives on Nietzsche and the Trans-human Condition*. London: Routledge.

Ansell Pearson, K. (ed.) (2006). *A Companion to Nietzsche*. Malden, MA: Blackwell.

Ansell Pearson, K. (2011). 'Multimodal', *Radical Philosophy*, 167, pp. 46–48.

Arendt, H. (1970). *On Violence*. New York, NY: Harcourt.

Aristotle (1996). *Poetics*. London: Penguin.

Aristotle (2004). *The Nicomachean Ethics*, edited by H. Tredennick. London: Penguin.

Auerbach, E. (1991). *Mimesis: The Representation of Reality in Western Literature*, trans. Wr Trask. Princeton, NJ: Princeton University Press.

Austin, J.L. (1970). Agathon and Eudaimonia in the Ethics of Aristotle, in *Philosophical Papers*. Oxford and New York: Oxford University Press, pp. 1–31.

Babich, B. (1994). *Nietzsche's Philosophy of Science: Reflecting Science on the Ground of Art and Life*. Albany, NY: SUNY Press.

Babich, B. (2004). Nietzsche's Critique of Scientific Reason and Scientific Culture: On Science as a Problem and Nature as Chaos, in Moore, G. and Brobjer, T.H. (eds.) *Nietzsche and Science. Nietzsche and Science*. Aldershot, Hampshire: Ashgate, pp. 133–153.

Bachelard, G. (1943/1988). *Air and Dreams: An Essay of the Imagination of Movement*. Dallas, TX: Dallas Institute Publications.

Badiou, A. (2003). *Saint Paul: The Foundation of Universalism*, trans. R. Brassier. Stanford, CA: Stanford University Press.

Bakewell, S. (2016). *At the Existentialist Café: Freedom, Being, and Apricot Cocktails*. London: Chatto & Windus.

Barber, D.C. (2014). *Deleuze and the Naming of God: Post-Secularism and the Future of Immanence*. Edinburgh: Edinburgh University Press.

Bataille, G. (1945/1992). *On Nietzsche*, trans. by B. Boone. New York: Paragon House.

Bataille, G. (1943/2014). *Inner Experience*, trans. by S. Kendall. Albany, NY: SUNY Press.

Bazzano, M. (2006). *Buddha is Dead: Nietzsche and the Dawn of European Zen*. Eastbourne: Sussex Academic Press.

Bazzano, M. (2011). 'Empathy for the Devil: A tribute to Jean Genet', *Existential Analysis*, 22(1), pp. 150–159.

Bazzano, M. (2012a). *Spectre of the Stranger: Towards a Phenomenology of Hospitality*. Eastbourne: Sussex Academic Press.

Bazzano, M. (2012b). 'Immanent Vitality: Reflections on the Actualizing Tendency', *Person-Centered & Experiential Psychotherapies*, 11(2), pp. 137–151.

Bazzano, M. (2013a). 'On becoming no one: Phenomenological and empiricist contributions to the person-centered approach', *Person-Centered & Experiential Psychotherapies*, 13 (3), pp. 250–258. DOI: doi:10.1080/14779757.2013.804649.

Bazzano, M. (2013b). 'This very Body, the Buddha', *Sexual and Relationship Therapy*, 28(1–2), pp. 132–140. DOI: doi:10.1080/14681994.2013.770143.

Bazzano, M. (2013c). 'Togetherness: Intersubjectivity revisited', *Person-Centered & Experiential Psychotherapies*. DOI: doi:10.1080/14779757.2013.852613.

Bazzano, M. (2014). 'The Poetry of the World: A Tribute to the Phenomenology of Merleau-Ponty', *Self & Society*, 41(3), pp. 7–12.

Bazzano, M. (2015). 'Therapy as Unconditional Hospitality', *Psychotherapy and Politics International*, 13(4–13). DOI: doi:10.1002/ppi.1342.

Bazzano, M. (2016a). Changelings: The Self in Nietzsche's Psychology, in Bazzano, M. and Webb, J. (eds.) *Therapy and the Counter-tradition: The Edge of Philosophy*. Abingdon, Oxfordshire: Routledge.

Bazzano, M. (2016b). 'Exile on Main Street: Towards a Counter-existential Therapy', *Existential Analysis*, 28(1), pp. 48–64.

Bazzano, M. (2017a). 'A bid for freedom: The actualizing tendency updated', *Person-Centered & Experiential Psychotherapies*, 16(3).

Bazzano, M. (2017b). *Zen and Therapy: Heretical Perspectives*. Abingdon, Oxfordshire: Routledge.

Bazzano, M. (2018a). 'Grace and Danger', *Existential Analysis*, 29(1), pp. 16–27.

Bazzano, M. (2018b). Meditation and the Post-secular condition, in Farias, M., Brazier, D. and Lalljee, M. (eds.) *Oxford Handbook of Meditation*. Oxford and New York: Oxford University Press. In press.

Bazzano, M. (2018c). Beauty and the Cyborg, in Bazzano, M. (ed.) *Re-visioning Person-centred Therapy: Theory and Practice of a Radical Paradigm*. Abingdon, Oxfordshire: Routledge, pp. 28–45.

Bazzano, M. and Webb, J. (eds.) (2016). *Therapy and the Counter-tradition: The Edge of Philosophy*. Abingdon, Oxfordshire: Routledge.

Behler, E. (1991). *Confrontations: Derrida, Heidegger, Nietzsche*, trans., with an afterword by Steven Taubeneck. Stanford, CA: Stanford University Press.

Benjamin, W. (1992). *Illuminations*. Introduction by Hannah Arendt. Waukegan, IL: Fontana.

Benjamin, W. (1996). *Selected Writings: 1913–1926*, edited and trans. by M.P. Bullock. London: Verso.

Benjamin, W. (1997). *Charles Baudelaire: A Lyric Poet in the Era of High Capitalism*. London: Verso.

Benjamin, W. (2006). *Berlin Childhood around 1900*. Cambridge, MA: Belknap.

Benjamin, W. (2007). *Walter Benjamin's Archive: Images, Texts, Signs*, trans. E. Leslie. London: Verso.

Bennett, J. (2010). *Vibrant Matter: A Political Ecology of Things*. Durham, NC: Duke University Press.

Berman, M. (2010). *A Question of Values*. http://morrisberman.blogspot.co.uk/2011_01_09_archive.html?m=0 (accessed 3 March 2017).

Blake, T. (2016). *Guattari's Lines of Flight (2)*. https://terenceblake.wordpress.com/2016/01/09/guattaris-lines-of-flight-2-transversal-vs-transferential-approaches-to-the-reading-con tract (accessed 18 January 2018).

Blanchot, M. (1969/1993). *The Infinite Conversation*, trans. Susan Hanson. Minneapolis, MN: University of Minnesota Press.

Bloch, E. (1959/1995). *The Principle of Hope*. Cambridge, MA: MIT Press.

Blondel, E. (1991). *Nietzsche, the Body and Culture: Philosophy as Philosophical Genealogy*, trans. by S. Hand. London: Athlone.

Bollas, C. (2007). *The Freudian Moment*. London: Karnac.

Bollas, C. (2011). *The Christopher Bollas Reader*. Hove, Sussex: Routledge.

Bollas, C. (2015). *When the Sun Bursts: The Enigma of Schizophrenia*. New Haven, CT: Yale University Press.

Borges, J.L. (2000). *This Craft of Verse*. Cambridge, MA: Harvard University Press.

Boscovich, R.J. (1763/2015). *Theory of Natural Philosophy*. London: Forgotten Books.

Bowie, M. (1987). *Freud, Proust, Lacan: Theory as Fiction*. Cambridge University Press.

Braidotti, R. (2008). 'In Spite of the Times: The Postsecular Turn in Feminism', *Theory, Culture & Society*, 25(1), pp. 1–24.

Brown, R.S.G. (2004). Nietzsche: 'That Profound Physiologist', in Moore, G. and Brobjer, T.H. (eds.) *Nietzsche and Science*. Aldershot, Hampshire: Ashgate.

Buber, M. (1961). *Between Man and Man*. London: Fontana.

Buber, M. (2004). *I and Thou*. London: Continuum.

Bull, M. (2014). 'Pure Mediterranean', *London Review of Books*, 36(4), 20 February, pp. 21–23. www.lrb.co.uk/v36/n04/malcolm-bull/pure-mediterranean (accessed 25 September 2017).

Canestri, J. (2011). On Negation: Some reflection following in Freud's wake, in O'Neil, M. K. and Akhtar, S. (eds.) *On Freud's 'Negation'*. London: Karnac, pp. 39–51.

Caputo, J.D., Hart, K. and Sherwood, Y. (2005). Epoché and Faith: An Interview with Jacques Derrida, in Sherwood, Y. and Hart, K. (eds.) *Derrida and Religion: Other Testaments*. London and New York: Routledge.

Carter, A. (2006). *The Bloody Chamber*. London: Vintage.

Chamberlain, L. (1996). *Nietzsche in Turin: The End of the Future*. London: Quartet.

Clark, T.J. (2016). 'At the Royal Academy: James Ensor', *London Review of Books*, 38(23), 1 December, pp. 16–17.

Colli, G. (1974). *Dopo Nietzsche*. Milano: Adelphi.

Colli, G. (1975). *La Nascita della Filosofia*. Milano: Adelphi.

Collini, S. (2016). 'Imagining Universities: New Worlds, Old Ideas', The Ashby Lecture, Clare Hall, Cambridge, May. www.clarehall.cam.ac.uk/files/Ashby_Lecture_transcript_2016.pdf (accessed 23 February 2018).

Collini, S. (2017). *Speaking of Universities*. London and New York: Verso.

Conway, D. (1999). The Birth of the Soul: Towards a Psychology of Decadence, in Golomb, J., Santaniello, W. and Lehrer, R. (eds.) *Nietzsche and Depth Psychology*. New York: State University of New York Press.

Conway, D. (2006). Life and Self-overcoming, in Ansell Pearson, K. (ed.) *A Companion to Nietzsche*. Malden, MA: Blackwell, pp. 532–547.

Coole, D. and Frost, S. (eds.) (2010). *New Materialisms: Ontology, Agency, and Politics*. Durham, NC: Duke University Press.

Cox, C. (1999). *Nietzsche: Naturalism and Interpretation*. Los Angeles, CA: University of California Press.

Cox, C. (2006). Nietzsche, Dionysus, and the Ontology of Music, in Ansell Pearson, K. (ed.) *A Companion to Nietzsche*. Malden, MA: Blackwell, pp. 495–513.

Davies, W. (2015). *The Happiness Industry: How the Government and Big Business Sold Us Well Being*. London: Verso.

De Beauvoir, S. (1948). *The Ethics of Ambiguity*, trans. B. Frechtman. New York: Kensington Publishing.

Deleuze, G. (1968/1990). *Expressionism in Philosophy: Spinoza*, trans. Martin Joughin. New York: Zone Books.

Deleuze, G. (1994). *Difference and Repetition*, trans. P. Patton. New York: Columbia University Press.

Deleuze, G. (2001). *Pure Immanence: Essays on a Life*, trans. A. Boyman. New York: Zone Books.

Deleuze, G. (2004). *Desert Islands and other Texts*, edited by David Lapoujade, trans. M. Taormina. Cambridge, MA: Semiotext(e).

Deleuze, G. (1962/2006). *Nietzsche and Philosophy*, trans. Hugh Tomlinson. London: Continuum.

Deleuze, G. and Guattari, F. (1972/1982). *Anti-Oedipus: Capitalism and Schizophrenia*, trans. R. Hurley, M. Seem and H.R. Lane. Minneapolis, MN: University of Minnesota Press.

Deleuze, G. and Guattari, F. (1994). *What is Philosophy?*, trans. G. Birchill and H. Tomlinson. London: Verso.

Derrida, J. (1974). 'White Mythology: Metaphor in the Text of Philosophy', *New Literary History*, 6(1). www.jstor.org/stable/468341 (accessed 21 April 2017).

Derrida, J. (1967/1978). *Writing and Difference*. London: Routledge.

Derrida, J. (1981a). *Disseminations*, trans. B. Johnson. Chicago, IL: Chicago University Press.

Derrida, J. (1978/1981b). *Spurs: Nietzsche's Styles*, trans. B. Harlow. Chicago, IL: Chicago University Press.

Derrida, J. (1982). *Margins of Philosophy*, trans. A. Bass. Chicago, IL: Chicago University Press.

Derrida, J. (1999). *Adieu to Emmanuel Levinas*. Stanford, CA: Stanford University Press.

Derrida, J. and Dufourmantelle, A. (1997/2000). *Of Hospitality*, trans. R. Bowlby. Stanford University Press.

Deutsch, H. (1942). 'Some forms of emotional disturbance and their relationship to schizophrenia', *Psychoanalytic Quarterly*, 11, pp. 301–321.

Dews, P. (1986). 'Adorno, Post-Structuralism and the Critique of Identity', *New Left Review*, I(157), pp. 28–44.

Dostoyevsky, F. (1866/2003). *Crime and Punishment*, trans. D. McDuff. London: Penguin.

Doubrovsky, S. (1986). *Writing and Fantasy in Proust: la Place de la Madeleine*, trans. C. Bove and P.A. Bove. Lincoln, NE: University of Nebraska Press.

Ehrenreich, B. (2010). *Smile or Die: How Positive Thinking Fooled America*. London: Granta.

Failla, S.G. (2016). Tears of Joy: Pascal's Night of Fire, in Bazzano, M. and Webb, J. (eds.) *Therapy and the Counter-tradition: The Edge of Philosophy*. Abingdon, Oxfordshire: Routledge, pp. 58–64.

Farias, M., Brazier, D. and Lalljee, M. (2018). *The Oxford Handbook of Meditation*. Oxford and New York: Oxford University Press.

Ferenczi, S. and Rank, O. (1924). *The Development of Psychoanalysis*. New York: Dover.

Feuerbach, L. (1841/2008). *The Essence of Christianity*. New York: Dover.

Fink, E. (1960/2003). *Nietzsche's Philosophy*, trans. G. Richter. London and New York: Continuum.

Foucault, M. (1983). 'Structuralism and Post-structuralism: An Interview with Michel Foucault', *Telos*, 55, p. 200.

Foucault, M. (1967/1990). Nietzsche, Freud, Marx, in Ormiston, G.L. and Schrift, A.D. (eds.) *Transforming the Hermeneutic Context: From Nietzsche to Nancy*. Albany, NY: State University of New York Press.

Foucault, M. (1966/1994). *The Order of Things: An Archaeology of the Human Sciences*. New York, NY: Random House.

Frankel, M., Sommerbeck, L. and Rachlin, H. (2010). 'Rogers' concept of the actualizing tendency in relation to Darwinian theory', *Person-Centered & Experiential Psychotherapies*, 9, pp. 69–80.

Frey-Rohn, L. (1988). *Friedrich Nietzsche: A Psychological Approach to his Life and Work*, trans. G. Massey. Zurich: Daimon Press.

Gell, A. (1998). *Art and Agency: An Anthropological Theory*. Oxford: Oxford University Press.

Gillispie, C.C. (1960). *The Edge of Objectivity: An Essay on the History of Scientific Ideas*. Princeton, NJ: Princeton University Press.

Goethe, J.W. (1808/1949). *Autobiography: Poetry and Truth from My Own Life*, trans. R.O. Moon. Washington, DC: Public Affair Press.

Goldhill, O. (2015). 'A philosopher's guide: How to have a beautiful midlife crisis', *The Telegraph*. www.telegraph.co.uk/men/thinking-man/11494791/A-philosophers-guide-How-to-have-a-beautiful-midlife-crisis.html (accessed 27 April 2017).

Goldstein, K. (1939/1995). *The Organism*. Foreword by Oliver Sacks. New York: Urzone.

Grant, M. (1960). *The Myths of Hyginus*. Lawrence: University of Kansas Press.

Guattari, F. (2015a). *Psychoanalysis and Transversality: Texts and Interviews 1955–1971*, trans. A. Hodges. Cambridge, MA: Semiotext(e), MIT Press.

Guattari, F. (2015b). *Lines of Flight: For Another World of Possibilities*, trans. A. Goffey. London: Bloomsbury.

Hegel, G.W.F. (1807/1977). *Phenomenology of Spirit*, trans. A.V. Miller. Oxford, MA: Oxford University Press.

Heidegger, M. (1982). *The Question Concerning Technology and Other Essays*. New York, NY: Harper.

Heidegger, M. (1961/1991). *Nietzsche. Four Volumes*, trans. and edited by D.F. Krell. San Francisco, CA: Harper & Row.

Heidegger, M. (2001). *Zollikon Seminars*. Evanstone, IL: Northwestern University Press.

Hesiod (2012). *The Theogony*. London: CreateSpace.

Hillman, J. (1997). *Re-visioning Psychology*. New York: Harper & Row.

Hillman, J. and Ventura, M. (1992). *We've Had a Hundred Years of Psychotherapy and the World's Getting Worse*. San Francisco, CA: Harper.

Hölderlin, F. (2010). *Bread and Wine*. http://coriscopoems.blogspot.co.uk/2010/05/frie drich-holderlin-bread-and-wine.html (accessed 20 August 2017).

Horkheimer, M. (1931). *The Present Situation of Social Philosophy and the Tasks of an Institute for Social Research*. www.marxists.org/reference/archive/horkheimer/1931/present-situa tion.htm (accessed 22 December 2016).

Horkheimer, M. (2002). *Critical Theory: Selected Essays*. New York: Continuum.

Huskinson, L. (2004). *Nietzsche and Jung: The Whole Self in the Union of Opposites*. Hove and New York: Brunner-Routledge.

Husserl, E. (1928/1990). *On the Phenomenology of the Consciousness of Internal Time*, trans. J.B. Brough. Dordrecht: Kluwer.

Husserl, E. (1931/2013). *Cartesian Meditations: An Introduction to Phenomenology*, trans. D. Cairns. Dordrecht: Kluwer.

Hyland, A. (1990). *Equus: The Horse in Roman Times*. Abingdon, Oxfordshire: Routledge.

Icke, R. (2015). *Aeschylus' Oresteia*, Almeida Theatre, London, 12 June–18 July.

Ignatieff, M. (2018). 'Who Killed Frank Olson?', *New York Review of Books*, LXV(3), 22 February, pp. 42–43.

Jacobi, J. (1968). *The Psychology of C.G. Jung*, trans. K.W. Bash. London: Routledge.

Jaffé, A. (1970). *The Myth of Meaning in the Work of C.G. Jung*, trans. R.F.C. Hull. London: Hodder and Stoughton.

Jankélévitch, V. (2005). *Forgiveness*. Chicago: University of Chicago Press.

Jantz, F. (1980). *Friedrich Nietzsche: Biography*. Rome: Laterza.

Jay, M. (1993). *Downcast Eyes: The Denigration of Vision in Twentieth-Century Thought*. Los Angeles, CA: University of California Press.

Jeffries, S. (2016). *Grand Hotel Abyss: The Lives of the Frankfurt School*. London: Verso.

Jung, C.G. (1928). The Relation between the Ego and the Unconscious, in Read, H., Fordham, M., Adler, G. and McGuire, W. (eds.) *Collected Works*, 20 vols, trans. R.F.C. Hull. London: Routledge.

Jung, C.G. (1963/1995). *Memories, Dreams, Reflections*. London: Fontana.

Kant, I. (1800/1963). *Introduction to Logic*, trans. T.K. Abbott. New York, NY: New York Philosophical Library.

Keats, J. (2009). *Selected Letters*. Oxford and New York: Oxford University Press.

Kierkegaard, S. (1843/1992). *Either/Or: A Fragment of Life*, trans. A. Hannay. London: Penguin.

Kierkegaard, S. (1847/2005). *Fear and Trembling*. London: Penguin.

Klinkenborg, V. (2018). 'A Horse is a Horse, of Course', *New York Review of Books*, LXV(3), pp. 46–47.

Klossowski, P. (1969/1997). *Nietzsche and the Vicious Circle*, trans. D.W. Smith. London: Athlone.

Kofman, S. (1972/1993). *Nietzsche and Metaphor*, trans. D. Large. London: Athlone.

Kramer, R. (1995). 'The Birth of Client-Centered Therapy: Carl Rogers, Otto Rank, and Beyond', *Journal of Humanistic Psychology*, 35(4), pp. 54–110.

Krell, F.K. and Bates, D.L. (1997). *The Good European: Nietzsche's Work Sites in Word and Image*. Chicago, IL: Chicago University Press.

Kristeva, J. (1987). *Tales of Love*, trans. L.S. Roudiez. Columbia University Press.

Kuzminski, A. (2008). *Pyrrhonism: How the Ancient Greeks Reinvented Buddhism*. Lanham, MD: Lexington.

Lacan, J. (1994). *Seminar XI: The Four Fundamental Concepts of Psychoanalysis*, trans. A. Sher-idan. London: Karnac.

Lamarck, J.B. (1809/2012). *Zoological Philosophy: An Exposition With Regard to the Natural History of Animals*. London: Forgotten Books.

Land, N. (2011). *Fanged Noumena: Collected Writings 1987–2007*. Falmouth: Urbanomic.

Large, D. (2001). *Nietzsche and Proust: A Comparative Study*. Oxford and New York: Oxford University Press.

Leibniz, G. (1704/1982). *New Essays on Human Understanding*, trans. P. Remnant and J. Bennett. Cambridge and New York: Cambridge University Press.

Lévi-Strauss, C. (1987). *Introduction to the Work of Marcel Mauss*. London: Routledge.

Levinas, E. (1961). *Totality and Infinity: An Essay on Exteriority*. Pittsburgh, PA: Duquesne University Press.

Levinas, E. (1963/1998). Existence and Ethics, in Ree, J. and Chamberlain, J. (eds.) *Kierkegaard: A Critical Reader*. Oxford: Blackwell, pp. 26–38.

Levinas, E. (1999). *Alterity and Transcendence*. New York, NY: Columbia University Press.

Linley, A. and Joseph, S. (2004). *Positive Psychology in Practice*. Hoboken, NJ: Wiley.

Lippitt, J. (ed.) (1999). *Nietzsche's Futures*. Basingstoke: Macmillan.

Loeb, P.S. (2006). Identity and Eternal Recurrence, in Ansell Pearson, K. (ed.) *A Companion to Nietzsche*. Malden, MA: Blackwell, pp. 171–189.

Løgstrup, K. (1997). *The Ethical Demand*. Introduction by Hans Fink and Alastair MacIntyre. Notre Dame, Indiana: University of Notre Dame Press.

Magee, B. (1983). *The Philosophy of Schopenhauer*. Oxford and New York: Oxford University Press.

Mann, T. (1947/1999). *Doctor Faust: The Life of the German Composer Adrian Leverkühn as told by a Friend*, trans. J.E. Woods. London: Vintage.

Marx, K. and Engels, F. (1845/1998). *The German Ideology: Including Theses on Feuerbach and an Introduction to the Critique of Political Economy*. Amherst, NY: Prometheus.

Masini, F. (1978). *Lo Scriba del Caos: Interpretazioni di Nietzsche*. Bologna: Il Mulino.

Maslow, A. (1962). *Toward a Psychology of Being*. Princeton, NJ: Princeton University Press.

Maslow, A. (1997). *Motivation and Personality*. London: Pearson.

Massumi, B. (1996). The Autonomy of Affect, in Patton, P. (ed.) *Deleuze: A Critical Reader*. Oxford: Blackwell, pp. 217–239.

Massumi, B. (2014). *What Animals Teach us about Politics*. Durham, NC: Duke University Press.

May, R. (1969). *Love and Will*. New York: Norton.

McDougall, J. (1980). *Plea for a Measure of Abnormality*. New York: International Universities Press.

Mearns, D. and Cooper, M. (2005). *Working at Relational Depth in Counselling and Psychotherapy*. London: Sage.

Merleau-Ponty, M. (1968). *The Visible and The Invisible*. Evanston, Ill: Northwestern University Press.

Merleau-Ponty, M. (1942/1983). *The Structure of Behaviour*. Pittsburgh, PA: Duquesne University Press.

Merleau-Ponty, M. (1945/1989). *Phenomenology of Perception*. London: Routledge.

Millar, A. (2015). 'Socratic Dialogue and Adlerian Therapy', *Self & Society*, 32(2), pp. 17–21.

Moore, G. (2004). Introduction, in Moore, G. and Brobjer, T.H. (eds.) *Nietzsche and Science*. Aldershot, Hampshire: Ashgate, pp. 1–17.

Moore, G. and Brobjer, T.H. (eds.) (2004). *Nietzsche and Science*. Aldershot, Hampshire: Ashgate.

Moreira, V. (2012). 'From person-centered to humanistic-phenomenological psychotherapy: The contribution of Merleau-Ponty to Carl Rogers's thought', *Person-Centered and Experiential Psychotherapies*, 11(1), pp. 48–63.

Moreno, A. (1974). *Jung, Gods and Modern Man*. Notre Dame, IN: University of Notre Dame Press.

Nagel, T. (1981). What is it like to be a bat?, in Miller, F.D. and Smith, N.D. (eds.) *Thought Probes: Philosophy through Science Fiction*. New Jersey: Prentice Hall, pp. 179–191.

Nagy, M. (1991). *Philosophical Issues in the Psychology of C.G. Jung*. Albany, NY: SUNY Press.

Nehamas, A. (1990). *Nietzsche: Life as Literature*. Cambridge, MA: Harvard University Press.

Nietzsche, F. (1962). *Philosophy in the Tragic Age of the Greeks*, trans. M. Cowan. Washington, DC: Regnery Gateway.

Nietzsche, F. (1968). *The Will to Power*, edited by W. Kaufmann, trans. W. Kaufmann and R.J. Hollingdale. New York: Vintage Books.

Nietzsche, F. (1969). *Selected Letters of Friedrich Nietzsche*, edited and translated by C. Middleton. Chicago, Ill: Chicago University Press.

Nietzsche, F. (1882/1974). *The Gay Science. With a Prelude in Rhymes and an Appendix of Songs*, trans. W. Kaufmann. New York: Random House.

Nietzsche, F. (1886/1978). *Beyond Good and Evil: Prelude to a Philosophy of the Future*, trans. R.J. Hollingdale. London: Penguin.

Nietzsche, F. (1871/1979). *Philosophy and Truth: Selections from Nietzsche's Notebooks of the early 1870s*, edited and trans. by D. Breazeale. Atlantic Highlands, NJ: Humanities Press International.

Nietzsche, F. (1874/1983). *Untimely Meditations*, trans. R.J. Hollingdale. Cambridge: Cambridge University Press.

Nietzsche, F. (1878/1984). *Human, all too Human: A Book for Free Spirits*, trans. J.R. Hollingdale. Cambridge: Cambridge University Press.

Nietzsche, F. (1887/1996). *On the Genealogy of Morals: A Polemic*, trans. D. Smith. Oxford and New York: Oxford University Press.

Nietzsche, F. (1881/1997). *Daybreak: Thoughts on the Prejudices of Morality*, trans. J.R. Hollingdale. Cambridge: Cambridge University Press.

Nietzsche, F. (1888/1998). *Twilight of the Idols or How to Philosophize with the Hammer*, trans. R. Polt, introduction by Tracy Strong. Indianapolis: Hackett.

Nietzsche, F. (1872/2000). *The Birth of Tragedy*, trans. D. Smith. Oxford and New York: Oxford University Press.

Nietzsche, F. (1883/2006a). *Thus Spoke Zarathustra: A Book for All and None*, trans. A. Del Caro, edited by A. Del Caro and R. Pippin. Cambridge University Press.

Nietzsche, F. (1872/2006b). Homer's Contest, in Ansell Pearson, K. and Large, D. (eds.) *The Nietzsche Reader*. Malden, MA: Blackwell, pp. 95–113.

Nietzsche, F. (2006c). *The Nietzsche Reader*, edited by K. Ansell Pearson and D. Large. Malden, MA: Blackwell.

Nietzsche, F. (1895/2007a). *The Anti-Christ*, trans. H.L. Mencken. London: FQ.

Nietzsche, F. (1908/2007b). *Ecce Homo: How to Become What You Are*, edited and trans. D. Large. Oxford and New York: Oxford University Press.

Nietzsche, F. (1872/2015a). *Anti-Education: On the Future of our Educational Institutions*, trans. D. Searls. New York, NY: NYRB.

Nietzsche, F. (1888/2015b). *Twilight of the Idols or How to Philosophize with the Hammer*, trans. W. Kaufmann and R.J. Hollingdale. London: Createspace.

Nussbaum, M. (2001). *Upheavals of Thought: The Intelligence of Emotions*. Cambridge: Cambridge University Press.

Ogden, T.H. (2005). 'On psychoanalytic supervision', *International Journal of Psychoanalysis*, 86(5), pp. 1265–1280.

Orbach, S. (2017). *In Therapy: The Unfolding Story*. London: Wellcome.

Ortega y Gasset, J. (1961). *The Modern Theme*, trans. J.F. Moza. New York, NY: Harper & Row.

Padesky, C.A. (1993). 'Socratic questioning', Keynote address, European Congress of Behavioural and Cognitive Therapies, 24 September, London. https://padesky.com/newpad/wp-content/uploads/2012/11/socquest.pdf (accessed 4 January 2018).

Paglia, C. (1991). *Sexual Personae: Art and Decadence from Nefertiti to Emily Dickinson*. London: Vintage.

Park, J.Y. (ed.) (2006). *Buddhisms and Deconstructions*. Lanham, MD: Rowman & Littlefield.

Parkes, G. (1994). *Composing the Soul: Reaches of Nietzsche's Psychology*. Chicago, IL: Chicago University Press.

Parkes, G. (1999a). Staying Loyal to the Earth: Nietzsche as an Ecological Thinker, in Lippitt, J. (ed.) *Nietzsche's Futures*. Basingstoke: Macmillan, pp. 167–188.

Parkes, G. (1999b). Nietzsche and Jung: Ambivalent Appreciation, in Golomb, J., Santaniello, W. and Lehrer, R. (eds.), *Nietzsche and Depth Psychology*. State University of New York Press, pp. 205–227.

Parkes, G. (2005). Introduction, in Nietzsche, F., *Thus Spoke Zarathustra*, edited and trans. by G. Parkes. Oxford: Oxford University Press, pp. ix–xxxiv.

Perls, F. (1973). *The Gestalt Approach and Eye Witness to Therapy*. New York, NY: Bantam Books.

Phillips, A. (2001). *Darwin's Worms: On Life Stories and Death Stories*. New York: Basic Books.

Pippin, R.B. (2006a). *Nietzsche, Psychology, and First Philosophy*. Chicago, Ill: Chicago University Press.

Pippin, R.B. (2006b). Agent and Deed in the Genealogy of Morals, in Ansell Pearson, K. (ed.) *A Companion to Nietzsche*. Oxford: Blackwell, pp. 371–386.

Plato (1951). *The Symposium*, trans. W. Hamilton. Aylesbury, Bucks: Penguin.

Plato (1993). *Sophist*, trans. N.P. White. Indianapolis, IN: Hackett.

Plato (2005). *Phaedrus*. London: Penguin.

Plato (2011). *The Apology*. London: Createspace.

Popkin, R.H. (1980). *The High Road to Pyrrhonism*. Indianapolis: Hackett Publishing Company.

Popper, K. (1945/2002). *The Open Society and its Enemies*, 2 volumes. Abingdon, Oxfordshire: Routledge.

Proust, M. (1923/1996). *The Captive and the Fugitive*, trans. C.K.S. Moncrieff, D.J. Enright and T. Kilmartin. London: Vintage.

Proust, M. (1913–1927/2003). *In Search of Lost Time*, 6 volumes. London: Modern Library.

Proust, M. (2016). *In the Shadow of Young Girls in Flower*, trans. C.K. Scott Moncrieff, edited and annotated by W.C. Carter. New Haven, CT: Yale University Press.

Rampley, M. (2000). *Nietzsche, Aesthetics and Modernity*. Cambridge: Cambridge University Press.

Rank, O. (1932). *Modern Education*. New York: Knopf.

Rank, O. (1958). *Beyond Psychology*. New York: Dover.

Rank, O. (1978a). *Will Therapy: An Analysis of the Therapeutic Process in Terms of Relationship*, trans. J. Taft. New York: W.W. Norton.

Rank, O. (1929/1978b). *Truth and Reality*, trans. J. Taft. New York, NY: WW Norton & Company.

Rank, O. (1996). *A Psychology of Difference: The American Lectures*. Selected, edited and introduced by R. Kramer. Princeton, NJ: Princeton University Press.

Raskin, N. (1948). 'The development of non-directive therapy', *Journal of Consulting Psychology*, 12, pp. 92–110. www3.telus.net/eddyelmer/Tools/ndtdev.htm (accessed 1 October 2015).

Raulff, U. (2018). *Farewell to the Horse*, trans. R.A. Kemp. London: Penguin.

Reitter, P. (2018). 'The Business of Learning', *New York Review of Books*, LXV(3), pp. 30–33.

Rethy, R. (1991). 'Schein' in Nietzsche's Philosophy, in Ansell Pearson, K. (ed.) *Nietzsche and Modern German Thought*. London and New York: Routledge, pp. 59–87.

Ricoeur, P. (1970/2008). *Freud and Philosophy: An Essay on Interpretation*, trans. D. Savage. New Haven, CT: Yale University Press.

Rimbaud, A. (1871/1986). *Collected Poems*, trans. Oliver Bernard. London: Penguin.

Robinson, M. (2012). *When I Was A Child I Read Books*. Hachette.

Rogers, C.R. (1961). *On Becoming a Person*. Boston, MA: Houghton Mifflin.

Rogers, C.R. (1980). *A Way of Being*. Boston, MA: Houghton Mifflin.

Rorty, R. (1989). *Contingency, Irony, and Solidarity*. Cambridge: Cambridge University Press.

Rose, J. (2011). *Proust among the Nations: From Dreyfus to the Middle East*. Chicago IL: Chicago University Press.

Rose, J. (2018). 'I am a knife', *London Review of Books*, 40(4), 22 February, pp. 3–11.

Rud, C. (2016). 'The philosophical practice of Spinoza and the person-centered paradigm', WAPCEP Conference, 20–24 July 2016, New York City, Cuny Graduate Center, 23 July.

Russell, J. (2017). *Nietzsche and the Clinic: Psychoanalysis, Philosophy, Metaphysics*. London: Karnac.

Safranski, R. (2003). *Nietzsche: A Philosophical Biography*, trans. Shelley Frisch. London: Granta.

Said, E.W. (2001). *Reflections on Exile and Other Literary and Cultural Essays*. Granta Books.

Schacht, R. (1988). Nietzsche's Gay Science, or How to Naturalize Cheerfully, in Solomon, R.C. and Higgins, K.M. (eds.) *Reading Nietzsche*. New York: Oxford University Press, pp. 68–86.

Schaverien, J. (2007). Framing Enchantment: Countertransference in analytical art psychotherapy supervision, in Schaverien, J. and Case, C. (eds.) *Supervision of Art Psychotherapy: A theoretical and practical handbook*. London: Routledge, pp. 45–63.

Schaverien, J. (2017). *Erotic Transference and Countertransference in Psychotherapy and Supervision*. Seminar in Central London, 5 May.

Schopenhauer, A. (1965). *On the Basis of Morality*, trans. E.F.J. Payne. Indianapolis: Bobbs-Merrill.

Schopenhauer, A. (1966). *The World as Will and Representation*, trans. E.F.J. Payne. New York: Dover.

Schrift, A.D. (1990). *Nietzsche and the Question of Interpretation: Between Hermeneutics and Deconstruction*. New York and London: Routledge.

Shaw, T. (2016). 'The psychologists take power', *New York Review of Books*, LXIII(3), 25 February, pp. 38–41.

Smith, W.L. (2017). *Solo: Reflections and Meditations on Monk*, CD music album. Pohjankuru, Finland: TUM.

Solomon, R.C. (1989). *From Hegel to Existentialism*. Oxford and New York: Oxford University Press.

Spiegelberg, H. (1964). *The Socratic Enigma*. Indianapolis, IN: Bobbs-Merrill.

Spinelli, E. (2007). *Practising Existential Psychotherapy: The Relational World*. London: Sage.

Spinelli, E. (2016). 'Relatedness: Contextualizing Being and Doing in Existential Therapy', *Existential Analysis*, 27(2), pp. 303–329.

Spinelli, E. (2017). 'Kierkegaard's Dangerous Folly', *Existential Analysis*, 28(2), pp. 288–300.

Spinoza, B. (1677/1996). *Ethics*, trans. E. Curley. London: Penguin.

Stack, G.J. (1983). *Lange and Nietzsche*. Berlin and New York: De Gruyter.

Stern, D.N. (2004). *The Present Moment in Psychotherapy and Everyday Life*. New York: W.W. Norton.

Stevenson, A. and Waite, M. (eds.) (2011). *Oxford English Dictionary*. Oxford and New York: Oxford University Press.

Strong, T.B. (2004). Wonder, Science, and the Voice of Philosophy, in Moore, G. and Brobjer, T.H. (eds.) *Nietzsche and Science*. Aldershot, Hampshire: Ashgate, pp. 197–214.

Taylor, M.C. (1987). *Altarity*. Chicago, IL: University of Chicago Press.

Tarr, B. (2012). *The Turin Horse*. A film directed by Bela Tarr, written by B. Tarr and L. Krasznahorkai. Budapest: Másképp Alapítvány Cirko Film.

Tedeschi, G. (2000). *L'Ebraismo e la Psicologia Analitica: Rivelazione Teologica e Rivelazione Psicologica*. Firenze: Giuntina.

Tortorici, D. (2017). 'Reckoning with a culture of male resentment', *The Guardian*, 19 December.

Townsend, C. (2017). 'Nietzsche's Horse', *Los Angeles Review of Books*, 25 April. https://blog.lareviewofbooks.org/essays/nietzsches-horse (accessed 25 February 2018).

Ure, M. (2008). *Nietzsche's Therapy: Self-cultivation in the Middle Works*. Lanham, MD: Lexington Books.

Vaidya, D. (2016). Amor Fati: Suffering to Become the Person One is, in Bazzano, M. and Webb, J. (eds.) *Therapy and the Counter-tradition: The Edge of Philosophy*. Abingdon, Oxfordshire: Routledge, pp. 179–190.

Van Hove, I. (2016). *Hedda Gabler*. National Theatre, London.

Vattimo, G. (2005). *Dialogue with Nietzsche*, trans. W. McCuaig. New York: Columbia University Press.

Vickers, B. (ed.) (1996). *Francis Bacon*. Oxford and New York: Oxford University Press.

Viriasova, I. (2016). 'The refugee's flight: Homelessness, hospitality, and care of the self', *Journal of Global Ethics*, 12(2), pp. 222–239. DOI: doi:10.1080/17449626.2016.1182935.

Voller, D. (2016). John Keats and Negative Capability: The Psychotherapist's X-factor?, in Bazzano, M. and Webb, J. (eds.) *Therapy and the Counter-tradition: The Edge of Philosophy*. Abingdon, Oxfordshire: Routledge.

Von Frantz, M.-L. (1975). *C.G. Jung: His Myth in Our Time*, trans. W.H. Kennedy. New York: Putnam.

Webb, J. (2018). Therapy as an Accident Waiting to Happen, in Bazzano, M. (ed.) *Re-visioning Person-centred Therapy: Theory and Practice of a Radical Paradigm*. Abingdon, Oxfordshire: Routledge. In press.

White, A. (1991). *Within Nietzsche's Labyrinth*. Abingdon, Oxfordshire: Routledge.

Whitehead, A.N. (1933). *Adventures of Ideas*. New York: The Free Press.

Williams, L. (1993). 'A Feminist Interview with Friedrich Nietzsche', *Philosophy Now*. https://philosophynow.org/issues/5/A_Feminist_Interview_with_Friedrich_Nietzsche (accessed 10 February 2018).

Wirth, N. (1976). *Algorithms + Data Structures = Programs*. Upper Saddle River, NJ: Prentice Hall.

Xenophon (2012). *Cyropedia*. London: Createspace.

Yoder, J.H. (1994). *The Politics of Jesus: Vicit Agnus Noster*. Grand Rapids: Eerdmans.

Žižek, S. (2013). 'The absolute recoil', paper presented at the conference: The actuality of the absolute: Hegel, our untimely contemporary. Birkbeck Institute London, 10–12 May.

INDEX

Abbey, R. 121
Acampora, C.D. 51, 86–87, 122–123, 141–142
Adler, A. 15, 83
Adorno, T.W. 69, 93, 148
Aeschylus 16, 21–24, 34, 38, 42
Agamemnon 22–24
Ansbacher, H.L. 83
Ansell Pearson, K. 37, 87, 118
anti-education 88
anti-Semitic 11, 63, 143
Apollo 21, 24, 33–36, 38–42, 72, 104, 150–152
archetypes 6, 53, 61, 78, 116, 150–151, 154–156, 174
Arendt, H. 45
Aristotle 26–27, 34–35, 53, 62, 76, 113, 139–140
Aristotelian thought 26, 53, 113–114, 116, 139, 151
atheism 17, 78–79, 82, 120, 150
Auerbach, E. 91
Austin, J.L. 53

Babich, B. 124, 140
Bachelard, G. 105, 121
Badiou, A. 88
Bakewell, S. 147
Barber, D.C. 17, 81
Bataille, G. 156
Bazzano, M. 3, 16, 27, 29, 37–38, 42, 50, 54, 56, 63, 66, 69, 72–73, 79, 84, 90, 96, 120, 148, 154, 166–167, 176

beehive 101, 103–104, 116
Behler, E. 92, 147
'Being' 16, 20, 79, 90, 92, 129, 136, 143–148, 151; of beings 144
Benjamin, W. 1, 53, 93, 178
Bennett, J. 114
Blake, W. 10, 46
Blanchot, M. 143
Bloch, E. 69
Blondel, E. 105–106, 132, 148
Bollas, C. 32, 110
Borges, J.L. 26
Boscovich, R.J. 64–65, 120, 141, 163
Bowie, M. 59
Braidotti, R. 81
Brown, R.S.G. 123–124
Buber, M. 16, 167, 176
Buddha 17, 20, 55, 120, 149, 166, 168, 170
Bull, M. 11
butterfly 168–169

Canestri, J. 35
case studies: Ahmed 73–74; Dan 18–19; Joanna 14–15; Joe 54–55; Karen 132; Michael 44–46
Central Intelligence Agency (CIA) 139, 159
Chamberlain, L. 12–13
chaos 63, 71, 77, 79, 106, 112, 140–141
Christianity 6, 16–18, 53, 56–57, 60, 64, 70, 77, 79, 85–87, 119, 130–131, 155–156; see also Judaeo-Christian
Clark, T.J. 63

cognitive behavioural therapy (CBT) 15, 56, 95, 119–120, 158
Colli, G. 20, 33–35, 90
Collini, S. 89
columbarium 101–102
consciousness 32, 39, 61–63, 68, 91, 99, 103, 105–108, 110, 112, 117, 119, 125–126, 147–148, 154, 156–158, 163, 175–176; self- 54, 137, 150, 167
Conway, D. 168
Coole, D. 114, 118
Cox, C. 30, 37–41, 65, 111, 114, 118–120
Cronos 22–23

Darwin, C. 14, 79, 87, 109, 112, 118, 121
Davies, W. 138
De Beauvoir, S. 85, 87, 169
decadence, 16, 18, 42–43, 77
Deleuze, G. 3–5, 7, 18–20, 39–41, 60, 62, 70–71, 80, 82, 87, 93–95, 97–99, 107–108, 110, 135, 143, 146, 165–167, 172–173, 178
Derrida, J. 17, 69, 86, 90, 92, 130, 147–148, 159, 167
Descartes, R. 68, 90, 133; Cartesian 63, 66, 70, 72, 90, 123, 125, 147, 149
Deussen, P. 7
Deutsch, H. 32
devil 61, 139, 177
Dews, P. 148
Dionysus 16–18, 20–21, 29, 33, 36–42, 56, 61, 76–77, 82, 90, 104, 137, 140, 150–152, 155–156, 163
dividuum 5, 69
Dostoyevsky, F. 12–13
Doubrovsky, S. 126

Ehrenreich, B. 138
enigma 21, 34–35, 76, 132
eternal recurrence 64, 84, 143, 170–173, 175–178
Euripides 42
evolution 19, 32, 78, 87, 90, 109, 115, 117–118, 122, 141, 156, 167–168

felt text 32, 123–125
Ferenczi, S. 157
Feuerbach, L. 79–81, 174
Fink, E. 81, 105
forgetfulness 54
Förster-Nietzsche, E. 11, 100, 143
Foucault, M. 145–148
fragmentation 16, 66, 70, 84, 161
Frankel, M. 118

Freud, S. 3, 25, 52, 59, 62–63, 71, 80, 83, 98, 102, 124, 131–132, 139, 145–147, 157, 166–167, 174
Frey-Rohn, L. 6, 154
fully living 52, 118

Gast, P. 170
Gell, A. 115
genealogy 66, 74, 91, 97, 109, 115, 140, 148
Gillispie, C.C. 65
God: death of 3, 6, 17, 80, 82, 85–86, 111–112, 121–122, 146, 154; shadows of 2, 80, 120, 122, 146–147, 154
gods 21–22, 24, 29, 34–35, 51–52, 81, 140, 150; new 22–23; old 22–23
Goethe, J.W. 48, 123, 143
Goldhill, O. 174
Goldstein, K. 32, 40
Grant, M. 18
Greek: culture 27–29, 35–36, 75; drama 16, 26; tragedy 15, 22–23, 26, 28, 38, 89, 151, 158; world 41, 43
Guattari, F. 40, 146

Hedda Gabler 72–73
Hegel, G.W.F. 17, 30, 38, 48, 79, 85, 109, 133, 145, 156, 167
Hegelian 46, 79, 161; dialectics 16–17, 39, 90
Heidegger, M. 7, 9, 31, 68, 92–93, 104, 123, 129–130, 143–148, 154, 156, 164
Heraclitus 18, 20–21, 30–31, 34–35, 67, 86, 90, 123, 142, 177
Hesiod 140
Hillman, J. 34, 152
Hölderlin, F. 8, 155
Homer 35; *see also* Nietzsche's cited works
homo natura 103–104, 111–112, 133
homo neoliberalis 27, 138–139
humanism 6, 43, 76–77, 81, 85, 147–148, 174
Huskinson, L. 151, 154–155
Husserl, E. 30, 68, 120, 136, 145, 162, 176
Hyland, A. 13

Icke, R. 24
Ignatieff, M. 159
individualism 5, 84–85, 95, 169
individuation 4–5, 7, 36, 41, 79, 81–82, 84, 120, 137, 139, 149, 151–155, 157

Jacobi, J. 154
Jaffé, A. 154
Jankélévitch, V. 17

Jay, M. 123
Judaeo-Christian 21, 29, 31, 63, 90, 122, 130, 140, 142
Jung, C.G. 6, 78, 151, 153–156, 164

Kant, I. 30, 37–39, 66, 68, 116, 120, 146, 151, 162
Keats, J. 150, 171
Kierkegaard, S. 45–46, 70–71, 78, 93, 136, 155
Klinkenborg, V. 13–14
Klossowski, P. 6
Kofman, S. 100–102, 104
Kramer, R. 157
Krell, F.K. 9
Kristeva, J. 71, 169

labyrinth 6, 78, 131–132, 134, 140, 156
Lacan, J. 4, 90
Lamarck, J.B. 118
Land, N. 62
Large, D. 68, 125–126, 161–163, 165
last human 27, 73, 76–77, 80–81; *see also homo neoliberalis*
Leibniz, G. 106, 120
Levinas, E. 17, 69, 155, 167
Lévi-Strauss, C. 96
lifedeath 42
Løgstrup, K. 50, 69
love of wisdom 20, 35

madness 14, 20–21, 33, 38, 155
Magee, B. 164
magnificent monsters 26, 48–49, 55, 172
Marx, K. 3, 131, 145, 159, 165, 174
Masini, F. 75, 77–82, 90, 99n1, 134, 150
mask 6, 42, 57, 72, 78, 82, 96–98, 104, 137, 141, 165–166, 170; un- 6, 47, 68, 98, 140–141, 149, 162–163
Maslow, A. 82, 168
Massumi, B. 33, 115, 139
May, R. 57, 61–63, 69, 96
McDougall, J. 32
Mearns, D. 176
Merleau-Ponty, M. 57, 93, 119–120, 124
metaphysics 2–3, 28, 30, 32, 37, 39, 43, 59–60, 64–65, 70, 79–80, 82, 84–85, 87–88, 92, 102–105, 111–113, 116, 118–119, 121–123, 128–130, 133, 137–139, 141–145, 147–150, 156, 160, 162, 166, 169–171; anti- 37, 82, 112, 144; post- 81; quasi- 37; semi- 41
Millar, A. 15
Moore, G. 121

morality 2, 7, 17, 32, 51, 55, 61, 68–70, 77, 81, 84–87, 90, 99, 104, 110, 117, 122, 128–129, 133, 135, 155; Christian 9, 19, 51, 60, 69, 85, 90; noble 99; slave 99, 167
Moreno, A. 154
multiplicity 6, 18–20, 30, 40–41, 63–65, 70–71, 77, 81–82, 84, 91, 95, 100, 106, 112, 116, 148, 154, 163, 169

Nagel, T. 124
Nagy, M. 151
naturalism 31, 105, 111, 118, 120–123, 125
Nazism 10, 100, 143, 145
negative psychology 148–149
Nehamas, A. 58
Nietzsche, F.: house 170–171; ideas 5, 18, 95; influence 7, 157; mental collapse 12; philosophy 4, 72–73, 82, 95, 98, 111, 123, 143–145, 148; psychology 43, 45, 69, 123, 133–134, 144–145, 157, 174; thought 3, 6, 10, 12, 40, 43, 45–49, 62, 71–72, 76, 88, 93, 95, 105, 121, 123, 131, 143–145, 152, 162, 177
Nietzsche's cited works: *Anti-Education: On the Future of our Educational Institutions* 89; *Beyond Good and Evil: Prelude to a Philosophy of the Future* 10, 21, 40–41, 43, 47–48, 64–65, 73, 99, 103, 107, 112, 115, 119, 121, 168; *Daybreak: Thoughts on the Prejudices of Morality* 50, 121, 124–126, 131–132; *Ecce Homo: How to Become What You Are* 38, 144, 160; *Homer's Contest* 16, 50–51, 76; *Human, all too Human: A Book for Free Spirits* 9, 37, 68–69, 121, 161; *On the Genealogy of Morals: A Polemic* 54, 67–68, 76, 85–86, 94, 97, 99, 101, 108–109, 122; *Philosophy and Truth: Selections from Nietzsche's Notebooks of the early 1870s* 66; *Philosophy in the Tragic Age of the Greeks* 31; *Selected Letters of Friedrich Nietzsche* 36; *The Anti-Christ* 106, 113, 127, 162; *The Birth of Tragedy* 16–17, 29, 36–38, 41–43, 151–152; *The Gay Science. With a Prelude in Rhymes and an Appendix of Songs* 6, 12, 19, 37, 40, 63, 67–68, 79, 85, 103, 106–107, 110–113, 117–119, 121–123, 168; *The Will to Power* 2, 9, 11, 48, 65–66, 71, 104–105, 107, 113, 116, 118–120, 129–130, 139, 154, 162–164, 169, 176–177; *Thus Spoke Zarathustra: A Book for All and None* 20, 116, 125, 133, 149, 154, 166, 173–174, 178; *Twilight of the Idols or How to Philosophize with the Hammer* 1, 30, 43, 49, 143; *Untimely Meditations* 54

nihilism 3, 47, 63, 73, 77, 79–81, 84, 87, 102–103, 127–135, 137, 144, 149, 151, 154; active 127, 129–130, 135–137; passive 127, 129–130, 135–136, 144
nonhuman 76, 114
noontide 173–174
Nussbaum, M. 49, 53–54, 56–59

Oedipus 34, 104, 146
ontology 36–37, 90, 111, 114, 148
Orbach, S. 162
Orestes 23–24, 33, 159
organism 5, 7, 31–32, 40, 57–58, 62, 65, 92, 98, 107–111, 113, 117, 123–124, 126, 133, 139–140, 149, 161, 168–169, 174; human 14, 31, 62, 115, 174; living 14, 141; micro- 117
Ortega y Gasset, J. 160
overhuman 3, 16, 32, 69, 76–77, 82, 84, 87–90, 118, 134, 147, 154, 174
Oxford English Dictionary (OED) 160

Padesky, C.A. 15
Paglia, C. 33
Park, J.Y. 20
Parkes, G. 123, 154, 171
Perls, F. 40
perspectivism 4, 111, 120, 150, 156, 159–163, 165
philistine 27, 43, 75–76, 89, 138, 167
Phillips, A. 118
philology 8–10, 36, 105, 132–133
Pippin, R.B. 47–48
plane of immanence 39–40
Plato 20–21, 29–30, 33–34, 47–48, 51–52, 112, 151
Platonism 15, 17, 21–22, 48, 55–57, 61, 77–78, 81, 116, 130–131, 133, 151, 155, 171
players 143–144; bad 19–20, 71; good 19, 71
plaything 143–144
pluralism 5–6, 18, 30, 40, 62, 81, 84, 86, 91, 93–94, 98, 106–107, 132, 154, 160–161, 163–164
positivism 31, 39, 41, 120–121, 126, 163; humane 31; neo- 1, 4, 42, 98, 103
Prometheus 22, 110
Proust, M. 55–59, 64, 66, 126, 161, 169
pyramid 101–102, 170; rock 170

queen of the sciences 10, 43, 121

Rank, O. 4, 10, 56, 59, 62, 83–84, 110, 135, 157–158
Raskin, N. 56, 158

Raulff, U. 13
Reitter, P. 89
religion 2–3, 7, 19, 21, 23, 28–29, 32, 46, 60, 70, 74, 77–79, 81–82, 84, 86, 97, 100, 117, 119, 122–123, 128–129, 133, 135, 138, 142–143, 153, 162, 172; anti- 95
ressentiment 3, 32, 60, 93, 99, 134
revenge 2, 24, 60, 133; instinct of 2–3, 60, 81; spirit of 18, 55, 60, 87, 99, 117, 166
Ricoeur, P. 145
Rimbaud, A. 82, 100, 134
Ritschl, F.W. 36–37
Robinson, M. 74
Rogers, C.R. 31, 40, 79, 82, 87, 91, 117, 157
Rorty, R. 59, 83–84, 169
Rose, J. 45, 63
Rousseau, J.-J. 85
Rud, C. 88, 118
Russell, J. 32, 72–73, 152, 177

Safranski, R. 8, 121
Said, E.W. 74
Schacht, R. 122
Schaverien, J. 25–26
Schopenhauer, A. 8, 17, 21, 37–39, 71, 73, 78, 98–99, 121, 132, 164
Schrift, A.D. 102, 143–146
Shaw, T. 139
Smith, W.L. 72
Socrates/Socratism 15–18, 20–22, 29, 35, 39, 42, 47, 51–52, 56–57, 62, 75, 77, 88, 123
Solomon, R.C. 69
spider's web 101–104, 116
Spiegelberg, H. 52
Spinelli, E. 80, 93, 149, 155, 176
Spinoza, B. 16, 67, 105, 107, 115, 154
spiritualization 49–50
Stack, G.J. 64
Stern, D.N. 176
Strong, T.B. 26–29

Taft, J. 4
Tarr, B. 12
Tedeschi, G. 6
Tortorici, D. 46
tower 101; of Babel 101

unconscious 7–8, 25, 39–41, 45, 62–63, 72–73, 79, 103, 106, 110, 126–127, 132–133, 136, 154, 157–158, 169
Ure, M. 121

Vaidya, D. 31–32
Van Hove, I. 72

vanity 7, 50, 86, 169
Vattimo, G. 42–43, 69–70, 85, 90, 128–129, 135, 148, 173–174
Vickers, B. 162
Viriasova, I. 3
virtual 39, 41
Voller, D. 150
Von Frantz, M.-L. 154

Wagner, R. 8, 36, 42–43, 71, 75, 121, 134
Webb, J. 16
White, A. 29, 132
Whitehead, A.N. 115
will to power 7, 41–42, 59, 64–66, 84, 95, 104, 108–109, 113, 115, 144, 161–164,

166–169, 176; *see also* Nietzsche's cited works
Williams, L. 47
Winnicott, D.W. 4
Wirth, N. 175
World Wars 13

Xenophon 14

Yoder, J.H. 17

Zarathustra 7, 60, 70, 82, 89, 166; *see also* Nietzsche's cited works
Zeus 18, 22–23, 155
Žižek, S. 156